A Little Light Friction~

A Little Light Friction ~

Val Hennessy

HARRAP
London

To Gordon McKenzie and Laurie Sharples —
two wily old buffers who have kept me on the rails.

First published in Great Britain 1989
by HARRAP BOOKS Ltd
19–23 Ludgate Hill, London EC4M 7PD

© Val Hennessy 1989

ISBN 0 245–54786–X

Designed by Rupert Kirby

Printed and bound in Great Britain by
Bookcraft (Bath) Ltd.

PICTURE CREDITS
Chris Barker (*Elizabeth Smart*); Ed Barber (*Wendy Perriam*); Nic Barlow (*Les Dawson*); Jerry Bauer (*Martin Amis, Anita Brookner, Ralph Steadman*); Martin Black (*Heather Ray, David Hebditch and Nick Anning, Hilary Norman*); Steven Champion (*Howard Jacobson*); Alan Davidson/Alpha (*Marsha Hunt*); Joyce Edwards (*Ivor Cutler*); Mark Gerson (*Laurie Lee, Andrew Sinclair*); Tara Heinemann (*Jeremy Reed, Fay Weldon*); Frank Herman/Camera Press, London (*Germaine Greer*); Jonathan King Enterprises (*Jonathan King*); Bob Knight (*James Herbert*); Helmut Koller, New York (*Pat Booth*); Niel Libbert (*Fiona Pitt-Kethley*); Chris Lord (*Erica Jong*); Steve Lyne (*Robert Shelton*); Mail Newspapers PLC (*Guy Playfair*); John Minihan (*Jeffrey Bernard*); Alistair Morrison (*Claire Rayner*); Tessa Musgrave (*Sue Townsend*); Palardo Photo (*Melissa*); Ryan Peregrine (*Aeron Clement*); Popperfoto (*David Bailey, Bob Geldof*); Nick Powell (*Kingsley Amis*); Press Association (*Joan Collins, Dee Presley, Fiona Richmond*); Peter Pugh-Cook (*Frank Jakeman*); Francesco Scavulo (*Barbara Taylor Bradford*); Terry Smith/ Camera Press, London (*Mandy Rice-Davies*); Horst Tappe/Camera Press, London (*Alison Lurie*).

CONTENTS

ACKNOWLEDGEMENTS

The articles which comprise this book first appeared in the following newspapers and journals and are published here with permission.

YOU (The Mail on Sunday Magazine)

Aeron Clement
Anita Brookner
Anna Ford
Barbara Taylor Bradford
Bob Geldof
Fiona Pitt-Kethley
Heather Hay
James Herbert
John Francome
Jonathan King
Les Dawson
Marsha Hunt
Nancy Roberts
Robert Shelton
David Hebditch and Nick Anning

Guy Playfair
Henry Root
Mandy Rice-Davies
Melissa
Pat Booth
Richard Sheridan
Wendy Perriam

SHE Magazine

Hilary Norman
Jeffrey Bernard

HONEY Magazine

Fiona Richmond

THE TIMES

Jeffrey Archer (8 November 1985)
Laurie Lee (18 February 1986)

TIME OUT

Alison Lurie
David Bailey
Erica Jong
Fay Weldon
Germaine Greer
Howard Jacobson
Jeremy Reed
Jill Tweedie
Martin Amis
Sue Townsend

THE DAILY MAIL ('Femail')

Joan Collins
Shirley Conran

THE EVENING STANDARD

Elizabeth Smart

THE EVENING NEWS

Dee Presley
Ralph Steadman

THE LITERARY REVIEW

Andrew Sinclair
Brian Patten
Claire Rayner

CATALYST (quarterly magazine for Austin Rover, Vol.1, No.1)

Frank Jakeman

INTRODUCTION

Hats off to all the people you are about to meet in this collection. Love them, loathe them, come to the conclusion that one or two of them are puffed up frauds, the fact is that for the last 10 years, thanks to them, I have been able to keep the wolf from the door whilst working as a freelance journalist. Or 'journo' as some of us now call ourselves in the post-Murdoch era. All the writers (and one photographer) in this collection have two things in common: they have produced a book and they have made themselves 'available for interview' in order to plug that book. Two of them were reluctant to be interviewed but were bullied into it by insistent agents who convinced them that interviews help sell books. The rest called me, via their agent, via my editor. I didn't call them.

Half a dozen of them are *real* writers. They are masters of their craft, inspired, driven to write, intoxicated by the magic of words. These you can spot for yourself shining like headlamps through fog. Some of the others are so talentless, so lacking in literary gifts, so unaware that their books are terrible that you marvel at their cheek. You wonder why they aren't skulking shamefaced, lying low or walking round with brown-paper bags over their heads rather than pushing themselves forward, eagerly volunteering to do interviews, and flaunting themselves on radio and TV chat-shows where they witter fraudulently on about what makes a writer tick.

As if they had the least idea! The thing that makes a writer tick, in my experience, is a fat advance, and fat advances tend to be paid (on the whole) for the sort of books that insult the trees chain-sawed to produce them. Yet these books, these banal, meretricious books are what readers these days rush out to buy. They soar to the top of the best-seller list. They are thumbed and enjoyed by millions. They may not be here to stay, as the great classics have stayed, but they simply cannot be ignored. Neither can their authors. Yet because I occasionally interview authors of atrocious (and, it must be said, *popular*) books, I have been castigated, labelled a 'hooligan journalist' and attacked by certain snooty, elitist book-page people.

Not that I let it get me down. If you don't learn to take the knocks, you rapidly go under in the world of journalism. Once, for example, at the NCR book award dinner I tried to strike up a conversation with Sebastian Faulks, Literary Editor of *The Independent*. When I introduced myself he looked jumpy and scuttled off as if he'd got a wasp in his knickers. 'Why was he so unfriendly?' I asked a man from *Punch* magazine. 'He wouldn't want to be seen at a do like this talking to a tabloid journo like you, that's why,' replied the man from *Punch* with an unmistakable sneer, 'particularly one who takes people like James Herbert, Sue Townsend and Barbara Taylor Bradford *seriously*, if you don't mind my mentioning it.' Oh well, a cat may look at a queen . . . if Sebastian Faulks hasn't, at some point, got stuck into a blockbuster or some irresistibly trashy read and found that he's actually hooked on it, then he has no business being a literary editor. Only po-faced, pretentious literary bores never read trash. Only pain-in-the-arse highbrows consider blockbuster authors unworthy of attention.

I can't *begin* to tell you how pompous these highbrows can be when you bump into them *en masse* at literary launches or at the Booker Award dinner, for instance, where they swan about sipping champagne, discussing books with magisterial seriousness, dropping names like 'Salman' and 'Kingsley' and making out they've actually read all the shortlisted titles. Windbags some of them, ratbags the rest. As a token common reader at the feast, I feel rather out of my depth. You can take it from me that it is instant social suicide if you make a remark like 'I couldn't get beyond page 10 of *The Bone People*,' at a Booker Award dinner. 'Don't smile, you might crack your face,' is something you feel like saying to the worst of them as, spraying the air with champagne and hors d'oeuvres crumbs, they drone drearily on in academic jargon, particularly those who review books for *The Times Literary Supplement* and *The London Review of Books*. Miserably bunch. Never let their hair down or have a good giggle.

Anyway, to return to author interviews. These are contrived by publicity people who swing into action several months before publication date. The publicity person sends proof copies of a book to magazines and newspapers with a long, effusive letter saying things like: 'This is a stunning debut from the most lucid, exciting writer of her generation, ignore this book at your peril . . .' or 'This author has taken the west coast of Venezuela by storm, his talent is breathtaking . . .' and they usually include, painstakingly typed, the blurb from the book's dust-jacket (which as often as not has been written by the author him/herself) and which you are perfectly capable of reading on the dust-jacket without a publicity person having typed it out again and having highlighted various parts of it with those hideous day-glo felt-tip marker pens they all use.

If the author to whom they are trying to draw your attention has written previous books, the publicity person will include fragments of book critics' supportive reviews. These are never to be trusted. When I tell you that there exists a Pan paperback by Richard Compton Miller entitled *Who's really Who* upon whose cover I am quoted as saying: 'People will rush out and buy this book,' and when I tell you that what I *really* wrote in my review was 'only totally moronic people will rush out and buy this book', need I say more? Snippets of notices should never be taken seriously, particularly when the critic happens to be a chum of the author as frequently happens amongst up-market Oxbridge novelists. The publicity person's letter invariably ends with the phrase: 'This exciting, fascinating, stunningly gifted author will be available for selected interviews around publication date, but please hurry as we are anticipating huge media interest.'

Sometimes gimmicky free gifts are included with the book that is being hyped. T-shirts, funny hats, badges and so forth. A velvet jewellery roll arrived with Sally Beauman's *Destiny* (Bantam Press); a small tin containing fish hooks, compass, sail-maker's needle, water purifying tablets and a condom for Martyn Forrester's *The Survival Skills Handbook* (Sphere); a can of Foster's lager and a boomerang for Alan Whicker's *Whicker Down Under* (Hodder); a silk pouch containing several hunks of rose quartz for Magda Palmer's *The Healing Power of Crystals* (Rider) and a lace handkerchief with a heart-shaped tag with the words 'a book to make you weep' arrived with Mildred Cram's *Forever* (Collins). (This book's accompanying P.R. letter promised '*Forever* holds you until the last gleam of its unearthly light has vanished, until the last whisper of its ghostly voice is lost . . .'.)

As soon as an editor has been persuaded of a book's story-worthiness, and as soon as I've been commissioned by a newspaper or magazine editor to interview the author, I find myself bombarded with phone-calls (always at home because I'm a freelance and work from home) usually about 5.p.m. as I'm starting to cook. The publicity person is always yuppie-sounding, pushy, gushy, breathless, keen, uses first names, never takes 'no' for an answer and wears a pair of two-tone tinted spectacles pushed on top of her head. (You *know* this, even though you only meet on the phone.) Basically they spend their working lives chatting up journalists to secure thousands of pounds worth of free advertising. It doesn't bother them that their authors are frequently vile and insulting to journalists and occasionally downright loony. Publishers' publicity people have no conscience and very few – if any – of them have actually read the book by the author they are trying to plug.

In my many dealings with publishers' publicity people I have only known one to crack. Her name was Sheila and she had spent 15 minutes raving about a Methuen novel. 'Oh come off it Sheila, a bright girl like you must *know* that the book's a load of crap,' I snapped in exasperation as my fried onions were starting to burn. 'Actually. I think you are right,' replied Sheila with a strangled sob, 'but I'm only doing my job.'

Fair dos. She was. And when people like Sheila rev up their engines for the big publicity build-up, we journalists become putty in their hands. Forget about literary merit. It is publicity that sells books (with one or two noble and miraculous exceptions). Chat shows sell books. Sign-in session sell books. (Kirk Douglas sold more than 900 signed copies of his autobiography *The Ragman's Son* (Simon and Schuster) in a two-hour session at Harrods.) Author interviews sell books. I was on holiday when a magazine editor telexed me urging me to cut short my holiday by three days and rush home to interview Derek Jameson (the man famous for introducing nipples to the *Daily Express*), described as 'one of Britain's best-known and best-loved figures' by his publicity person, in connection with his autobiography *Touched by Angels* (Ebury Press). 'This is an interview not to be missed,' read the telex, 'this book will be number one.

Two weeks of serialization in the *Daily Mirror*. Major TV advertising. Feature in *Woman's Own*. Profile in *Good Housekeeping*. Paperback rights have been bought by *Penguin* for a 6-figure sum. Jameson is undertaking a nationwide tour of radio programmes and book-shop sign-ins. Life-size Derek Jameson cut-outs will be on display in all bookshops as well as giant copies of *Touched by Angels* . . .' I decided to give this one a miss. Derek Jameson was obviously doing very nicely without me to give him a double-page spread. Frankly I wouldn't cut short my holiday to interview Graham Greene himself. But it is interesting, alarming even, to consider the sort of whiz-kid, big business strategies employed these days by ruthless publishers pulling out all the stops to engineer a best-seller.

An intriguing example of a high-power sales campaign was the one mustered to market first-time author Aeron Clement's best-seller *The Cold Moons* – 'a simple tale of woodland creatures caught in the maelstrom of an act of human folly' (see page 14 for interview with Aeron Clement). After the book had been rejected by two large publishers, Clement and his partner Bernard Kindredson decided to go it alone. They produced the book with a local printer, threw a modest launch party at their local pub, The Cottage Inn at Llandeilo in Dyfed, Wales, and personally distributed copies of the book to Welsh branches of W.H. Smith. The book sold out. They reprinted and brought in a small newly established distribution firm. They decided that the publishing lark was a piece of cake. They then decided that they could use someone with 'know-how' to promote *The Cold Moons* across the UK. Enter Vikki Stace Associates to undertake the promotion. In an article in *The Bookseller*, Clair Harrison of Vikki Stace Associates tells the story of the rise and rise of *The Cold Moons*: 'The combination was challenging. First-time author, first-time publisher, new distributor and two months for Vikki Stace Associates to make a novel about badgers into a best-seller . . .' begins Harrison, who in her long, eye-opener of an article never once mentions (a) whether *The Cold Moons* has any literary merit or (b) whether it is worthy of Vikki Stace Associates ferocious, frenzied, high-speed sales pitch.

Harrison describes how a syndicated publicity tape was sent out and used by six radio stations. How advertisements for *The Cold Moons* were placed in *The Bookseller, Publishing News, Guardian, Times, Natural World,* London International Book Fair catalogue and countless provincial newspapers. 'It was a gamble,' Harrison concedes, 'there are a number of factors which contributed to the success of the venture' . . . (note that none of the factors she goes on to list include whether or not *The Cold Moons* was a smashing, unputdownable, compulsive read or whether, indeed, it was actually any good) . . . 'the key factor was team work. All our energies were channelled into one project, decisions were made quickly and groundwork was laid in preparation for a success. Aeron was prepared to go anywhere and do anything . . . all the reps were kept informed of promotion plans and advertising bookings . . . we drew up a tight schedule, with dates for review copy mailing, telephone chasing and trade and consumer advertising.'

A few paragraphs further on we learn that the UK publication date and the paperback auction were fixed for the same day. The second booster launch was timed to coincide with the London International Book Fair. A regular update was circulated to all concerned keeping them informed with cuttings, plans and Aeron Clement's personal promotion schedule; press packs with author details were distributed. Publishing, sales history and Welsh press agencies were mailed with the review copies months before launch date. 'No advertisement appeared without a badger head,' boasts Harrison (the friendly badger head having been drawn by Aeron Clement's wife, Jill, to minimize expense), 'it was used on notepaper, envelopes, postcards, bookstands and posters.'

And here comes the crunch. *Lateral Thinking.* As Harrison explains 'Lateral Thinking' came powerfully into play at Vikki Stace Associates as they scrabbled through conservation directories for badger-related organizations, products and supporters. Every UK badger preservation group was sent posters and a review copy for their newsletter. (Books about badgers being few and far between, it is hard to imagine any badger preservation group when presented with a free hardback entirely about badgers being so churlish as to give a negative or indeed objective review, to my way of thinking.) A 'The Cold Moons' stand was organized at the RSPCA's annual conference. A 'The Cold Moons' window display was set up in the Welsh Development Agency conveniently situated opposite Hatchards Bookshop in Piccadilly. Badger estate agents were persuaded to display 'The Cold Moons' posters. Crisp packets with World Wildlife save-the-badger appeal on them were given away with every signed copy of *The Cold Moons* at the London International Book Fair. Fluffy, winsome, cuddlesome toy badgers were sent out for use in bookshop window displays.

As Harrison sums it up: 'As with any gamble, luck was a vital ingredient. Spring was in the air, wildlife is popular.' Meanwhile Aeron Clement postponed a heart by-pass operation in order to 'go anywhere and do anything' in the cause of self-promotion. This was exactly the sort of human interest touch to appeal to national newspapers. Consequently there can't be a person in the UK who hasn't read the rags-to-riches story about the shy, ailing, welsh badger-enthusiast living on borrowed time and an invalid pension whose book about badgers zoomed to the top of the best-sellers and made him a millionaire. *Wind in the Willows* it may not be, but *The Cold Moons* certainly hit the jackpot, although few people are acquainted with Vikki Stace Associates' extraordinary role in creating this sensational brockbuster (whoops, sorry . . .).

However, it is all very well for me to carp about crass books topping the best-sellers. It is all very well to scoff and sneer at the standards of certain so-called writers, but at least they have actually managed to get a book together, get it published, see their name on the spine, which is more than I've yet achieved (apart from this collection which is not, let's not beat about the bush, in the same league as a gutsy, pulsating novel). The truth is that inside every journalist is a novelist fighting to get out. Our work, you see, is circumscribed and limited by the constraints and restraints imposed by the editorial line of the publications we write for. In the world of paid pen-pushers writing a novel separates the wheat from the chaff. Journalism has a short shelf-life. One day the piece you've sweated over, sat up with all night in order to make your deadline, is in the columns of a newspaper or magazine. Next day it's wrapped round someone's Brussels sprouts. In the past 10 years I've had as many words published as Leo Tolstoy had but they've all been lost – ephemeral outpourings, used to soak up dog's pee, mop up suds from overflowing washing machines, light fires . . .

Which brings me to my ex next-door neighbour, Pete. He was a willow basket-maker, blond, be-jeaned, soft of speech, loud of record-player, who often used to pop in between baskets. Three years ago he let slip that he had just started writing his first novel. I've heart that one before. Hundreds of times, from hundreds of people. 'Oh yes?' I replied, muffling a yawn and began talking about a reporting assignment I'd just completed at a 4-day Yamaha Electronic Organ convention in Blackpool for *You* magazine. Pete chipped in that he was stuck on chapter 6 and I murmured, with cynical disregard: 'Really? That's tough. Best stick to baskets. Bad news, Pete, now if you don't mind I've got a deadline to reach . . .'

Some days I'd hear jubilant, frisky typing sounds coming from Pete's work shed. 'Still at it?' I'd inquire whenever we bumped into each other in the butchers. Sometimes Pete would lean out of his shed window and make the 'thumbs up' sign. Sometimes he'd lean over the hedge and say 'I've nearly finished, hope the sound of my typewriter isn't disturbing you at night?' Disturbing me? It was driving me demented. I hadn't had any work for three weeks. What was he up to in there? Who did he think he was, Ian McEwan? Several weeks later, whilst helping me down the steps with my dustbin, he remarked that his novel was finished. Finished? I nearly dropped dead. Stone me, Pete-the-basket had finished his novel. This was a slap in the eye, make no mistake. 'Know anything about publishers?' asked Pete. It shames me to recall that I suggested various Vanity publishers and told Pete how notoriously difficult it is to place a first novel, how big boy publishers junk 500 unsolicited manuscripts a week and so forth and asked him whether he could fix my fence which had blown down in a gale. He fixed it. Very badly as a matter of fact.

A few weeks later, Pete's novel *The Levels* (about a basket-maker) arrived in the post. Published by Constable. Fait accompli. Peter Benson's name across the spine. To make matters worse, there across the dust-jacket was a quote from no lesser literary giant than John Fowles who described *The Levels* as being 'as cool and sharp as a glass of cider'.

Pete's production was certainly several up on a magazine article about the Yamaha Electronic Organ Convention in Blackpool. I never again asked him to help me down the steps with my dustbin. *The Levels* won The Guardian Fiction prize, the authors Club First Novel award, a Betty Trask award and was short-listed for the Whitbread Prize and the David Higham Fiction prize. Good old Pete.

Yet did we see life-sized Peter Benson cut-outs on display in the nation's bookshops? Was every basket-related association mailed a willow basket and a review copy of *The Levels*? Were syndicated tapes sent out, telephones chased, press packs distributed? Did lateral thinking come into play? No it did not. If the creative force of Vikki Stace Associates had backed Benson (and maybe if Benson had postponed something like a colon transplant operation) perhaps a charming novel as cool and sharp as a glass of cider might have stormed the bestseller lists and raked in mega-bucks.

There are two points to this anecdote. One is to indicate that in the arbitrary world of publishing, the quality of a book has little bearing on its success. The second is that Benson's book made manifest, instilled in me an ambition to write a novel of my own. Being a journalist is invigorating, hilarious, agonizing, often insane. But it is only second best. Like I said, a novel separates the wheat from the chaff. In conducting the interviews in this collection, I have met some vile, extraordinary, marvellous – even special people. Occasionally there has been a little light friction. On the whole I've got on with them like a house on fire. It's been a privilege. I would never have met them other than through my work. They have caused me pain, sweat, tears, indignation, hilarity. I'm grateful to all of them, even the ones that rubbed me up the wrong way. Even the ones that treat journalists like some malodorous item brought in by the cat.

Whilst choosing which interviews to include, I've been indulging in a little fantasy in which I'm hosting a literary dinner where Martin Amis, Les Dawson, Anita Brookner, John Fowles, Mandy Rice-Davies and Claire Rayner are all sitting round a table in some privately-hired dining room at The Ritz, merrily tucking in and discussing the future of literature. 'A big hand for Val,' says Amis, kissing me on both cheeks (and maybe pinching my bottom) and raising his glass of Rioja red, 'This woman is doing for British literature what Intersun did for Mallorca . . .' (Leonard Cohen's 'Bird on a Wire' moans gently from hidden speakers. A waiter tops up everyone's glass.) 'Bless 'er,' booms Rayner, playfully hurling a bread roll across the room. 'Right on,' murmurs Brookner, making the thumbs-up sign. 'Hear, hear. Wonderful woman,' says Fowles through a mouthful of Poussin-au-poivre, 'Why isn't she literary editor of *The Independent*? Why isn't she a Booker judge?'. Les Dawson blows me a kiss and pokes Fowles in the ribs with a French stick. Ah, 'the weight of the world is love,' as Allan Ginsberg once wrote . . .

Lack of space and escalating publishing costs meant that there was not room for all the interviews I would have liked to include. You won't find my interview with the late Lord Mancroft which took place when he was publicizing his collection of essays *Bees in Some Bonnets* (Bachman & Turner). His agent delivered me to Lord Mancroft's Chelsea home where I was just lowering myself into a Parker Knoll armchair in front of a Magicoal one-bar electric heater when Lord Mancroft (who was wearing carpet slippers and matted woollen socks) thundered 'Don't damn well park your backside there, my girl,' which startled me terribly. I sprang up, dropped my pen, then realized that he'd been addressing his dachshund. During this interview Lord Mancroft beckoned me to the window and pointed sadly to a builder's skip parked outside his front gate. 'You see that skip?' I nodded. 'You're probably wondering why it's draped with a sheet?' Again I nodded. 'It is draped with a sheet because some philistine has scrawled FUCK OFF in red paint across it, twice, and I'm expecting European royalty to visit today on family business of a romantic nature . . . obviously I felt that the scrawl was hardly appropriate in the circumstances.'

Neither will you find an interview with delightful actress Beryl Reid, when she was promoting her autobiography *So much love* (Hutchinson). On this occasion she was laid up with a broken arm beneath a turquoise bedspread surrounded by cats and champagne bottles. 'I feel such a fool,' she said, wearing a satin nightie, black angora stole and, with her hair elaborately coiffed and tinted, looking like Madame de Pompadour awaiting a visit from Louis XV, 'and please, no photos. You see I can't put my bra on while I'm in this sling and I'm certainly not going to foist photos of a bra-less Beryl on to the British public.' As it happens, the interview started on a note of friction due to a misunderstanding. When Beryl mentioned that, these days, she always seemed to be falling over 'because I get so tired', I thought she said 'because I get so tight'. *'Tired*, dear, I said *tired'* hissed Beryl a trifle waspishly, and then went on to regale me with wonderful stories about how she had her knickers eaten by rats at the Palace Theatre, Attercliffe (Yorks) (she wasn't wearing them at the time), and worked 84 hours a week in her youth at London's Cine-Variety living on hope and spaghetti. She also recalled the time she lunched with the Queen: 'At a Buckingham Palace lunch, you have a drink first to make you relax, then the corgies come in, followed by the Queen and you get all ready to curtsy and say "thank you for having me Ma'am . . ." '

You will not find my interview with Douglas Fairbanks junior (who was in London to discuss his in-progress autobiography) because he was too boring, or my interview with John Fowles, which, alas, has never taken place. For 8 years I lived five minutes walk away from John Fowles in Lyme Regis. Both the *Guardian* and the *Evening Standard* asked me to arrange interviews with Fowles but his agent informed me that he dislikes being interviewed by women. I even posted a friendly note through his letter-box saying 'Dear John Fowles, how about me taking you for a little snorter in the Cobb Arms sometime seeing as how we are neighbours', which elicited a dismissive reply (posted in London) along the lines of John Fowles having no wish to meet me. Ever. Point taken. I did bump into him once in the greengrocers where we had a brief discussion about fossils and the rising cost of cucumbers. I don't think he knew who I was. I once heard him on 'Desert Island Discs'. If his choice of gramophone records is anything to go by, I don't think we would have hit it off in the Cobb Arms. The owner of the local bookshop told me he grinds his 'blackened teeth' and gets flustered, even paranoid, about the groupie-type people who stop him in the street with requests for autographs.

Neither is there space for my interview with the marvellous Major Ronald Sinclair who, as this collection goes to press, is about to publish his *Adventures in Persia* (To India by the back door) (Gollancz). It is his first book, written at the age of 99. He is currently at work on his second. *Adventures in Persia* tells the story of how he drove a Model A Ford 3,000 miles from Beirut to India in 1926. In Beluchistan he was maanœuvring the Ford through a narrow ravine and found his way blocked by a putrefying camel. He had to build a ramp of rocks up over the camel and down the other side and as he drove over (one hand clasping a handkerchief to his nose) he feared that the carcass would explode, leaving him stuck on top. Incidentally, he survived the journey on a diet of hard-boiled eggs, water and the local bread which came in soggy sheets the size of a newspaper. He would spread a sheet over his chest and drive along with it drying off and crisping up (like biscuit) in the sun. Do you think John Fowles would be such fun to talk to as Major Sinclair? When I interviewed the Major at his Plymouth rest home he mistook me for meals-on-wheels, told me he was 'nice and peckish, thank you,' and then wanted to know why I kept asking him so many questions. 'Radiator caps have a fatal fascination for the unwary,' he said, a propos of nothing, sipping a large brandy. 'I remember once, on an Assam tea plantation, an elephant stuck its trunk on a boiling radiator cap. Lost its temper. Smashed the car to pieces.'

Among the conversations reprinted here, I hope you will find something to entertain, to enlighten, and to indicate how diverse and fascinating is the assortment of people writing and selling books in the 1980s. Many people think it is amazing that anyone reads books any more, what with radio and TV, comics, magazines and newspapers stealing the time we once set aside for book reading. George Steiner, writing recently in the *T.L.S.*, doesn't hold out much hope for the future of books and concludes that these days 'our parchment is the wall, on which ephemeral graffiti have their brief and strident moment (or, as Simon and Garfunkel first sang it 15 years ago so much better, 'The words of the prophets are written on the subway walls . . .').

Personally, I think that Steiner's view is too gloomy. People still enjoy books. Books are still valued. Furthermore I now intend to write one. Having interviewed so many authors, I've decided if you can't beat them, join them. I'm determined to crack it. I want to see my name triumphant on the spine. The first blank page is on the typewriter. Will it be about lust? intrigue? boiling passion? Or will it be some simple tale of a woodland creature caught in the maelstrom of an act of human folly? All I hope is that like Mildred Cram's *Forever* it will hold readers until the last gleam of its unearthly light has vanished, until the last whisper of its ghostly voice is lost. Whatever I decide to write about, it will be *mine*, all mine. Vikki Stace Associates, I'll be in touch. Booker here I come. Oh yes, the stars look down.

VAL HENNESSY, London 1988

*   *   *

Each interview that follows took place between 1980 and 1988 at the time the interviewee's book was published.

A E R O N
CLEMENT

I STILL CAN'T ACCEPT THAT BY PUTTING WORDS ON
PAPER YOU GET REWARDED WITH WEALTH. I'M FINDING
IT DIFFICULT TO COME TO TERMS WITH.

Don't mention stuffed badgers to Aeron Clement. He has lost count of the number of stuffed badgers he's been obliged to pose with in recent weeks. Fame, as he points out, has its drawbacks. All Aeron wants is a quiet life, time to go badger-spotting, plant his hanging baskets, play darts with the Llandeilo darts team and bounce his baby grandson on his knee. Instead his first novel *The Cold Moons* ('a simple tale of badgers caught in the maelstrom of an act of human folly') soars to the top of the best-sellers. It earns him half a million pounds (so far) and the soubriquet 'a famous author' and suddenly the world's media (all carrying stuffed badgers) are beating a path to his remote Welsh bungalow.

'It's all happened so sudden-like', admits Clement in his bardic Welsh lilt, similar to Neil Kinnock's with a smidgeon of Dylan Thomas's. He leads the way up his front garden path, round a motor-bike, past a concrete badger and a couple of gnomes. Next door the net curtains twitch. Aeron waves and says 'That's Tom, first person to read the manuscript and suggest I'd written a winner. I still can't accept that by putting words on paper you get rewarded with wealth. I'm finding it difficult to come to terms with.'

Aeron Clement is a publishing phenomenon. He is the literary equivalent of the 'primitif' painter. One year ago, 52, depressed, recovering from a series of heart attacks and struggling on sickness benefit of £3,500 a year, he sat in the very same chintz armchair in which he is sitting as we speak, took out his biro and wrote: 'The evening air lay heavy with the drifting fragrance of new leaf incense which sent shivers of expectant pleasure through the inhabitants of Yellow Copse. . .'

Little could he foresee that this Blyton-esque sentence would change his life. Little could he guess that it would herald the sort of fame and fortune that must make deposed best-selling authors like Catherine Cookson, Noel Barber and Stephen King (all pipped to the post by *The Cold Moons*) want to spit. Ten months and many foolscap pages later Clement had a feeling in his bones that he'd written a masterpiece. Friends and family went wild. 'You'll hit the jackpot with this, boyo,' the darts team enthused. But did the Big Publishing Boys in London want to know? No they did not. Hutchinson, then Macmillan rejected the manuscript outright. In a fit of independence Aeron's pal, Bernard Kindred, Landlord of the Cottage Inn, declared 'We'll publish and be damned' (in Welsh), set up his own publishing company, Kindredson, and the rest is history. The initial print-run of 2,000 copies sold out in a week. Penguin bought the paperback rights for £140,000. Delacourt bought the US hardback rights for £250,000. Film and book club rights have been sold for undisclosed sums. (Clement: 'I am flabbergasted. The amounts I've been offered are enough to shake anyone. I've done nothing rash, mind. I've bought a new suit, and when the gearbox went on my Chrysler Sunbeam I splashed out on a Ford Granada automatic. People tell me I should go on a world cruise but I don't fancy it because I don't like to put the dog in kennels . . .') Sweden, Finland, Holland, Denmark, Norway, Italy, Australia and South Africa are currently bidding. 'Clement the badger', as he's known at the Cottage Inn, is now a literary celebrity.

'To tell the truth I'm finding it all a bit embarrassing,' he says, as we sip tea in his front room. His wife, Jill, who illustrated *The Cold Moons* ('I'm not trained but I love drawing badgers') is preoccupied with the spin-offs. Her artwork is being incorporated into badger tea towels, wall charts, key fobs and tea-pot covers just like *The Country Diary of An Edwardian Lady* ones and to be honest it's taken her by surprise. The Clements' bookcase bulges with nature books. There are miniature porcelain badgers on the window ledge, and on top of the telly. Framed photographs of badgers glint on the sideboard. In the hallway there's a stuffed badger mounted on oak with a brass plaque reading 'pregnant badger road casualty', doubtless left behind by some photographer. Clement is even wearing a black-and-white striped tie with a badger head motif.

Ask him about the price of fame and he sighs. What with sign-ins, chat shows, rotary club dinners and presenting prizes at the Swansea short-story competition he is in a whirl from dawn to dusk. Jill interrupts to say that being a man who likes his chips and black forest gateau, his health is not what it was and he has postponed a heart by-pass op until after the furore has died down. Clement twangs his braces: 'I've been invited to sponsor two Welsh rugby teams, I've been asked to the Institute of Bankers' Dinner which is ironic, mark you, because I'd had terrible trouble getting an overdraft until my book took off. Not that I'm crying pauper, but what I'd saved when I retired early from Management soon went . . . It's a new world I'm into. I was presented to the Duchess of York at the London Book Fair. She said: "Your book is one I'm taking away from this event even if I have to kick someone's ankle to get a copy." Fair play. I gave her one, signed.'

One TV producer asked me to shout down the sett to encourage the badgers to come out. You'd be amazed how few of these people have read the book.

Here let me describe the book that so captivated Fergie. It opens with two badgers Bamber and Dainty 'in the first blush of life' being hounded by humans. When Dainty is gassed Bamber's eyes 'blur with tears' and he 'sobs with wretched desolation'. The badger community in their woodland grove 'brushed with hundreds of snow-flossed plumes' face the prospect of dying in the valley they have inhabited for hundreds of generations and setting off on a perilous quest for freedom. Far be it from me to spoil the plot, but in case you are chewing your nails, I assure you it has a happy ending. It also has a few of Clement's poems. 'When strolling along a country road/Stop a while should twilight bode . . .', and 'The day will shortly come, when in a sheltered bower/A leaf will unfurl to reveal a splendoured flower . . .' and so forth. A cursory perusal of these poems may possibly have been the reason for Hutchinson's and Macmillan's peremptory rejections. The fools. They must be kicking themselves. How grossly they underestimated the taste of the book-buying public . . .

Not that Clement holds a grudge. If his book can do its humble bit to draw public attention to the cruelties of badger baiting and gassing then he doesn't care who published it. And it's in order to get his message across that he's prepared to put up with being hounded by the media: 'They come here with their stuffed badgers, they make me traipse through the woods in the rain, they expect me to crouch in wet leaves for photographs, they don't know the first thing about badgers. They've probably never seen one in their lives – only dead ones on the roads. They are utterly ignorant about the ways of nature. One TV producer asked me to shout down the sett to encourage the badgers to come out and be filmed. You'd be amazed how few of these people have read the book. The Americans never discuss the story, only how much money I've made. Then there was Radio Birmingham. They wanted me to go there to do a 3-minute interview squeezed between two pop records. I said 'It's a long way to go for 3 minutes' but I went. The interviewer took me aside before it started and said: 'I'll tell you straight. I can't stand animal books. Specially when the animals speak to each other.' I had a good answer to that. "There's no dialogue in my book, see?" The interview lasted 17 minutes.'

Which is understandable because Clement in full flow is unstaunchable. Puffing copiously on filter-tips he reveals his writing methods: 'If I'm not in the mood I pack it in, it's as simple as that.' He reveals his literary influences: *Watership Down*. Full stop. The description of the death of the rabbit Hazel is the best thing I've ever read.' He voices his hatred of badger baiters: 'I've just assisted with a TV report on badger baiting. The hooligans we picked up said they do it for fun. The *League of Cruel Sports* showed us a film where a badger, ripped apart by dogs, took 4 hours to die. At the end the baiters decapitate the animal, mount its head as a trophy to hang on the wall to remind themselves of a pleasant day for years to come. As far as I'm concerned it's not a sport, just a sadistic lust for blood.' He recalls his book launch at the Cottage Inn: 'Tom, my neighbour, announced "Aeron will make a million before the end of the year" and a chap from *The Western Mail* took up the remark and headed his report "Local author set to make millions". We hadn't at that stage sold a single book, but there's the power of the Press for you.'

And finally he has a word to say about book critics: 'Only one chap slated it, from *The Birmingham Post*. All I can say is that he lacked the perceptiveness of imagination appropriate to appreciate a good story. I can't accept that such a person is a critic of fiction. He wrote that the idea of 340 badgers setting out on a quest for freedom was nonsense. My book is fiction, mark you, not documentary.'

Later Clement kindly offers to drive me the 25 miles to Swansea station. Can you see Jeffrey Archer doing this? Or Kingsley Amis? Or any other famous

All I want is a house of my own with a bit of land in badger country.

author? We wind along the leafy lanes with Aeron imparting natural history information: 'Those two beech trees are a calendar shot in autumn' he effuses, whizzing round a double-bend. 'A very nice man lives there, loves his animals, he's got a little pets' cemetery in his tulip bed . . .' Pointing to a house on a hill he says 'That's a house we're considering buying. That's a piority at the moment, to move from our rented bungalow. I can't take it in when people tell me how much money I'm making. I like to know where I am with money, to tell the truth. All I want is a house of my own with a bit of land in badger country.' Over a humped-back bridge: 'That's the Tovy, best salmon river in Britain . . .' and past a flock of sheep: 'Look at that view of the Brecon Beacons, we've got lots of owls up there . . .', out onto the motorway and past the new MFI complex: 'The more the concrete jungle spreads the more badgers there are that get crushed by bulldozers . . .'

Halting smoothly outside Swansea station he guides me to the ticket office, pausing at a news-stand to check the current bestseller list. 'Still number one,' he notes gleefully, then lowering his voice he adds: 'Here's a scoop for you. I'm close to half way finished a sequel. It's to be called *The Spirals of Light*.' Badger fans (and Fergie) will be thrilled to learn that it is about badgers. It will be published at Christmas. It is, according to Clement, the best thing he's written. It will doubtless take the bestseller lists by storm again. You have been alerted.

The Cold Moons (Kindredson, 1988).

Most writers sometimes feel
themselves to be witches or
warlocks, somehow peculiar
or damaged.

Alison Lurie

T

he last thing Alison Lurie wants to talk about is her new novel, *Foreign Affairs*. Tell her that it is selling well in Britain and she says 'Huh Huh' and nothing more. Mention that it is considerably more tender and compassionate than what we have come to expect from the writer labelled, by Gore Vidal, as the 'Queen Herod of modern fiction' and she simply stonewalls. She starts talking about her three grown-up sons, the Laura Ashley shop ('it drives us Americans *wild*'), the weather and the Tissot exhibition at the Barbican Centre where tiny, frail, bird-like Lurie was almost ground underfoot by the throng.

We are drinking in the Chelsea Arts Club. Lurie's huge eyes, which have been darting ceaselessly round the bar where several noon drunks morosely slurp, suddenly focus with disconcerting intensity upon mine. She grips the table and rasps: 'Who are these *amazing* people? They look so *interesting*, so bohemian, so extremely *visual* . . .' To me they look like a bunch of middle-aged pissheads trying very hard to look like artists in their unravelling Fair Isle handknits, baggy corduroys and art-deco cravats. Several even have paint splashed on their suede shoes. 'Terrific,' enthuses Lurie, pencil poised, notebook at the ready, 'I wish I'd seen this place before I finished the book. It represents *exactly* what the Americans find so seductive about London . . .'

Which brings us, circuitously, back to her new novel *Foreign Affairs*, her seventh, in which she mocks the rose-tinted expectations of American tourists in Britain. Lurie plots, with some wit and dexerity, the progress of two Anglophile academics on sabbatical leave. There is tall, dark, handsome, somewhat boring Fred (28) compiling a study about eighteenth-century writer John Gay. Fred walks everywhere, regardless of weather or distance, in deference to his hero whose epic poem 'Trivia, or the art of walking the streets of London' castigates all users of public transport.

And there is snobby unloved Vinnie (54). She specializes in children's folklore and playground chants, is well 'in' with the London cultural élite and is as captivating as an old cardigan. The two spend a great deal of time researching in the British Museum Reading Room, referred to by Fred as the 'Bowel Movement' (British Museum=BM=Bowel Movement. Rather a schoolboy sense of humour has Fred). Their various disenchantments with London are the result of what Lurie terms 'tourist disorientation'.

Lurie loves England. Like Fred for whom a slag heap means DH Lawrence, a pawnshop George Gissing, a Sussex pylon WH Auden and a sooty south London slum Doris Lessing, she once saw literary allusions in all things English. As she explains, Americans create the most ludicrous London fantasies: 'There's a particular kind of American English Lit. teacher whose images of London have totally evolved from Dickens, Shakespeare and Bloomsbury . . . Then there's the other non novel-reading sort of American whose vision of England is based on imported TV series like *Upstairs Downstairs* and *Brideshead Revisited*, or on movies like *Far From The Madding Crowd* and *The French Lieutenant's Woman*.' Here Lurie pauses to express her admiration of the author of the *French Lieutenant's Woman*, John Fowles. 'Great guy. Great writer. Very popular in the States.' It could be said, in fact, that Lurie owes some of her success to John Fowles. Some time ago he wrote – and where he wrote it and to whom she can no longer remember – 'I am convinced that Alison Lurie's fiction will long outlast that of many currently more fashionable names. There is no American writer I have read with more consistent pleasure and sympathy over the years.' This quote, naturally, continues to appear on the dust-jacket of each new Lurie novel. It is trotted out in all of Lurie's publicity blurbs. It has done her proud. It has made people sit up and take notice. I wonder whether John Fowles has ever had second thoughts? I wonder if Lurie's work went downhill whether he might be cheesed off to see his quote used as an on-going-puff?

How does Lurie feel about the quote resurfacing with each new book? 'It's fine by me. I'd like to meet John Fowles. Buy him a bottle of bourbon . . . anyway, as I was saying

There's a particular kind of American English Lit. teacher whose images of London have totally evolved from Dickens, Shakespeare and Bloomsbury.

about rose-tinted be-spectacled American tourists . . . both types I described expect England to be quaint, cosy, picturesque and roses-round-the-door, thatched cottages everywhere and comic characters making cockney asides. This is the England they want and come to see. Somehow they arrange not to notice the Wimpy Bars, and McDonald's and garish advertising hoardings – or if they *do* see these things they feel hurt, insulted, outraged and moan about England being ruined . . .'

Lurie describes herself as having been 'a skinny, odd-looking kid, deaf in one badly damaged ear with a paralysed face muscle that gave me a lop-sided sneery smile'. Making up stories is what she did for fun. With a pen she believed she could cast a kind of witch's spell and revise a hostile world where she was considered ugly, strange and too clever for her own good. 'I wrote constantly. I never stopped. But once I was out of college with a full-time job, writing got to seem like smoking, or biting one's nails, a bad habit, a waste of time. It was something my friends and lovers thought I was doing too much of, especially since I got so upset when the rejection letters came.'

She can remember sitting in a park sometime during the mid-fifties and taking stock of her spectacular lack of success. She decided to abandon her writing: 'I said to myself: you don't have to make up stories now. You're in the real world: you have real babies, a real husband and a real house.' Then, having made the decision she felt no better. It seemed like self-mutilation: 'As soon as I wasn't a writer the world looked flat and vacant, emptied of possibility and meaning . . . a kind of glossy, banal calendar photograph. To give up writing was *stupid*. I wheeled my baby home from the park, changed his diaper, fed him, put him down for a nap and went back to the typewriter.

'Most writers sometimes feel themselves to be witches or warlocks, somehow peculiar or damaged. This has been especially true of women, at least until recently. Women, in order to go on writing, have had to struggle with the fear that they are not "normal", however that word is currently defined. In the past it meant staying home and keeping house. Today, most often it means having an absorbing job. But in both cases the underlying demand is the same as it is for most men. It is a demand that is always fatal for writers: work, conform, succeed and forget your childish impulse to ''play'' with words, to reimagine the world.'

Lurie's fans will inevitably suppose that *Foreign Affairs* is autobiographical. Vinnie, the heroine, is an authority on children's folklore: so is Lurie. Vinnie is a raunchy divorcée not averse to the occasional carnal adventure. When you ask Lurie whether Vinnie's sexual experimentation is inspired by personal midlife experience, she grins that captivating, lop-sided grin and stalls by taking a swig of wine before replying: 'The heroines in all my novels have something in common with me ... I'm prepared to admit that my own situation of suddenly being a single woman again when I was 49 years old was an educational experience. Marvellous. At the moment I'm ''romantically involved'', very much, with a man 14 years younger and that's an educational experience too.'

Lurie has learnt that the middle-aged often do burst into robust and unexpected blossom. As she points out, a whole lot of us will one day be 50 and still eager to be hanging in there with our fingers on the pulse.

She stares again at the Chelsea Artists slouched by the bar. One of them, his chapped, paint-stained fingers protruding from fingerless gloves, waves and gives Lurie the eye. His left eyebrow slides quizzically up into the pleated forehead. It is a 'come on' of the commonest kind. Lurie grins. 'Hmm. The world is full of people over 50 who will be around and in fairly good shape for the next quarter century: plenty of time for adventure and change. If you get outside your ordinary environment things can happen that you never considered possible, and *that's* what my novel is about.'

Foreign Affairs (Michael Joseph, 1985).

*My two lightweight novels, Bumbo
and Judas, were both written in
four weeks when I was 22, and I've
been lumbered with them ever since.*

ANDREW
SINCLAIR

Everyone who is anyone has heard of 'The Apostles'. They were the best Heavy Metal Band in the history of Rock 'n' Roll. When a Weidenfeld PR person lets slip that writer Andrew Sinclair (author of *The Breaking of Bumbo* and *My Friend Judas*) used to be in The Apostles – well, I mean, you can't see me for dust. I'm banging on his front door before you can say *Suck My Truncheon* (title of The Apostles' greatest hit). I bang again. Ten years in journalism have taught me that legends in the flesh tend to be somewhat overwhelming. My knees are knocking like a young girl's. Then someone I assume is an Apostles groupie ushers me inside and into a vast, opulently furnished room. Surprisingly there are no perspex-framed gold discs hanging on the walls, no Gibson Humbuckers or Gretch Hollowbodies chucked across the shag pile, no Apostles' *Greatest Hits* albums, no roaches in the ashtrays . . . just this morose old-timer drinking a cup of tea with his feet up on a velveteen pouffe, looking more like a geography teacher than a guy who once gyrated through swirling dry-ice with his sweaty chest hair glistening in the crimson strobes.

'Hi, Andy,' I say, trying to play it cool, 'tell us about the Apostles, man.' Andy flattens his lips against his gums in an effort to convey good humour and replies: 'The Apostles is a self-electing Cambridge secret society which has run since the 1820s. It has attracted most of our best philosophers and poets including Tennyson, Rupert Brooke, Russell, not to mention Wittgenstein and the Bloomsburys . . .' Who? Wittgenstein and the Bloomsburys? Are they a reggae band? I am out of my depth, no two ways. Old Andy continues to rap on about Cambridge and how he was the youngest of the Angry Young Men apart from Colin Wilson, and how the Bloomsburys were vastly inflated, while I keep on saying 'Right on, Andy' having twigged at last that I'd got the wrong Apostle. No chance of this one twanging a live chorus of *Suck My Truncheon*. No way.

So, playing safe, I begin talking about his novels, *The Breaking of Bumbo* ('59) and *My Friend Judas* ('61) which became immediate best-sellers and established Sinclair (as I shall now call him) as 'a talented young novelist in the act of extending his range' (*Sunday Times*). These novels are packed with incomprehensible public-school slang expressions like 'sloppy wop', 'tophole tottie', 'blast my bollocks' and philosophical asides such as 'Pee on the waters before the waters pee on you' (a sentiment close to the heart of the Apostles Rock Group as it happens). Sinclair looks hurt when I suggest that the vocabulary of his working-class characters doesn't quite ring true. 'It is possible that I have rather a tin ear for working-class idiom,' he concurs, banging down his teacup, 'although I should point out that I'm a totally self-made man. I was one of the last of the abandoned colonial children. I gained a scholarship at Eton and my mother wrote historical fiction to support the family. Her book *I Struggle and I Rise* sold a quarter of a million copies . . . I was very much a war child, all black-out and rationing until mother hit it lucky when I was about ten.'

I interject that he obviously hasn't done too badly since if his sumptuous Chelsea abode and his titled third wife are anything to go by. *Bumbo* and *Judas* must have obviously come up trumps. Sinclair looks slightly shifty. The groupie (who turns out to be his secretary) tops up his teacup. 'The two lightweight books you mention were both written in 4 weeks when I was 22 and I've been lumbered with them ever since,' he grumbles, nipping across a Persian carpet or two and seeking out a bulky Curriculum Vitae. 'If you cast an eye over this you'll see that there's much more to Sinclair than *Bumbo* . . .'

And how! The man must have spent his every waking moment 'extending his range'. Apart from the definitive work on prohibition, *The Era of Excess,* and biographies on Warren Harding, Che Guevera, Queen Victoria and Dylan Thomas, plus a pioneering study of the American Women's Rights Movement which was awarded the Somerset Maugham Literary Prize and struck off radical feminist reading lists because its author was a man, Sinclair has written stage plays, TV plays, a concise history of the United States, a thriller called *The Surrey Cat* ('as gripping as *Jaws*', *Sunday Telegraph*) and over 40 screenplays. There's also his latest book, *The Red and the Blue,* a compulsive and authoritative account of the tensions between open scientific inquiry and political restraint. And that's just the tip of the Sinclair iceberg. 'Oh yes, I've scribbled quite a bit since Cambridge,' Sinclair acknowledges, pulling up his Marks & Spencer socks above which an expanse of pallid shin is exposed. 'Mention my name and people always think of *Bumbo*, yet when I was 25 I wrote all Gaitskell's speeches, you know . . . I have always been, and still am, a loner. I rarely see any of my contemporaries unless I bump into any of them by chance, I've never been one to court publicity. I do my own thing, go my own way . . . thus nobody knows what I've been writing . . .' At this point Sinclair springs up, paces about the room and comes to a halt by the drinks cupboard. He fiddles tantalizingly with his cocktail shaker whilst holding forth on how he has written 'one wild,

I still believe in one all-inclusive love in which bed, brains, beauty and even boredom will all mix. I like to be totally involved with one woman. When I'm in love, I just want to be with that woman all the time. Promiscuity is a failure of romantic love . . .

ranting, romantic novel' called *Gog* ('67), and that this is the book he'd like to be remembered for. Handing me an extremely liberal gin he explains that *Gog* was written at a time when he was 'anti' the whole contemporary English literary tradition, and so he plunged impulsively into a 'bardic novel' dating back to Homer, a novel which Robert Nye in *The Guardian* called 'a randy romp'.

Speaking of which, and after Sinclair has knocked back a couple of swift vodkas, the conversation turns to sex. Sinclair, you sense (in spite of the crusty academic veneer) has been a bit of a lad in his time. 'Oh, how I've always hated D.H. Lawrence,' he begins, refilling our glasses. 'I simply do not understand his sexual feelings. The sex in his novels is farcical, ridiculous. . .' 'You must mean all that verbal foreplay and "tha's got a lovely cunt, lass" sort of thing?' I suggest, trying to picture Sinclair frolicking about in the woods, forget-me-nots entwined in the pubes, John Thomas at the ready and so forth. Not easy.

'Exactly, yes, the false feeling of folk love, and getting back to the loins of the race. I've parodied it all in *Gog* . . . You see, I'm a romantic. Like Bumbo, I still believe in one all-inclusive love in which bed, brains, beauty and even boredom will all mix. I like to be totally involved with one woman. When I'm in love, I just want to be with that woman all the time. Promiscuity is a failure of romantic love . . .'

Sinclair has started pacing again and waving his hands about a good deal. He looks as if he is about to shout 'blast my bollocks' or some similar upper-class expostulation. Then, without warning, he fixes me with a glittering eye and rasps: 'I'm no fool! Oh no. Your editor Auberon Waugh sent you round here to take the piss. And I can tell you why. I once slagged him off and he's still licking his wounds. He's as vulnerable as the next writer, despite his facetious veneer. The rift started when we were both young novelists and my notices were better than his. He immediately began taking swipes at me and nicknamed me "Jesus Sinclair". As a consequence I wrote a famous letter to *The Spectator* pointing out that everything he says is untrue, that he was miffed because I'd been more often compared to his father than he had, and that it is a sad fact that literary gifts often skip a generation . . . however, that was during my chippy days. I don't fire back any more even though he violently slagged my last novel.'

'Andy,' I say, slurring my words slightly, 'I don't give a toss about the ludicrous literary vendettas all you old fogeys wager amongst yourselves.' 'Quite right too,' says Andy, 'I think there's a certain virtue in being a loner and not engaging in literary wars. Most of those at the top spend their whole time going around influencing critics and giving readings and pushing themselves forward. My great friend William Golding never attends parties, has never consciously promoted himself, and yet he won the Nobel Prize. He won *unsolicited* support from a host of influential people, and that's how it should be. I've always loved him for being a loner. Ted Hughes is another one. He works and behaves like Heathcliff, he shuns publicity, avoids his fans, and yet he has been made Poet Laureate. I'm glad those two have got to the top spots. I think they both have true genius.'

We finish this interview listening to Andy's *Velvet Underground* LP. We discuss, with conspiratorial chuckles, a certain ex-Cabinet Minister who, Andy quips, was born with a silver spoon up his nose. 'A great line, Andy,' I say, 'a great line.'

The Red and the Blue (Weidenfeld & Nicolson, 1986).

Anita Brookner

All of my books are impossibly
romantic. And if I have an
overriding theme in my novels it
is innocence and what brings it
down.

I once bumped into Anita Brookner outside Waitrose. Recognizing her from her dust-jacket photograph, I was overcome. I began gushing and burbling fan-like things like 'Oh, it's Anita Brookner, *hello*, I thought that *Hotel du Lac* was brilliant, and I was ever so thrilled that you won the Booker prize . . .' while she stood uneasily shifting foot to foot, wide-eyed and fearful, like a trapped hare. 'Thank you. Thank you so much,' she said, and hurried away. I *did* feel a fool.

About a year later she suddenly sat next to me on a number 14 bus. 'I thought it was you,' she said, friendly as anything, and I nearly passed out with surprise. This time I refrained from gushing and burbling even though she is one of my literary heroines, *and* I have every one of her eight clever novels on my bookshelves.

We discovered that we were both going to buy something to wear for New Year's Eve. We got off the bus at the same stop. Brookner went into The Scotch Wool House where she planned to buy 'something tweedy and dull'. I went into Jane Norman where I bought a scarlet satin frock slashed to the thigh and rather inappropriate for someone of my advancing weight and years.

I was recalling the chance encounter when I rang the doorbell of Brookner's Chelsea flat. During a phone conversation the previous evening she had expressed alarm and consternation about being interviewed. She said that she finds it 'an ordeal', but she promised to do her best.

When she opened the door I was reminded again of the trapped hare. Brookner's enormous, intelligent eyes are her most striking feature. They gaze unnervingly into you rather than at you. You begin to imagine that she's probably thinking that you look a bit thick so you start talking too much and uttering banalities like 'terrible weather' or 'nice flat you've got' and 'isn't your garden looking green'.

'Nice flat you've got,' I say, sitting nervously down in a room which is serene, tidy and predominantly beige. Through the kitchen door I can glimpse a bed-sit sort of kitchen, with a forlorn-looking Baby Belling on legs. 'Oh, it's too small,' replies Brookner, scurrying into the kitchen and putting the kettle on. 'Only one bed-room. I long for another room. My dream would be to have a large house, full of family which I haven't got, and lots of children, and if I had that I'd never have written a single word.'

And *that* would have been a major loss to literature. Brookner's novels are un-putdownable. Her prose is elegant, concise, beautiful and spell-binding. Critics have described her as 'a writer of bewitching readability' and 'one of the greatest writers of contemporary fiction'.

The snootier, more pretentious elements of the London literati were rocked and shocked when someone so *readable* won the prestigious Booker Prize (1984). Brookner was pretty shocked too. When asked to describe her emotions that evening she reflects for several minutes before replying 'A primitive delight mixed with the know-ledge that it would rebound.

Let's get away from the simplistic idea that my novels may be read as autobiographical, *please*. I'm energetic, happy, not at all the miserable woman I've been made out to be by people who think I write about myself in my books.

'*Hotel du Lac* was an unpopular choice; a lot of people let me know that – oh yes – it was very hurtful.' She pauses to light a cigarette. She takes several thoughtful puffs before continuing. 'So I've been very cautious since then. I've made myself obscure. Nothing has changed in my life. The nicest thing of all was that my students were so pleased for me when I won.'

These students, however, at the Courtauld Institute of Art where Brookner is an internationally renowned authority on eighteenth-century painting, are soon to lose their tutor. She has decided, after 25 years, to give up teaching. She de-scribes how she recently woke one morning and thought 'this particular life is over. I've loved every minute of it, but teaching for me is finished. I might get another job. I might try charity work. I might do more writing. I hope so, but with twice as much time I'll probably do half as much work. I'd rather like to do a paper round.'

And if that sounds exactly like a Brookner heroine speaking you'd better not say so because Brookner gets rather impatient with such observations. 'Let's get away from the simplistic idea that my novels may be read as autobiographical, *please*,' she beseeches. 'I'm energetic, happy, not at all the miserable woman I've been made out to be by people who think I write about myself in my books. I *do* live alone. I would say that I'm not gregarious, that I receive more invitations than I accept, but this is largely because I'm pretty tired in the evenings. The so-called "Brookner-woman" has been exaggerated. The one thing all my characters have in common is that they are inexperienced in the ways of the world; I am certainly not.'

Brookner's latest novel, *A Friend from England*, is a skilfully crafted study of the rapport between two young women with nothing in common apart from a long-standing acquaintanceship. Rachel is worldly, hard-up, cynical and self-possessed. Heather is spoilt, silly, indulged and schoolgirlishly romantic. It says much for Brookner's skill that the reader becomes compulsively caught up in what are fairly humdrum lives and events. And, as with all Brookner's novels, sexuality permeates every page yet there are no sexually explicit scenes.

In this subtlety and restraint Brookner is reminiscent of that other great, passionate writer Colette, a fact that she acknowledges gracefully, smiling for the first time during our conversation, before replying: 'There is a misapprehension that women describing sex is attractive. It isn't. The best-selling sexually explicit blockbuster phenomenon is to do with money, nothing to do with literature. I long for a blockbuster that's also good writing – voluminous, satisfying and touching on all aspects of experience.'

When I try to encourage her to discuss *A Friend From England* she shrugs. She says that she dislikes both Rachel and Heather. 'I don't like Rachel because she's the sort who believes that you can have any man you want when you want and control the whole thing, which is, of course, an illusion. And I don't like Heather who allows herself quite passively to get married and is rather indiscriminating. The point of the book is the growing dislike they share for each other.' Each book takes about six months to write. When she finishes she feels 'glad to have got it over with'. She celebrates by going out for a long walk, then usually succumbs to a virus. As she explains: 'Being a writer is not a healthy way to live. I began writing fiction in 1980 without warning. When my first (*A Start In Life*) was accepted I was delighted, extremely happy.

... If I have an overriding theme in my novels it is innocence and what brings it down.

'All of my books are impossibly romantic. And if I have an overriding theme in my novels it is innocence and what brings it down. The interesting thing is that everyone loses innocence in a different way. It's nothing to do with sex, it's to do with morals. It's knowing whether or not to take a step which you feel is ill-advised, or even wrong. It's not only a problem for women, men have it too. You know, I'm finding this interview worse than a tutorial . . .'

What with her unease and my own fear of saying something crass, the tension in the room is almost palpable. I break an uncomfortable pause by remarking that she looks younger, smaller, softer in life than in her photographs. 'Good,' she says, smiling again, 'I'm doomed to look terrible in photographs. But I was plainer as a young girl, very plain. I could never get by on looks. I've always envied women whose appearance did the work for them.'

Getting up to leave I ask whether she remembers our meeting on the number 14 bus. 'Of course I do. What did you buy to wear?' I describe the scarlet frock which my daughter says makes me look like a barmaid from *EastEnders*. Brookner looks serious and says that she expects I feel terrific wearing it and that she, boring as usual, bought something tweedy and dull.

I say that I know it's a cheek for me to suggest it but I'd like to see her all glammed up for once in a scarlet dress, and what would she have done if I'd dragged her into Jane Norman and made her buy one. She reflects for several minutes, then replies: 'I'd have bought it, thanked you for your advice, and taken it back next day.' Which is *exactly* how a Brookner heroine would behave.

A Friend from England (Jonathan Cape, 1987).

A ^ N ^ N ^ A

F ˅ O ˅ R ˅ D

I don't think I want to talk about money.

W hen Anna Ford used to read the *News At Ten* I noticed that the male viewers in my household would gaze intently at her mouth and never take in one word of what she was actually saying. Wars were breaking out, nuclear reactors were leaking, mutilated female corpses were being dug up from shallow woodland graves, Ethiopians were starving, but all the male viewer was taking in was Anna Ford's perfectly asymmetrical features and her wide-apart eyes. Doe-like, it must be said, and yielding.

Anna Ford certainly had what it took to make male TV viewers sit up in front of their tellies and drool. When I went to interview her I paced uneasily about her sitting-room clutching my copy of her book *Men*, peering at gilt-framed oil paintings, family snapshots and political cartoons by her husband Marc Boxer, and wondered if she might think me trivial if I mentioned these matters. Outside, the Boxers' cherubic toddler stamped her tiny wellies, and from somewhere upstairs the famed Ford voice instructed 'Nanny' to organize a cup of tea for me. As 'Nanny' proffered milk and sugar, and shovelled smokeless fuel on the fire, I was also wondering how Anna Ford would react if I repeated the unkind things people are saying about her first book.

This work is being hyped by its publishers as 'a controversial and compelling work' in which Anna Ford 'pierces the masculine mystique'. However, in the pubs and wine bars where media folk and publishers hang out I have heard cynics snigger unkindly behind their hands and saying things like 'Oh Christ It's a load of totally embarrassing shit, and from someone who calls herself a *social anthropologist*, well, I mean . . .' and 'My *dear*, have you *read* it? Talk about *pathetic* . . .'

Before this interview I spent two days leafing through the book's 300 pages, studying the voluntary (edited) out pourings of 120 pseudonymous men. I also prepared a list of relevant interview questions along the lines of: Is modern man rebelling against the dominant role? Does he feel threatened by women's equality? Is traditional masculinity a myth?

I had been planning to fire away in-depth, but then Anna Ford herself, wide-apart-eyed and as stunningly beautiful as ever, strode across the kelim rugs wearing high red leather boots, and put me off my stride. She began chatting about motherhood, pregnancy and the new baby due in May and handed me a photograph of 3-year-old Claire who is, as Anna Ford explained with that thrilling intake of breath that used to send male TV viewers into a trance, 'a real Boxer through and through'. She was so disarming, so natural, so *nice*. How could I suddenly come on the heavy interviewer? How could I say 'Well, yes Ms Ford, but a lot of people are suggesting that you and your chums made up most of these "confessions" after a few drinks', or 'In some people's view, it's the rude bits that leave you open to accusations of leaping on the lucrative soft-porn band-wagon in the guise of "social research".' Instead, and forgive me for being such a wimp, I told her how charming her hair looked in its stylish new bob. We also discussed how a strategic rinse does wonders for the odd grey hair, and it wasn't until the conversation had meandered to the antique wood-panelling on Anna Ford's walls that I took the plunge and inquired whether it was true that she received a £60,000 advance payment for *Men*.

Anna Ford nibbled thoughtfully on a biscuit proffered by 'Nanny' before replying: 'I don't think I want to talk about the money. I will just say that the advance was far less than the figure you mention, and besides, the book actually cost me £16,000 to write, what with all the travelling expenses, research and secretarial fees involved over a period of three years.

'When my book was originally up for auction I accepted the highest figure I was offered. Naturally. I was slightly hurt to learn that people were going about saying "Why the hell should she get a vast advance never having written a book before?" But it would be silly for me to say to my publisher, "As it's my first book just pay me five pence," wouldn't it?' Anna smiled her imperturbable smile before adding that the rancour arose mainly because she's a woman. 'It's like everyone complaining about how much Selina (Scott) earns without commenting on the fact that Frank (Bough) earns double.'

She went on to explain how when she quit breakfast television she missed the 'buzz' and the 'adrenaline charge'. But her energies were soon deployed in completing *Men*, which arrived at the publishers a year or so late due to the birth of Claire and the TV–AM contract.

'I'd had the idea of writing a book about men some years ago. I was interested to find out about men beneath their layers of camouflage. I had a lot of experience of men – I grew up with 4 brothers, had lots of men friends, a few lovers, and I've worked exclusively in organizations run by men. **I don't want people to imagine that I wrote the book because I think men are awful. I don't. The book is the hardest thing I've ever done in my life.**

'Writing something that long was a tremendous satisfaction. It became an obsession. I'd have supper, then disappear to my study to edit the taped transcripts until 2 a.m. My husband was extremely supportive. One of my problems was that I collected far too much material and I had to cut out a lot of stuff I was really attached to.'

And there were setbacks. When she began interviewing her cross-section of English males (which included diplomats and dustmen, MPs and meths drinkers) four declined to take part. These were Denis Thatcher, the Archbishop of Canterbury, Sir Freddie Laker and Oliver Reed. They all wrote charming refusals apart from Oliver Reed. Denis Thatcher's was particularly sympathetic. And you can't help wondering what he will make of the Margaret Thatcher fantasies of several middle-aged men in Chapter 9. There's a 'well-known city figure' who admits that he finds the combination of Mrs Thatcher and her power 'quite tantalizing'. And a fifty-year-old security officer who muses 'She's not a cuddly woman. I used to think she was, but now I think you'd probably have to ask permission.'

Most of the men were extremely keen to have their 'masculine mystique' pierced by Anna Ford. As she explains: 'I interviewed men whose ages ranged from 18–94, from all socio-economic classes, at length on tape. I had no formal questionnaires, my idea was to encourage men to talk with "as little inhibition as possible" about the things they chose. *They* arranged the locations for the meetings, usually their workplace or a bar nearby, rarely at home. Some found it difficult to tell their wives about the interview, and in order to allow them to speak without fear of identification I promised to change all names and locations.'

One man who might have found it difficult to tell his wife about the interview is naughty old 'Clive' – a 26-year-old policeman, whose spicy revelations in Chapter 9 are of such a pornographic nature that the suspicion crossed my mind that he might have been having Anna Ford on. When I mentioned my hunch that Clive probably went back to the lads at the station after his session and sniggered 'Cor, strewth, I didn't half pile on the filth, talk about lead her up the garden path, laugh . . .?' she didn't so much as smile. She merely raised her finely arched eyebrows, gazed long and calculatingly at me and emphatically shook her head: 'I am utterly convinced of the authenticity of the tapes. When you are an experienced interviewer you know when someone is hoodwinking you. By just listening, by making absolutely no judgements, men begin to open up to you and say things that surprise even themselves.

'I am amazed when people suggest that the tapes are fantasies. Someone attacked me at a dinner party recently saying "Don't trust men, none of them have told you the truth, it's all a pack of lies" and so forth. But I *know* they were being completely honest. Many of them told me they had never talked so frankly before and I was astonished how many said "This has been very interesting, can we have another session." '

Maybe that's because they fancied her, I suggested, with a slightly bitchy sniff. Anna Ford sniffed, too: 'That's too obvious. Of course there were the ones that said "Give us a kiss, dear" ' but that's life. It happens to women all over the place. No. The men simply wanted another opportunity to pour out their deepest, most primitive feelings.' Here I was about to point out that Anna Ford, being *Anna Ford*, who was once nearly as big as Princess Di and Charlotte Rampling with the British male population, has certain advantages when it comes to interviewing. I wouldn't mind betting that many men's notion of heaven would be to pour out their deepest, most primitive feelings, whilst she sat listening sympathetically and making no judgements. But before I voiced these thoughts Anna Ford had turned solemn. What she was about to say was important, she said. Her three years' travail had taught her that with a few obvious differences men and women were much alike, human beings with similar talents, anxieties, capacities and failings. 'What surprised me most about listening to so many men talking about themselves was how completely insular they are, as a species, compared to women.

'Behind the facade, behind the pinstripe suits and the boilermakers' dungarees, are a lot of question marks and confusions. There is fear and worry, and often nobody to share it with. Many men lack the basic skills of communication in some important aspect of their lives, be it at work, at home, with others or with themselves. I was surprised by the sense of detachment that men can exhibit in their sexual affairs, surprised by the fact that men have just as many anxieties as women about their looks. I was also interested to discover that men are not yet used to independent women. One of the men I interviewed actually told me: "I wouldn't care to be married to a woman like you".'

At this point 'Nanny' came in with Claire to remind Anna Ford of a luncheon appointment. I took the hint. There was no time to suggest that 120 men out of England's total of 23,873,000 are, perhaps, rather few to provide any sound generalization about their sex. But I did just manage to ask Anna Ford whether she truly believed that our knowledge of mankind has been greatly enriched by reading about the factory foreman's propensity to break wind in public (p.50), by another's technique of prolonging bedroom performance by focusing his thoughts on what needs doing in the garden (p.143), or by the musings of a gay member of the House of Lords who used to think that women were 'totally different creatures – monkeys' (p.169).

Anna Ford did feel that such revelations are enriching in so far as they help us all to understand the effects of the dominant male, assumptions which underlie our society. She said that a re-evaluation of the masculine role would surely be as beneficial to some men as the feminist revolution has been to some women. Quite honestly, I don't know how she managed to keep a straight face.

Men (Weidenfeld & Nicolson, 1985).

I DON'T THINK MINE IS GREAT LITERATURE, BUT I DO THINK I'M AMONG THE WORLD'S BEST WRITERS OF POPULAR LITERATURE, IF NOT *THE* BEST.

BARBARA TAYLOR BRADFORD

You saw the mini TV series. You read the book. Now you can tackle the bulky, 542-page sequel to Barbara Taylor Bradford's *A Woman of Substance*. This eagerly awaited novel, *Hold the Dream*, is being hyped as 'one of the decade's most glamorous, most eagerly awaited publishing events'.

It is, according to Mrs Taylor Bradford's agent, 'more than a sequel; it is a powerful novel, tremendously moving in its own right'. And it will doubtless do its pulsating bit to ensure that Mrs Taylor Bradford retains her position as one of the three highest-earning novelists in the world.

Yes, but is it actually literature? This was the question I put to Mrs Taylor Bradford as we whizzed up in the lift to her luxury penthouse at London's exclusive St James's club.

The internationally acclaimed author, wearing a mink coat, several diamond rings and an asphyxiating perfume, smiled good-naturedly and replied: 'I don't think mine is great literature, but I do think I'm among the world's best writers of popular literature, if not *the* best. I don't mean this to sound arrogant, but people really do think my books are wonderful . . .'

She is only telling the truth. People are avid for her books. *A Woman of Substance* sold 11 million copies worldwide. It was translated into ten languages and became the world's fastest-selling novel. It earned Mrs Taylor Bradford a cool £1.5 million and her delighted publishers paid her an unprecedented $8 million advance for her next three books. Which is quite remarkable when you consider that it was Mrs Taylor Bradford's first novel, and she waited until she was 43 years old to produce it.

As we entered her penthouse suite, where the air was heady with the scent of a dozen ornate flower-arrangements, and sank into sumptuous sofas, I asked Mrs Taylor Bradford to reveal the secret of her astonishing success.

'I think people like my books because basically they are good entertainment, and that's what a popular novel is meant to be,' replied Mrs Taylor Bradford, in the sort of brisk, bossy, no-nonsense manner one associates with Margaret Thatcher. 'They also enlighten people a little bit, touch them, move them, and they have a good strong story which is, of course, the formula that made Dickens so successful as a popular novelist.'

Not that she compares herself to Dickens, she added modestly, but his books, too, were all rollicking good reads with a message. *And* they weren't full of tedious, explicit sex. 'Personally I can't stand all that sleazy sex. I write about feelings and emotions rather than the physical act. Sure, I *do* have scenes of sexual intimacy but they are the sort of scenes that my fans write to tell me are *beautiful* rather than steamy. We all know what people do in bed so there is no need for a writer to dwell upon vulgar details. I bring in sex where it is natural for it to occur between people. All right, my heroine Emma Harte did have numerous men in a sense, but she came out smelling like a rose . . .'

When I asked Mrs Taylor Bradford what it is like suddenly to find yourself successful and a multi-millionaire she paused. She patted her stiffly lacquered blonde hair, smiled and said that there was just one thing she'd like to make very clear. There was simply nothing 'sudden' about it. Far from it. She was a well-paid and highly successful Fleet Street journalist for several action-packed years until she met and married wealthy film producer Bobby Bradford, and moved to New York in 1964. Bobby, if Mrs Taylor Bradford's jewellery, furs and lifestyle are anything to go by, is certainly not short of a bob or two, and the royalty cheques fluttering through the letterbox of their Manhattan penthouse aren't, you gather, exactly crucial to the family budget.

'The fact is I was comfortably off anyway. I don't need to write to earn money. I've never written for money. But I do have to write for my own sense of well-being. If someone said, "You cannot ever write again," I'd go slightly crazy. Writing gives me a sense of satisfaction and fulfilment that nothing else gives me. It was Colette who said that love and work are the most important things in life, and I agree.'

She described her work-routine as 'fairly rigorous'. 'I'm always up early, after Bobby has brought me the cup of coffee in bed which is my one great luxury in life. I go to my desk at about 6.30 a.m. and write until 6 p.m. with two short breaks for snacks and to walk the dog. *Hold the Dream* took only a year to write, and after the first three months my routine became more intensive. I'd work from 5.30 a.m. until 7 p.m. Towards the end of the book I was getting up at 4.30. The pressure of getting the story told wouldn't let me sleep.

'I am utterly grateful to the understanding of my husband who knows that I must do this for my own peace of mind. A lot of men wouldn't put up with the life I lead when I'm writing.'

I don't need to write to earn money. I've never written for money. But I do have to write for my own sense of well-being.

She went on to explain that there is only 'so much' a person can do with money. She's always had jewellery. Bobby has just bought her a sensational diamond-and-ruby necklace. She's always had mink coats because Bobby wouldn't want the sort of wife who goes around in denim. She does, however, splash out on expensive evening clothes, her most recent purchase being an extravagant little silk dress and jacket by Fabrice which set Bobby back $35,000. In general the Bradfords' money is invested in stocks, bonds and real estate. And their penthouse apartment, of course.

Mrs Taylor Bradford showed me a copy of American *House and Garden* ('the magazine of creative living') featuring the Bradfords' 47th-floor penthouse in an article entitled 'A Glamorous Garret'. If the Georgian crystal chandelier, Italian linen walls, the Hepplewhite and the Hermes leather-lined bookcase are any indication, Mrs Taylor Bradford has come a long, long way from her native Leeds.

'I suppose so,' she agreed, patting the blonde hair again, laughing a trilling laugh,. 'But I'm still exactly the same person as I was when I married Bobby 21 years ago. Even though I've lived in New York for 20 years my Englishness is very deeply engrained. I'm still very English.

'I must make it clear that people are quite wrong to assume that the rags-to-riches theme of *A Woman of Substance* echoes my own life. I was never Emma Harte. I never scrubbed floors. Gracious me no. I came from a very middle-class home. I was an only child, very pretty, very spoilt, I had a great deal of love and attention. I was always scribbling in penny notebooks and at the age of 12 sold a short story to a children's magazine for which I received ten shillings and sixpence. Just seeing my own name in print thrilled me. I became hooked. I left school at 16 and became a cub reporter on the *Yorkshire Evening Post*; at 20 I went to Fleet Street and then became the fashion editor of *Woman's Own*.'

She said that she is 'very proud' of having worked as a journalist but that she always had this yearning to write a novel. She made several false starts, hiding them away in her filing cabinet after a successful novelist advised her, 'Don't try to write a novel until you're at least 35. You've got to live a little first. In the meantime practise by writing a thousand words each day.'

It was astute advice. In 1975, when she'd lived more than a little, she decided the time was ripe. She began *A Woman of Substance*, writing each chapter by hand, typing, editing, and rewriting for two-and-a-half years. It was, as she recalled, 'bloody hard work'. The finished manuscript was 1,520 pages long and weighed 16½ pounds. 'Thank goodness *Hold the Dream* didn't take as long. I've now tightened up my style a bit. There's less description. It's so much more pacey. And there's a *marvellous* love story in it . . . '

As she refused to give the plot away, allow me to whet your appetite by quoting from *Publishers' Weekly* which predicts that Mrs Taylor Bradford's latest work is certain to become another million dollar bestseller. 'At the centre of this spell-binding novel of ambition and betrayal, politics and power, passion and love is Paula McGill Fairley. Emma Harte's granddaughter and heir, Paula is married to a descendant of Emma's enemies. As Paula's struggle "to hold the dream" entrusted to her unfolds, we are taken into the world of the rich and privileged, to lush country estates, to the boardrooms of the powerful. Like Emma, Paula will capture the imagination of millions, mirroring as she does the contemporary struggles with ambition and success, with love and its loss . . .'

As Mrs Taylor Bradford pointed out, her fair, finely pencilled eyebrows meeting in a slight frown, it is very easy to sneer at romantic fiction, but sales figures indicate that this is the genre of literature that people actually want to read. She has certainly turned the writing of it into a commercial art. She added: 'I have grown quite accustomed to being mocked by the highbrows. I always tell my detractors that at least my books have a good sense of moral values, and that my heroines are strong characters in their own right which must be a good thing in these days of sexual equality. I write about women as survivors and achievers. Not victims. I'm sick of reading about poor, helpless females. You're only a victim in this life if you permit it.

I write about women as survivors and achievers. Not victims. I'm sick of reading about poor, helpless females. You're only a victim in this life if you permit it.

'I'm not exactly a feminist. I do think women are entitled to equal rights because women are not second-class citizens, but I can't abide these women's lib organizations. Those bra-burning militants drive me insane. They ought to read my books and see how the world really is.'

It can only be conjectured how the bra-burning militants might react to such passages as: 'Responding to her ardent kisses he ran his hand over her body, her hand went into his hair and he heard the faint moan in her throat . . .' (p.311), and 'Paula, Paula, I love you. Take all of me. All of my essence . . .'

Meanwhile Mrs Taylor Bradford revealed that she is already at work on the sequel to the sequel. The next sensational saga is already on the typewriter. 'It may be the North-country ethic in me,' she sighed, playing absent-mindedly with the diamond-and-ruby necklace, 'but I do have a strong sense of God. I always feel that He might very well strike me dead if I waste the talent He blessed me with . . .'

Hold the Dream (Grenada, 1985).

BOB GELDOF

*I realized there would be something
focking ludicrous about the sight of
a Nobel prize-winner hurling
himself round the stage with a
guitar.*

I had the privilege of meeting Bob Geldof back in 1983 when he was simply a Boomtown Rat and I had seen his star in the South East and had come to worship him. A newspaper had set up my visit to the Geldofs' medieval friary home in Faversham where the dazzling Paula Yates shoved a microwaved corn cob (Geldof grown) and a potato-in-its-skin under my nose and the effervescent Bob said 'You're focking welcome to stay the night'. I was entranced. He was so unstar-like. Love, of a Chernobyl intensity, radiated between Bob and Paula. When each walked the other's way a thousand lead guitars began to play. In the morning I was woken by Bob's flock of sheep bleating outside his mullioned windows and by Bob himself, like Albert Schweitzer on amphetamine, crashing in with a cup of tea and perching on the end of the spare bed in his shortie dressing gown to rage about injustice, bureaucracy, Apartheid, Mrs Thatcher and the 'focking slime' who write nasty items about Bob and Paula in *The Melody Maker*. I hung onto his every word. No flies on Bob. Later, he cooked me some toast and, at some point, threw a telephone across the kitchen.

Who could predict that 12 months later this anarchic Irishman would rally rock performers worldwide and inspire billions to raise millions for the starving people of Africa, that he would plead personally with world leaders for food and funds, and that he would tell Mrs Thatcher to pull her finger out with regard to the EEC butter mountain? Who could predict that his action-packed autobiography *Is That It?* would rocket to the top of the bestseller lists? A big hand for Bob!

'Parents and some other readers may find parts of this book offensive,' the publishers warn us on the book's dust-jacket. This must be a reference to page 248 on which the death agony of a starving Ethiopian boy is described. There is, of course, nothing more offensive and obscene than skeletal human-beings, their eyes clotted with blowflies, vomiting blood and intestinal tissue while we in the West guzzle on regardless ... However, easily offended readers may be relieved to learn that there are 247 pages to enjoy before they reach Ethiopia. We read about Bob's dismal Dublin boyhood, his cantankerous 'Da', the traumatic early death of his mother, and the manner in which he met his Magdalen at the age of 13 in the shape of 'Mrs Armstrong down the road' who pushed his jeans down to his ankles and told him afterwards that he was a 'good boy'. There follow Bob's battles with authority, his beatings, his masturbation anxiety, his habit of pinching money from slot meters, his way of smoothing his hair down with (shoplifted) Dippetty-Do hair gel, and then, the turning point, his discovery of The Rolling Stones: 'Suddenly my big mouth was acceptable. Suddenly my scruffiness became something to be emulated. The Stones looked and sounded like they were saying "Fuck you" to everything. They were my boys.'

For Bob there was no turning back. One suspects he has been saying 'Fuck you' to everything and everyone (apart from Prince Charles, and Mother Teresa and the starving Ethiopians) ever since. And like all aspiring rock stars he soon went to London, with his heart full of hope and his hair full of Dippetty-Do, to squat in Tufnell Park. Here he got into flared trousers, girls' sleeping bags, flower power, dope, LSD, anarchy, grew a Zapata moustache, hitch-hiked round Spain and Canada, got into rock journalism, got the clap, returned to Dublin and formed The Boomtown Rats. All this is rivetingly related in the book. Pow! Zap! Zoom! Bob hit the big time. You couldn't see him for angel dust. Or groupies. As he wryly observes: 'I had just become a pop legend and the world – and its legs – had opened up for me.'

However, along came posh pop-fan Paula (nicknamed The Limpet by Bob and the band) with her platinum punk hair do, eager to keep Bob's head screwed on while the Rats endured the death-defying hazards of gigging round the world. 'Japan: I had food poisoning and was on an intravenous drip until ten minutes before the gig . . . I came off half way through to be sick, went back on and collapsed afterwards,' and 'Bombay: with regret and diarrhoea I left the sub-continent.' Daughter Fifi Trixabelle was born. Bob saw a TV news report about famine in Ethiopia. The rest – Bob forcing the rest of the world to recognize famine and creating his Band Aid organization to relieve massive hunger – is world history.

For me Bob's autobiographical high-spots are his meeting with Mother Teresa ('I do not normally kiss strangers on a first meeting but it seemed like the right thing to do ... I found out later she only lets lepers kiss her'), his address to Strasburg Euro MPs when he tells them to 'fuck off back to school' and his conversation with the Prince and Princess of Wales in the Royal Box during the Live Aid concert at Wembley. Bob was wearing jeans with a broken fly he'd been wearing for a week. The Prince, Bob tells us, 'tapped his brogues spasmodically and clapped his hands hopelessly out of time'.

I don't want to talk about my book. I don't want to talk about the Band Aid thing. I'm keen to talk about my new album _Deep In the Heart of Nowhere_, that's all.

Impetuous, manic, Messianic, some say appalling, Bob Geldof is an unparalleled hero of our time. Yet he is a reluctant one. He is sick of all the fame and adulation.

Three years after our first meeting, I meet him again. This time in London. En route for his bijou terraced second home (worth half a million pounds if not more) in Chelsea, I was thinking how, as a consequence of his glory, the Boomtown Rat is now unable to jump anonymously onto a bus or nip quietly to the shop for a packet of fish fingers without having hundreds of admirers slapping him on the back, pumping his hand, thrusting money for Band Aid into his pockets and reaching out simply to touch his garments. 'Keep up the good work, lad' they entreat when all he really wants to do is jack in the good works and concentrate on being a rock singer.

All this he verifies as I enter a sitting-room cosily cluttered with Victoriana and toys belonging to Fifi Geldof. 'Call me Bob, none of this formal rubbish,' he says, hugging me and scratching the legendary stubble across my cheek in such a way that I suddenly understand how Mary Magdalen felt when she drew close to the wispy tickle of the Lord's beard. No wonder she anointed His feet with perfume. Speaking of which, Bob's own could do with a bit of anointing. Padding about as he is without any shoes, there is quite a noticeable whiff of sweaty socks. I mention this not as a criticism (far be it for me to cast the first stone) but to remind ourselves that Bob Geldof is but a mere mortal afflicted by the same mortal tribulations as the rest of us.

It kind of scares me that people may now be expecting only gravitas and integrity from me.

'I don't want to talk about my book. I don't want to talk about the Band Aid thing. I'm keen to talk about my new album *Deep In the Heart of Nowhere*, that's all,' begins Bob, sprawled across his settee and muffling the foot odour somewhat by pulling on a pair of black velvet slippers embroidered with scarlet roses, 'I'm kind of worried that after all the honours that have been heaped willy nilly on me people won't now accept me as a pop singer. The idea of doing a record again after so long a gap was nerve-racking. Without the Rats it was terrifying. A week may be a long time in politics but it's an infinity in pop. Haw. Haw.' He has a laugh like a cheerful donkey. I notice that his upper lip is afflicted by an open cold sore.

As he jerks his head back and forth – 'Haw. Haw' – I am struck by how young he looks. And exhausted. And thin. I resist an urge to say, 'What you need, my boy, is a nice milky drink, a plate of steak-and-kidney pud and a long holiday,' and inquire instead whether his new songs reflect his Ethiopian experiences. 'Not really. The prejudices I had before were just reinforced. Certain moods and atmospheres in these songs are without doubt a by-product of the last two years, but I don't write songs about starving children, for example ... This album came about because Dave Stewart from the Eurythmics said he'd be interested in doing something with me. He said, "Come to Paris where I'm mixing Mick Jagger's single" and I jumped at the chance because I think Dave's brilliant. I didn't know if I had any songs because my mind's been on organizational and logistical things for two years, you know?' I nod. 'So I said to Dave, "What if I want to sing 'Yummy yummy yummy I've got love in my tummy' sort of songs?" After all, what I sing now won't be much different from what I sang before. It kind of scares me that people may now be expecting only gravitas and integrity from me. Anyway, all my new songs came from bits and pieces I've been carrying round in my

mind for two years. I never write anything down, see?'

I nod again. I am beginning to feel like
one of those suedette dogs you see in
the back window of Ford Escorts, Nod,
Nod, Nod, as Bob goes on about Dave,
Midge, Daryl (who *are* those people?),
and his fear of having lost his credibility
in the fickle world of pop on the one
hand, and now losing the trust of establishment people who showered him
with accolade on the other.

I also have a very kneejerk reaction against anything I perceive as an institution. In that respect Mrs Thatcher and I have a lot in common.

'It has been very nice to be on the
receiving end of so much good will, but some people may
laugh out loud when they see me singing again and say
"Who's he trying to fool?" They might feel I've let them
down. I'm quite worried about it. Focking worried. I don't
want to let anyone down. But I must live my normal life
again, and for me that means being a pop singer.' He adds
that it was just as well he didn't receive the Nobel Peace
Prize. 'My being nominated struck me as bizarre, I wasted
no sleep over it – and that's not false modesty – I realized
there would be something focking ludicrous about the sight
of a Nobel prize-winner hurling himself round the stage
with a guitar at the Hammersmith Odeon. Haw. Haw. Haw.
An element in me knew that it would be better not to get the
prize because such an award carries a great deal of moral
baggage. A weight descends on one. I couldn't live up to it
or want to.'

Here Bob pauses, tentatively fingering his upper lip. He
remarks that he hopes I haven't noticed his cold sore. 'What
cold sore?' I reply diplomatically, turning the conversation
to recent suggestions that Bob's ultimate destiny lies in
politics.

'Oh no. Not in politics, I wouldn't want to become one of
60 voices subject to party whips telling me how to vote. You
have more chance of achieving things by kicking up a
focking fuss outside. I also have a very kneejerk reaction
against anything I perceive as an institution. In that respect
Mrs Thatcher and I have a lot in common. Change that to we
have *something* in common. Not a lot. Haw. Haw.'

Bob's discourse is peremptorily curtailed by young Fifi, a yo-yo in human form, who bounces in, hurls herself at Bob's legs, drags off his slippers, jumps on his lap, jumps off, does a backwards somersault and runs up and down the room several times before switching on the video. Bob's sock problem is making itself noticeable again. One thinks of Blake's 'And did those feet in ancient time' . . . Blasphemy. Fifi is collected by her nanny who takes her away for some lunch. Bob remarks that apart from his new album his chief passion is his family: 'It's very corny saying things like "My wife is brilliant, clever, fun and beautiful" and "My child's the most gorgeous thing there's ever been on this planet." But it's true.'

Picking up a pink plastic guitar belonging to Fifi, Bob twangs it thoughtfully and remarks 'I just hope that my new album will be judged on its own merit. I don't want people buying it because they approve of *me*. That would be patronizing. I thought they might do that with my book, but happily the reviewers said it was a good read. It's going to be on the A-level syllabus, by the way. Perhaps you'd better not write that down. It makes me sound like a focking creep writing a book suitable for sixth-formers' exams . . .' But then, like he said, he never *planned* to be a hero. He's always been a Boomtown Rat at heart. As he observes in *Is That It?* 'I've done as much as I am capable of doing. I will always try to avoid the cant and hypocrisy I loathe so much . . .' Suddenly, yes, Bob's big mouth is acceptable. Like Mrs Armstrong-down-the-road said, he is a good boy. Very good.

Is That It? (Sidgwick & Jackson, 1986).

B R I A N

P A T T E N

*All that 'being discovered' meant to me
was that poems of mine which had been
previously rejected suddenly became
publishable.*

Brian Patten lives in a west London basement with a black cat. He has extremely dark curly hair, murderous-looking eyebrows and the sort of intense penetrating blue stare that makes you forget to breathe. His Liverpool accent is irresistible. Not for nothing is he dubbed 'the pin-up poet' . . . Because he is *A Poet* and has been described by a *Times* critic as 'having the magic ability to run radiant imagination loose in the cities, streets and lonely bedsits of modern living,' you expect Patten, in the flesh, to be other-worldly and woe-begone. It comes therefore as something of a shock to find him cheerfully padding about his kitchen, doing mundane things like putting the kettle on, washing up two cups, and sprinkling Go-Cat into a rather filthy dish on the floor. There is a bottle of Jif on his draining-board. A packet of Daz. Something soaking in a bucket. Socks? Can you imagine Shelley washing his socks? Or Keats?

'I've just been burying a neighbour's cat in the communal gardens' says Patten, opening a 'fridge which is empty but for half a packet of margarine, one dessicated beefburger and a carton of milk. He sniffs the milk before pouring it into coffee mugs. '. . . she wanted it buried in an airtight plastic bag so that no dirt would get on it. I didn't like to upset her by pointing out how much more slowly decomposition takes place in an airtight plastic bag. One day in the future someone will be digging the communal garden, hit the cat and there'll be a gas-like explosion which will start off the second great plague of London . . .' When Patten laughs he gets crinkles round the eyes. Killer crinkles that might, one imagines, quite easily melt the susceptible heart.

Patten has published six volumes of poetry, four children's books, made numerous gramophone records of his readings, and written for stage, TV and radio. He is one of Britain's few genuine 'full-time' poets, earning his living entirely from his poetry and performances. In the space where it says 'occupation' on his passport he writes 'Poet' and he's not exaggerating. In his new collection *Love Poems* (Allen & Unwin) he composes rhapsodies and lamentations to the awesome bondage of human love. In an introduction, he explains that love colours every other human feeling, and that society brainwashes people into 'assuming that love is ours as an unassailable right so that we are thrown into anguish when we fail to find it'. He also believes that love-poetry 'helps us to understand and resolve these discords'.

Not that he's very keen to talk about it during this interview. 'The 'love-poet' label, he says, makes him sound like some morose, palely loitering wimp – on his brow 'anguish moist and fever dew' like Keats' knight in La Belle Dame Sans Merci. The *Liverpool Poet* label is just as irritating. Despite the fact that he left Liverpool in the 1960s it has been hanging round his neck like an albatross since he, Adrian Henri and Roger McGough appeared together in *The Mersey Sound* (1967) – a book that did for British poetry what the film score of Elvira Madigan did for Mozart. Suddenly poetry became *accessible*. It caught on. It captured the imagination of people who had previously thought poetry was posh or highbrow or only for aesthetes. For Patten (then 22 years old) *The Mersey Sound* meant panic: 'When it was about to come out I left Liverpool to avoid all the promotional razzmatazz. The media descended on Liverpool trying to get us to do readings and become part of the pop thing . . . I wanted nothing to do with publicity, I just wanted to write poetry.'

Not that the literary establishment was entirely impressed. Mersey verse came in for a great deal of castigation. 'The poets appear in drooping moustaches . . . but these merely emphasize the general mediocrity of the actual poems,' wrote one *Times Literary Supplement* critic. Stanley Reynolds spoke for all literary sceptics: 'The fact that the Liverpool people believe that *their* poetry is different from other bad poetry . . . does not make it so. Seven hundred and forty five thousand two hundred and thirty Scousers after all can be wrong.'

Reminded of these critical demolition jobs Patten shrugs. He points out that *The Mersey Sound* became the bestselling modern British poetry collection ever published, went into 12 reprints and sold more than 300,000 copies. It also had a triumphant, working-class ebullience greatly despised by aspiring Oxbridge poets. 'To be honest,' says Patten, lighting a strong-smelling cigarette, 'all that "being discovered" meant to me was that poems of mine which had previously been rejected suddenly became publishable. With the first bit of "recognition" I was able to escape from a very narrow, claustrophobic world, from a tiny house in a shabby street, the "slums" I suppose it would have been called then . . .'

Patten's work is included in the *Oxford Book of Twentieth Century Verse* and the Penguin Modern Poets Series. When a *Guardian* writer once patronizingly described one of his earlier collections as 'sensuous, erotic, intellectual even . . .' you can imagine how the scouser who left school aged 15 must have given way to a private, triumphant chuckle at the word 'intellectual'. About his education he recalls: 'I was in the C-stream at school, very late learning to read and always struggling three Beacon readers behind everyone else. I came from a bookless home. Can't remember my father, my mother was never a great one for books. I send her all my books when they come out and she keeps them on the mantelpiece like Christmas cards. I still can't spell. One of my poems was set for the GCE O-level paper. The question was "Why has the poet misspelt the word 'heared' ". I couldn't understand what the question was about at first. I'd spelt it wrong because I can't spell. And the book's editor hadn't noticed the mistake. Goodness knows what the kids made of such a question . . .'

He recalls that his first job, as junior newspaper reporter, involved 'doing write-ups about juvenile delinquents, boy scout's meetings and interviewing girls with holes in their hearts. When I was doing reporting I bought my first typewriter. I'd never been so proud of anything in my life. I left it at home on the floor and someone peed all over it. A while later I sold it to Adrian Henri.'

He began writing poetry, helped set up an alternative magazine in Liverpool at a time when pop music and poetry were fusing with exhilarating novelty, and published the then 'underground' poets Adrian Henri and Roger McGough. In the seventies Patten had a reputation for attracting poetry groupies to his readings. In fact you suspect that a track is still beaten to the London basement. However, casting a speculative eye round the bathroom you'll notice no signs of current female occupancy. No tell-tale drying tights, no hair-pins, no nail-varnish bottles. You also suspect that a hedonistic past inspired such lines as '. . . and bending here you are naked/wind from the half open skylight hardens breasts/Your blond hair falling is spread across me . . .' Although, as Patten reminds you, his poems are not autobiographical. 'No way,' he says, taking several long drags on the aromatic cigarette, 'never confuse the "I" in a poem with the poet who wrote it. These days I look back to some of my earlier work and think to myself "I couldn't write that now", but I don't dismiss the person who did write it. I believe that all poetry is a map of the emotions.'

> These days I look back to some of my earlier work and think to myself 'I couldn't write that now', but I don't dismiss the person who did write it.

Fidgety and restless, he doesn't sit still for long. He'll be back with you in a minute, as soon as he's nipped out for some more cigarettes. As soon as he's made more coffee. As soon as he's let the cat in. You get the impression that interviews are a tribulation. So, too, are people who use his work (occasionally without his permission) in anthologies: 'Jilly Cooper annoyed me when she included my poem *Party Piece* in her book *The British In Love*. ('Let's stay here/And make gentle pornography with one another . . . So they did/There amongst the Woodbines and Guinness stains' etc). Instead of finding beauty in the mundane which is the intention of my poem she saw only squalor. I am now powerless to explain to everyone who accepts her misinter-pretation that she got it all wrong . . .' Scowling, he asks whether I mind if he plays his Rolling Stones album to cheer things up. The Stones take him back, he says. And the Beatles, too. In fact he felt washed out for a week after Lennon's murder.

Lennon he reckons must have felt suffocated by adulation. Even 'small-scale' poets like himself get pursued – get phone calls, letters, bright-eyed enthusiasts begging for autographs after readings. He recalls one such admirer, a lonely homosexual who wrote to him praising his work. For 15 years a sporadic correspondence evolved. The men never met. Recently he was extremely moved to receive a final thoughtful letter explaining that fatal illness urged his fan to return the entire correspondence in case it was found after his death and false assumptions were made.

One topic that Patten avoids, even dodges, is the writing of poetry. 'The ideas come in flashes' he explains uneasily, 'something sparks off a line or a fragment . . . it's an act of self-discovery . . . ya-know-warr-I-mean. . ?' Well, no you don't, but you catch yourself thinking that Robert Nye's description (in *The Guardian*) of Patten's work as 'taut, beautiful and exact' rather well describes Patten himself. You also find yourself reconsidering Grevil Lindrop's review which claimed that Patten holds large audiences spellbound at readings not only because of 'the enormous passion' with which he reads but also because of a suspicion 'that at any moment he may be going to pick a quarrel with someone'. Tales are told on the poetry circuit that he has butted people on the chin with the black curly head. More than once. Nevertheless you still wouldn't mind bumping into him on a dark night.

More coffee is made. In the kitchen the cat clamours. You get the feeling that it is better fed than its owner. The same poet famed for such lines as 'We have translated each other into light/And into love go streaming' opens a tin of Co-op cat food and says: 'In my recent poems I seem to have become preoccupied with loss, "shades of the prison house" closing round the senses. The dulling of emotion scares me more than the physical ageing process. That was Stevie Smith's great quality, she retained a childlike wonder into old age.' Did he know Stevie Smith? 'Yes. Stevie was a great woman. She was with me on my first ever plane flight. I was terrified. After a safe take-off I leant back with a sigh of relief and she tapped me on the shoulder and said "it's the landing you have to worry about, Brian".'

The killer crinkle again. The demonic gleam in the eyes. Your stomach lurches. 'Nice things have been happening lately,' he says, foot tapping in time to the Rolling Stones album which is still pulsing away in another room. 'I was watching the floor show where a stripper had been performing. She came up to me afterwards and said she'd read my poems at school and thought they were smashing. She was a very classy stripper, an ex-ballerina who'd got too tall for the corps de ballet . . . recognition like that means everything to a poet.'

Love Poems (Allen & Unwin, 1984).

I've been writing for 25 years, 80
books, a lot of them non-fiction, and
none of the Literary bods has ever
been near me. Why?

Claire Rayner

What is the opposite to a shrinking violet? A bloated peony? A swollen rhododendron? Whatever it is, it describes Claire Rayner. Boisterous, ebullient, effervescent as liver-salts, she is certainly not the sort to interview if you're feeling depressed. I met her at the Michael Joseph office in Kensington after spending two terrible hours in C & A's changing rooms. How ignominious it feels to have one's frayed knickers and flab exposed to sniggering, unsisterly scrutiny in the brutal glare of fluorescent lights. How mortifying to be obliged to acknowledge that what was once size 10 is now 14.

In mild shock I arrived at Michael Joseph, where Claire (a reassuring size 20 if ever I saw one) pumps my hand, drags me onto a sofa in an extremely public corridor, and bursts forth with an astounding torrent of chat: 'So why is *The Literary Review* interested in me all of a sudden? Hey? Hey? I've been writing for 25 years, 80 books, a lot of them non-fiction, and none of the Literary bods has ever been near me. Why? I obviously made no impact. Don't think it doesn't hurt. It's one of my beefs that when my books land on their desks Serious Reviewers (here she wiggles her fingers in the air miming quotation marks) say to themselves sterotypically, "This is by that Agony Aunt woman", and then don't even bother to open it. But my books sell. They sell well. The readers love my books, bless 'em. They send letters saying "Dear Claire Rayner. I hate you. Your book kept me up till 4 a.m. Why aren't your books on telly? When's the next one coming out?" My beef is this. Why should literary types assume, damn cheek, that an Agony Aunt can't write reasonable prose, and construct reasonable characters, and interesting stories? A skill is a skill is a skill, I say. I get quite bothered by the thunderous silence of critics. Not so much bothered, as *irritated*. Only one reviewer mentioned my last novel, slamming it and ending up "of course, she's very readable". I thought "you squirt" . . .'

My mouth is hanging open. I tell Claire to hang on a moment while I get out my notebook and breathe on my biro to warm it up. I beg her to slow down. I explain that I'm recovering from a trauma, having just got my backside stuck in a pair of jeans. Don't expect sympathy from an Agony Aunt. She throws her hands in the air, inhales through mobile nostrils, and lambasts: 'Life's too short to be worrying about the size of your arse, *bottom*, I should say, do put *bottom*, Val, I don't want to come across as coarse. I don't give a damn about my bottom. I hate being defined by my size. I don't see why I should look as if I've been squeezed out of the same toothpaste tube as everyone else. The awfullest thing people ever said to me was, "My, you're a big girl for your age". I was. I am. Loomed over everybody else as a teenager. Knew every bald patch in London. Now I've come to terms with my size. I'm 57, I cannot be doing with people who lie about their age. I swim half a mile every morning. I'm deeply puffed up about it. People are wrong to assume that middle-aged women are only interesting if they're fizzy with oestrogen. Oh dear. I *know* what you're going to write. You'll put that you walked in and this wretched woman came down on you like a ton of bricks. Shut up, Rayner. I never shut up, that's my problem. Verbal, that's me. Acute logorrhoea. Just because I'm paranoid it doesn't mean you're out to get me. Ho hum. Old joke, that one. But very apt. Excuse me. May I kiss two rather nice men . . .'

> One thing that makes steam come out of my ears is people who waste my time. Life's too short to push dirt from one place to another. It's a long time since I did housework.

Here Claire sprints across the room and hugs two Michael Joseph employees who are wearing striped shirts and nervous smiles. 'Are you well, Roger, love?' booms Claire, 'bless him. Kiss, Kiss.' Roger, looking panicky, congratulates Claire for just having been voted the second most popular woman in Britain. From behind a partition someone calls 'Felicity Kendal came first. Shame!' Don't mind me, I feel like saying, sitting here a suicidal wreck, I'm only supposed to be doing an interview. I'm only supposed to be asking penetrating questions about Claire's prolific output and phenomenal success as an author.

Would John Fowles's publisher stick him in a draughty corridor for an in-depth interview? Would J G Ballard's? Just as I am about to voice my complaint Claire is off again at full throttle: 'Second most popular woman? I'm embarrassed. Gobsmacked. It's bloody ridiculous. It's a terrible responsibility. It saddens me that women say "I want to look like you, booby-do". They must learn to look inside *themselves*. I think they admire me because I live by the rules that I'm going to be what I am, do what I want, and if you don't like it, it's too bloody thing . . .'

Phew. Struth. As Claire bangs on a secretary arrives with cups of tea. 'No milk. No sugar', says Claire. She sips. I sip. When I whisper that mine is too strong she grabs it, chucks it over a pot plant, winks and declares, apropos of nothing as is her way: 'One thing that makes steam come out of my ears is people who waste my time. Life's too short to push dirt from one place to another. It's a long time since I did housework. Delegation, that's my secret!' The pot plant is made of silk. Tea drips from its imitation leaves. Claire jiggles her eyebrows. I leap in with my first question, and ask Claire to describe her latest novel, *Maddie,* described in the blurb as 'a racy and compelling novel set in London and New York about Maddie, blinded by her passion for Jay. Heedless of all warnings and oblivious to the cost, her hate becomes as strong as her love.' When I tell Claire that I'm on page 30 and finding it gripping she nods energetically. 'Readers do get gripped, bless 'em. I wanted to write a zonking great melodrama using the Medea theme. Jason of the Argonauts always struck me as an outsize wimp. *Maddie* is the story of a woman horribly tramelled by being a woman. it's also about obsessive love. A dreadful thing, obsessive love, as I've learnt from my readers, bless 'em. It's also about mental hospitals. They are a disgrace. It frightens the socks off me the way they are closing down. I used to be left-wing. Now I'm just an angora jumper – pink and woolly. Not original that one. Bad habit of mine, always quoting. But I'm moving left again. I had a go at Mrs Thatcher in print again this week. I get bitterly angry with a society that says the only ones who matter are the achievers. I might be in the top tax bracket but that doesn't stop me feeling disgusted with the budget. Guess how much of my income comes from books? No? You can't? 75 per cent. All my radio, television, journalism, lecturing, odds and sods mount up to a titchy 25 per cent. Books is where the money is. Ever since the Public Lending Right started I've been in the top band. When

Brigid Brophy and Maureen Duffy fought for PLR I kept my head below the parapet. I was concerned that it might adversely affect library users. I love libraries. The smell is wonderful. I learnt to read when I was three. Yes, I'm one of those I'm afraid. I write because I'm deeply, deeply nosey. Got a head like a ragbag. And I write *fast*. I bang it all down. Each novel takes four months. In the bath, in the loo, amazing how much plotting you can do . . .'

My second question is about explicit sex scenes in popular fiction. 'Sex?' bellows Claire, before I've even finished my question, 'there's always some sex, love. I hope it's real sex. My novels are not the inwardly, outwardly, downwardly, thrustingly sort. That's from *Seven Year Itch*, not original. I don't write the trembling inner thigh stuff. Ho hum. It gives me the giggles. I'm all for the erotic but bored by the titillating. I always say my only sexual problems come in envelopes. Agony Aunt letters, bless 'em. I love 'em all. I like to think I write like J.B. Priestley. He wrote zonking good stories. Howard Spring, marvellous. Daphne Du Maurier, terrific. That one she did about incest, what's it called? Can't remember. Anyway I thought to myself, no-one is going to be able to do it again, she did it to perfection.'

Roger, in the striped shirt, is hovering by the sofa. I think he has heard the sound of dripping tea and noticed the tannin-tinged leaves. He mentions that Claire is not an exclusively Michael Joseph author. 'Dear me, no,' roars Claire, 'I'm a bit of a tart literature-wise, I'm also with Weidenfeld, Hamlyn, Hutchinson . . . I'll have to leave shortly, Val, love. I've got to go and record a talking book at the BBC.'

She stands, helps herself to a dozen or so books, crams them into a bulky bag, taps her nose and remarks: 'I scrounge hardbacks. I make no secret of the fact. I reckon an author's perks are free books from her publisher.' She suddenly looks very much like her Spitting Image. When I tell her so she rolls her eyes and bellows: 'I haven't ever seen it. I'm not daft. The first time I knew I was on I went to bed with a book. But it gave me my best gag of 1988. Three weeks after Messrs Fluck & Law put me on their show, *Ronnie Barker*, bless 'im, got in touch to ask whether I'd mind if he impersonated me on *The Two Ronnies*. I'd much rather be Barkered than Flucked, I told him. Boom boom.'

Maddie (Michael Joseph, 1988).

DAVID BAILEY

This country is run
by bloody writers,
distorting facts,
making false
interpretations.

*I*f you have a copy of David Bailey's book *Nudes (1981–1984)* loitering to one side amongst the colour supplements on your kitchen table it excites all kinds of fervent and unsolicited responses. Such as 'Wor! Kinky bastard!' (Uncle Stan), 'Bloody waste of fifteen quid, if you ask me' (gas meter reader), 'Vile, woman-hating muck' (my friend Beryl), 'Looks like police photos of murder victims' (my son). The man from Curry's TV Rental arrears department looked through *Nudes (1981–1984)* cover-to-cover, twice, and raged: 'Cor, strewth! The geezer who took these disgusting pictures ought to be put away. Bleedin' headcase.' Ron the milkman took a long look and grumbled: 'What a blinking rip-off. No split beaver!' No split beaver? Do us a favour, Ron, this is a *work of art*. This is a work which according to the famed photographer's publicity person, 'constitutes a major new collection in which Bailey uses nudes to achieve a Goyaesque effect, one of his themes being ways of wrapping up women . . .'

Turn the large, glossy, sepia pages and you'll see nude women wrapped in bandages, latex, laundry bags and cooking foil. One is manacled with tinsel, another has a garter of barbed wire spiking her thigh. One woman, wearing just black stockings and suspenders, has her head wrapped in a balaclava (Ron the milkman quite liked this one), another is strapped by bandages to a bench and masturbates contemplatively in a room full of filing cabinets. A third, with her head shrouded in a sack, is about to tuck into two fried eggs and a rubber dildo.

In short *Nudes (1981–1984)* is, you could say, an example of violent pornography against women. In my view it could be said to expose a crazed, psychopathic imagination at work, and I was plucking up the nerve to tell David Bailey just that as I waited for him in his Primrose Hill house hallway with his dog sniffing round my legs and his parrots squawking from some far-off upstairs room. 'You ought to sock him in the gob, Val,' my friend Beryl had urged when I told her I was going to interview him, 'You tell him! Don't let the sadistic, trendy bugger get rich by exploiting the female form.' As I sharpened my biro for the kill, David Bailey himself, khaki-clad like an extra from *Mash*, poked his head round the door and said 'Hi Toots'.

Toots? *Toots*? I was livid. It was like pouring petrol on smouldering coals. I came on all supercilious and scathing. No messing about with this one. 'Well, I've looked at *Nudes (1981–1984)*, Mr Bailey' I snapped, my dignity dented somewhat by the dog that was still sniffing my legs, 'and it's my impression that the man who took these photographs *hates* women, he *enjoys* torturing, humiliating and inflicting gross indignities upon them . . .'

Bailey grinned, flashing fabulous white teeth. Those teeth were my downfall. 'Nah, just the opposite,' he replied, several cats streaking out of our path as we entered his studio,' And there's no need to call me "Mr", people just call me "Bailey".' Sensing he was certainly not the sort you'd call 'Dave' I hesitated and told him that I'd feel overfamiliar calling him 'Bailey'. It struck me as a bit pretentious like calling someone 'Shakespeare' or 'Picasso' or 'Christ'. Or, indeed, it was as awkward as being introduced to someone fat and horrible who insists that everyone calls him 'Binkie' and you can't possibly bring yourself to do so. Bailey chipped in to say that he didn't think 'Bailey' was in the least like 'Binkie' and what in God's name was I going on about. Grimly I steered the conversation back to Art.

'To return to the vile, mutilated images of women in your new book . . .' I began, as Bailey swigged Diet Pepsi straight from the can, looked disgruntled, bored even and replied: 'I haven't got much to say about my book. It's difficult putting words to a book like this one, that's why there aren't any words in it. I'm a photographer for Christ's sake, not a writer. You don't go up to Graham Greene and ask him to explain what his books are about by taking photographs of them do you? As soon as you put words to an image that image is altered. Look, if you see a picture of an old man with a pair of NHS glasses on the end of his nose, chiselling away at a bit of wood, you think, "Aah, sweet old bugger, it's Gippetto carving Pinocchio". But if someone writes a caption underneath it saying "A rare photograph of Adolf Eichmann" the image is totally changed.

'This country is run by bloody writers, distorting facts; making false interpretations . . . last week an Irish reporter turned up and I just happened to mention that when I was

All those big titties and stocking-top books have no message, no feeling, they're much more exploitative of women than my books . . .

photographing the Kray twins I had to keep reminding myself what horrible gangland killers they were because when I was with them they were great company, a laugh-and-a-half – just as Hitler was also reckoned to be a bit of a card, and I told the Irish reporter that he, too, was always considered to be the life-and-soul of a party. So what happens? Her article appears in the Irish Press headlined: "David Bailey says Hitler was a great bloke." It irritates me that a visual artist is always expected to explain himself in terms of *words*, he shouldn't *have* to, the reason I'm an image maker is because I'm explaining myself with images . . . here, I don't half like those sexy shoes you're wearing. Where d'you buy them?'

'Dolcis. £24.95,' I replied, having regrettably been caught off guard, disarmed by the white teeth. 'Wor! I go for pointed toes! Not half! They're the sort of shoes you can kick snakes up the backside with . . . anyway, about my book, I tell you this much, it's not meant to be entertainment. It's meant to provoke *thought*. There's a bloody big difference between entertainment and serious statement.'

Here I suggested, a trifle brusquely, that the thoughts it provoked were surely sadistic ones, and that maybe only *he* could define whatever 'serious statement' he is making with his collection of grotesquely spreadeagled, wrapped-up, victimized women. Bailey grumbled that his 'statement' was obvious to anyone with a shred of intuition. 'It's about women's lives, about love, car accidents, childbirth, sex and death.' Even the nude with the feathers stuck all over her naked body and an ostrich egg under her arm? 'Yes. That's right. You might have seen similar images in Hieronymus Bosch paintings, in Goya's war atrocity sketches, in Renaissance paintings of Christ being unwrapped after the crucifixion – the bandages are, of course, allusions to the shroud, and the nude standing in the sea with two dead fish hanging round her neck was inspired by Botticelli.'

Botticelli? Christ? Give over. I looked Bailey straight in the eye and suggested that *Nudes (1981–1984)* is, in fact, pornography posing as Art. It is just one more in a spate of glossy photographic publications suddenly flooding the bookshops in time for Christmas. It is in the same titillating category as David Hamilton's tacky, soft-focus *Dreams of a Young Girl* (Collins) and Bob Crichton's *Photographing Women* (Macdonald) in which Crichton asks 'What are the best ways of photographing female curves' and reveals the secret by means of provocative, full-frontal females posing in G-strings, camiknix, and wet T-shirts. On page 61 one of Crichton's photographed women takes a shower with a metal shower fixture between her thighs, and on page 130 a girl in a transparent leotard raises her right leg in the air, wisps of pubic hair bristle around the edges of her leotard gusset, and Crichton, in what the publicity blurb refers to as the 'clear and absorbing text', enthuses how 'the popularity of keep-fit routines has opened up a new market for glamour photographers'.

Bailey said that he hadn't seen Crichton's book. That he hates those glamour pictures anyway. 'All those big titties and stocking-top books have no message, no feeling, they're much more exploitative of women than my books; mind you if girls want to pose for them I'd never set myself up as a censor. I expect you're going to ask me next whether my models minded being wrapped in bandages? The answer to that one is not at all. They're all my friends, I wouldn't make anyone do anything they didn't want to.

'If I was a homosexual the models would probably all be men: these nudes are certainly not meant to be sexual, or erotic. All my work is autobiographical. I believe there's a collective visual gene bank shared by all of us, it surfaces in different people, how else can you explain a Blake or a Picasso? And Picasso never justified his paintings to journalists, he had the right answer, all right. He just said "Nobody questions the song of a bird . . ." '

I was growing alarmed. I hadn't managed to get in a snide remark or a reprimand for over 5 minutes. What was happening? I was beginning to succumb to Bailey's baggy-eyed charm, that's what was happening. The feminist in me was faltering reprehensibly before this Living Legend who has the world's most beautiful women slavering at his plimsolls. Forgive me, Beryl. I blew it. He was getting the upper hand. Definitely. A few seconds more of his charismatic conversation and I would have been begging him to wrap me in bandages, or cling-film, or spray me with liquid latex, to garland me in barbed wire, to hang dead fish round my neck ... ooh! The thought of it! Sorry Beryl. Pulling myself together in the nick of time I glowered at the man whose theme is always of wrapping up women and retorted 'Viewed from a feminist perspective your book is both shocking and vaguely obscene'.

'Cor Blimey,' snorted Bailey, putting his dog on the lead, 'I've been waiting for the feminists to start having a go. If you lot insist that *my* work degrades women, all I can say is go and have a look at what *female* artists are doing to women, and to men.'

So saying he handed me his copy (purchased that morning from the Arts Council shop) of *Female Artists* compiled by Nicholas Treadwell. Flicking quickly through, 'The Abortion' by Denyse Willem caught my eye. This was an acrylic on canvas painting of a woman wearing fetishistic high-heeled button-up boots, but otherwise naked, sitting spread-legged and pushing a knitting needle into her vagina. Equally eye-catching was 'Framed Figure' by Mandy Havers (leather and mixed media) of a male torso (minus head, hands and lower limbs) strapped by leather and metal springs to something resembling a sunbed frame, the skin of his belly peeled back and his genitals vulnerably a-dangle. 'Study for Kenneth B' by Cathy Fenwick (resin and mixed media) made an instant impact, too. It depicted a mangled, bloodstained, hermaphroditic torso, minus lower limbs, arms and head, dumped inside an open cupboard.

Yes. Well. These works of art made me feel like kicking a few snakes up the backside. As Bailey remarked there's no denying that these pictures by women all seem to be making violent, sadistic statements. What more could I say? Apart from 'Nice one, Bailey. Shame about the bandages. And shall we go down the pub for a quick drink?'

'Nah. No Thanks,' said Bailey, idly peering at a spool of negatives, 'I don't drink. I don't smoke. I've been a vegetarian since I was 12.' So was Hitler.

Nudes 1981–1984 (Dent, 1984).

Something that did surprise us is that women are becoming keen porn consumers as well as purveyors of porn.

David Hebditch & Nick Anning

David Hebditch and Nick Anning know more about hard-core porn than any other men in Britain. If not the *world*. For two-and-a-half daunting years these stalwarts have roamed red-light districts, delved into dirty mags, watched porn performers in action, pursued porn barons and baronesses, and snooped behind the windowless doors of massage parlours worldwide. From water-beds to peepshows, deep throats to shallow storylines, Hebditch and Anning have meticulously ex-amined the ins and outs of the hard-core porn industry. And all this vigilance has been in the cause of research.

Their resulting bulky book *Porn Gold* ('A startling inves-tigation into the $5-billion world trade in hard-core porn') blows the lid off the porn biz and reveals how modern technology and changing legal and social attitudes have turned porn into the world's biggest, most profitable indus-try.

Sensational fact! Sensational book! And a sensational way, if you ask me, for two solemn academic researchers to spend two-and-a-half years of their lives. Are they porn mad? Or merely serious investigators engaged on a socially relevant project? In fact, the prospect of meeting them in the flesh is somewhat intimidating. One imagines that after such a superabundance of porn Hebditch and Anning have become depraved-looking, steeped in vice, twitchy, with bloodshot eyeballs and dirty raincoats. Not at all. They both look as wholesome as compost-grown greens. They have that casual mode of dress (bomber jackets, track shoes) and head-nodding, eye-contact way of conversing that one associates with trendy social workers, Jehovah's Witnesses or SDP candidates.

It is quite difficult to imagine this homely-looking pair nosing around sex shops and sitting stiff upper-lipped, gritted teeth, through endless videos with titles like *Born Erect*, *Don't Get Them Wet*, and *Kinky Adventures of Casanova*.

Hebditch (41) has one child and lives 'in a stable rela-tionship'. Anning (46) is a father of three, 'divorced but I see my children on a regular basis'. They insist that the women in their lives felt few qualms about the nature of their project but drew the line at practical research.

'We would like to emphasise that we're not dirty old perverts who've suddenly decided to cash in on it,' says Anning. 'When we started our research we knew next to nothing about porn. Like most people we would have said Page Three girls and blue movies are pornography but if you call them that then you've run out of words to describe the real thing.

'Mention porn and everyone thinks of seedy Soho, cellophane-wrapped girlie mags, flickering projectors in smoky back rooms cranking out smutty images. The porn scene is just not like that any more. Nowadays there's no discernible porn trade operating out of Soho. Porn has become a highly structured international business controlled by wealthy people who have entered the ranks of commercial respectability.'

Hebditch chips in here, stabbing the air with his cigarette and gravely pursing his lips. 'Furthermore 90 per cent of hard-core porn is produced, distributed and sold *unhindered by law*. The vast majority of British people don't realise that throughout the rest of the world porn has become a thriving, above-board business.'

This fact may appal you. Or it may make you want to kick your feet in the air. That's the problem with porn. Is it vile and disgusting? Or is it a fun way to liven up our leisure hours? According to Hebditch and Anning, whenever porn is mentioned we British, with our sexual hang-ups and inhibitions, are incapable of rational discussion. They claim that the British Isles remains the last bastion of sexual censorship. Despite the fact that the porn industry proliferates worldwide due to popular demand, people like moral majority groups and Mary Whitehouse are determined to suppress it here.

Maybe they have a good point, you are thinking? So am I, and a right party-pooper I feel too. Hebditch and Anning, having sussed which side I'm on, are looking definitely jumpy.

So I pipe down, decide instead to let the experts bang on uninterrupted. Their demeanour is glum. In fact they look downright mopey when I mention having found *Porn Gold* rather heavy-going, not quite the sizzling shocker one might expect from its title. So let us allow them to get things off their chests and justify their hunch that Britain ('a quaint backwater with repressive porn laws and puritan attitudes') will soon be dragged by the rest of the world into the porn-pervaded 21st century. Sit up, open your eyes and think of England . . .

Hebditch: Neither of us feel defensive about our work. OK, we take an impartial stance. We haven't *judged* any of the pornographers we interviewed, we haven't taken a moral viewpoint and that might leave us open to criticism. We have simply allowed the pornographers to speak for themselves so that the readers can form their own judgements. I have to say that we met some delightful people. We also met a lot we would not invite home to dinner but they were in the minority. When we deal with such topics as sadism, bestiality, snuff movies and child porn we describe the material as little as possible. It doesn't need us to tell the reader that these things are disgusting. There is no way that anyone is going to become a convert to the idea that child porn is a good idea after reading our chapter investigating child porn rings. To describe the activities of Danish child porn pioneers Willy Strauss and Peter Theander is enough, as far as we're concerned, to totally condemn them.

Anning: Absolutely. As parents ourselves and as mature sexual beings we experienced strong revulsion towards the purveyors of child porn.

Do either of them feel, well, sullied or demeaned by their two-and-a-half years' research?

Anning: Not demeaned. Not in the least. I feel it was an educational, even liberating experience. The international porn trade is big business. It is no longer a scene of run-down sleaziness. We were often ushered into luxurious offices, into tasteful rooms, were greeted by charming secretaries who said, 'Here's our latest catalogue'. It was all very friendly, open and above board.

Hebditch: Some of the bigger porn companies in Scandinavia and Germany have pension funds, superb social clubs, staff canteens with Warhol prints on the wall, and even sponsor public buildings and the local ladies' handball teams. In Germany we visited a sumptuous porn company building which had been opened by the Lord Mayor. He'd received enough taxes from the industry to build a new town hall ... incidentally they're much more interested in booze than porn in Scandinavia.

Anning: Visits abroad demolished my English attitude to sex. For English people sexuality is something private, furtive, not to be talked about, a bit grubby. I now believe that this attitude has held back the healthy development of our society. There is no denying that we live in a country with a strong repressive element. I neither advocate nor denigrate porn. But I certainly can't see any sense in the law trying to prohibit it.

Hebditch: I agree.

Anning: Our research has shown that it is absolutely impossible, given modern technology, to prevent porn. It's not like controlling rabies, say, or foot-and-mouth disease. Human sexuality cannot be controlled. Something that did surprise us is that women are becoming keen porn consumers as well as purveyors of porn. Those that star in porn movies enjoy it, say it's a fun way of expressing themselves, take pride in their work.

Were Hebditch and Anning ever tempted to sample some of the 'pure erotic dynamite' they encountered? Were they ever seduced into giving it a whirl?

Anning: No, I was never tempted. We would like to make clear that *at no time* did we get any specific offers of sexual favours from the trade.

Hebditch: No way. Although I was tempted a bit. In Bangkok. When you're surrounded by 60 beautiful, virtually naked girls, all claiming to be 18, it is difficult to say 'no'. Very. But I did not succumb to temptation. It would have been unprofessional in a researcher. Another restraining factor was that Bangkok has been deliberately developed by the Thai government as a sex centre and we were concerned about the exploitation of Thai women. They call their work 'Going with rich men'. There is something reprehensible about the fact that 80 per cent of air passengers to Bangkok are unaccompanied males. All you can do these days in Bangkok is the Temple of the Emerald Buddha or the red light districts. Thai feminists have started protesting about the 'sex tours' organized via the tourism authority.

Anning: I was not tempted, even in Bangkok. The only person I felt really attracted to was the female editor of a Swedish porn mag. She was stunning. Our interview was interrupted by a dirty phone call from the Arctic Circle. Some lumberjacks fuelled up on vodka screamed, 'Will you walk all over us in high-heeled shoes?' She replied 'I'm too busy'. She had started off as a secretary and, in economic terms, worked herself up.

Hebditch: During our visits we were given a lot of free samples which we dumped with our lawyers. Didn't want to keep them at home.

Anning: No. They wouldn't have been well received at home ... While working on the project I found that my relationships with women as friends deepened. I found myself able to talk more openly about sexual attitudes, needs and fantasies. I also learnt a lot about women.

Hebditch: That's true of me too. Absolutely.

Have Hebditch and Anning become at all hooked on porn?

Anning: (loud laughter) No. Absolutely not. We are the living refutation of the idea that pornography is addictive. Boring is a better adjective. It is just terribly boring. You reach saturation level very fast. We came to the conclusion that if porn was legalized in Britain tomorrow there would be a tremendous initial interest, but it would be a ten-day wonder. After that people would get on with the real thing. Basically all you see in mags and videos are repetitive depictions of what happens in bed between two cohabiting adults but it's a bit more acrobatic. That's show biz!

Hebditch: (louder laughter) There was no way we got hooked by porn. We could take it or leave it. We left it. We were not turned on or turned off by our research. We were just a couple of blokes doing a job. We've already investigated phone tapping, gun running, code breaking, police corruption. When we came up with the idea of investigating porn it seemed like a great idea. After all, everyone is interested in sex. Everyone is intrigued and fascinated by pornography. Believe us, if they say they aren't, they're lying.

Porn Gold (Faber & Faber, 1988).

DEE PRESLEY

MY ACCOUNT OF LIFE WITH THE KING, WARTS
AND ALL, COMES STRAIGHT FROM THE HEART.

'I don't mind you focusing on my legs but just don't get too close up onto my face, okay? It's kinda crumpled these days . . .,' says the late Elvis Presley's stepmother, Dee Presley, patting her blonde hair for the photographer. She sucks in her cheeks, flutters fake lashes, sticks out her bust. She bares large Scrabble-piece teeth in a girlish simper, but the eyes stay wary. She is in London to launch the book with the worst title of all time, *Elvis We Love You Tender*. If the title makes you cringe then you'd certainly have to keep firm control of yourself if you had to watch Dee kissing the photograph of Elvis on the dustjacket cover (as she does for the photographer), leaving greasy kiss marks all over it.

Dee insists that her everyday story of Nashville folk is 'an honest account of the King's life and death as told by those closest to him, namely me and my three boys'. In this 'painfully honest memoir' (as it is billed by the publicity blurb) Dee never uses ordinary English where a ghastly cliché will do. She also has a technique of sprinkling the pages with ludicrous Biblical quotations such as 'The King's business required haste' (1 Samuel 21:8).

Perched on an armchair in a London hotel ('Say I'm 40-ish, okay?') Dee tells, in her deep Southern drawl, the amazing story of how 'humble little Dee' was destined to be caught up in the heady, insane world of Elvis Presley. When Dee married Elvis's father, Vernon, and found herself stepmother to the man 'with the voice that cut through Memphis like a razor' she had not anticipated the Presley pique.

'It was hard, very hard to cope with all that simmering hostility,' sighs Dee. 'Elvis you see was inconsolable after his mother Gladys' death from diet pills and alcohol abuse. When I first got to know Vernon his boy Elvis was still making daily pilgrimages to his mother's grave. He brooded. He mourned. He missed her more than Vernon did. It's true to say that Elvis was a broken man after his mother died. He never got over it. Her epitaph "She was the Sunshine of our Home" says it all. Gladys was an impossible act to follow.'

Dee pauses to sip champagne. The bubbles get up her nose and she starts coughing. She bangs her chest. Gasp, wheeze. 'Jeez! I was only 9 years older than Elvis, and I guess he had to make emotional adjustments when I married his father . . . I didn't think that he liked me at first.' What made her think that? 'Well, he wouldn't attend the wedding. He did give us quite a large sum of money as a present I'll admit, but his being at the wedding would have been a better present.' Later Elvis gave Dee mink coats, Cadillacs, and expensive jewellery like the two huge diamond rings she keeps rattling against her champagne glass. He also invited the newly-weds to share his appalling mansion Graceland, with its pools, fountains, pin ball machines, chandeliers, cocktail bars, kinky two-way mirrors, and the bathroom where one day the heavily drugged King (wearing blue cotton pyjamas) would expire while sitting on the lavatory.

Life at Graceland, according to Dee's book, was no picnic. Surrounded by a crazed and sycophantic entourage Elvis enjoyed macho roughhouse and practical jokes. As Dee recalls, his pet chimpanzee, 'Scatter', rampaged and defecated everywhere: 'Once Scatter was sitting at the dinner table and bit my finger real hard. Vernon and Elvis fell about the floor laughing before getting me to a hospital . . '. another time Elvis summoned me to the kitchen bar which he'd fixed up with crackers, the whole place exploded and the kitchen caught on fire . . .'

Dee admits that the truth of the matter, the *real* truth, is that Elvis always got on her nerves. 'No-one dares say so, but he was one almighty pain in the arse. He never knew when to stop. It could be 3 a.m., and if he decided to begin a 4-hour conversation, or wanted you to ride snomobiles, or take a 'plane somewhere to go and buy his favourite hamburgers you just didn't dare say "no" . . .'

Life at Graceland, if we are to believe Dee, was like living in a goldfish bowl. Hysterical fans peered in through the gold gates all day and night, and there was nothing to do but sit by the pool, watch movies, and pander to Elvis's every whim. 'Thankfully I moved out and was spared the agony and pain of Elvis's terrible decline,' says Dee, opening another bottle of champagne. There follows a two-minute silence. She sips with eyes downcast, murmuring that hers is a book which 'tells it like it really was'. In writing it she has released a lot of buried resentment. Not least her resentment at the way Elvis treated her three boys. And here Dee gets really wound up, scuffing up the twisted pile with her stiletto heels. Dee had ambitions for Billy, Rick and David, see. It drove her wild to watch the way they offered their total, but *total* allegiance to the King in exchange for expensive gifts.

No-one dares say so, but Elvis was one almighty pain in the arse. He never knew when to stop.

Pacing about and wringing her hands, Dee confesses: 'I hated the way Elvis interfered ... we had many harsh words because I was strongly opposed to my sons leaving Christian school. I wanted them to be preachers or doctors.'

Instead they became part of the 'Memphis Mafia', devoting their lives to 'Taking Care of Business' for the King. If Elvis leaned back they gave him a glass of water, if he leaned forward they lit him a cigar. They plugged his ears with cotton wool before he slept, switched on his humidifier, and fried his famed peanut and banana sandwiches. If he demanded a cheeseburger, Go-kart ride or woman they sprang to attention. If they forgot to put Thousand Island Dressing on the Presley baked potato he was likely to fire a round or two of bullets up into the chandeliers or at the TV screens. He once machine-gunned his pink Cadillac when it wouldn't start. In a way – a very small way – you can begin to appreciate Dee's dilemma ... TCB-ing for Dee's boys meant mixing Elvis's nasal douches, colonic irrigation fluids, and drugs. Later, when getting out of bed was a major achievement, it involved supplying Elvis's uppers, downers and suppositories, cramming his flab into spangled jump-suits and slapping him to get the circulation going before concerts. Later still it involved changing his incontinence pants, but Dee had moved out of Graceland by then. As she says, and you can see her point, 'I could feel that I'd lost my boys to Elvis, they no longer shared their lives with me ...'

Then Rick was arrested for drug dealing. Elvis however stormed into the police station announcing, with the legendary sullen twisted snarl and heavy eyebrows, 'Take them damn cuffs off him or I'll buy out this whole goddam city block.' No messing with the King. Them damn cuffs were gotten off pretty fast and so was Rick. But Dee was 'so crushed I almost fainted because it seemed I didn't even know my own son any more . . .'

Let us pause to consider our author's predicament. Not only were the boys lost to her, but Vernon (fed up with Dee) had joined them and was whooping it up 'on the road'. Vernon had become a rock 'n' roll raver. Dee decided to call it quits. There followed divorce plans. Then Vernon had his famed heart attack and an anguished Elvis phoned Dee sobbing 'Dee . . . I'm so worried about Daddy . . . nothin' worked out the way I wanted it . . . promise me you'll keep this thing outta court. God bless you Dee, you came in like a lady and you bore it like a lady.'

Dee says she was 'devastated' by Elvis's death on 16 August 1977. There followed a 'numbing haze of pain' exacerbated by the dawning realization that the King had left Dee and the boys out of his will. And yes, despite the fact that they all loved him so tender, a definite feeling of bitterness welled up. Unable to cope with their grief and with being left out of the will, the boys went off the rails. David turned to drink and drugs, swallowed a fistful of Valium, and as his stomach was being pumped out he swore he could feel Elvis in the room reproaching him. Billy, dazed and disoriented, felt as if Elvis was not dead but had just gone on tour again without him. And Rick became a born-again Christian. He began regularly addressing crowds at the Mississippi football stadium where revivalists greeted him with banners stating 'HE SERVED THE KING OF ROCK 'N'ROLL/NOW HE SERVES THE KING OF KINGS.' As Dee reminds us, young Rick will 'carry to the casket' his memory of Elvis's premonitory remark before his last concert. 'Know what, Rick?' Elvis had rasped, panting and coughing, with the black hair dye trickling down his temples, 'I may not look too good for my television special tonight but I'll sure look good in my coffin.'

Apart from the will, Dee has no regrets. (She came in like a lady and bore it like a lady.) God had his plans. Rick, David and Billy are now all born-again Christians and TCB-ing for the Lord. Vernon died two years after Elvis. Sighs Dee, 'I'm happy to know they're all there together in Meditation Garden right near the spot where Vernon proposed to me.' She doesn't care at all for the 50-ton bronze statue of Elvis in his jumpsuit cast in classical Greek pose and recently erected in Memphis. Pained as she was by both Presley passings

and despite Elvis's overwhelming gener-
osity to the family and herself, she feels
under no obligation to let him rest in
peace. Like she said, hers is a 'painfully
honest memoir' written not to make
money – heaven forbid – but to 'tell it
like it really was'. Anyway, some of the
more unpleasant memories (and here
she rolls her eyes and purses her
lips) are, like her teeth, still her own.
If perchance she should rake in a
few thousand dollars by spilling the Presley beans, well, she
sure won't suffer any sleepless nights. As she says, 'Believe
me, I was Elvis's greatest fan. But I understood how tired
he'd become of his Good Guy image – and my account of life
with the King, warts and all, comes straight from the heart.'

Believe me, I was Elvis's greatest fan. But I understood how tired he'd become of his Good Guy image . . .

Elvis We Love You Tender (New English Library, 1980).

ELIZABETH SMART

Getting up on stage reading my work and being the focus of attention is hell for me, utterly terrifying.

To reach Elizabeth Smart's Suffolk cottage – which is really two cottages knocked into one – involves travelling across a lunar landscape of gravel pits. For several miles the track snakes through puddles and ponds and mountains of grit, until suddenly mud sprouts grass, brambles and silver-birch trees. Through a five-bar gate, and across a lush stretch of lawn, and you're at The Dell, a cottage straight off a National Trust notelet with honeysuckle round the door and wonderful profusions of cow-parsley. Inside there'a a coal fire glowing (even though it's August) and a room lined with packed book-shelves. Mozart's Clarinet Concerto is playing on a tinny, portable cassette recorder. Smart is in the kitchen, glass in one hand and fish-slice in the other. Her hair is full of dandelion seeds because, she explains, she's spent the afternoon forking over the compost heap. I present her with the bottle which her publisher, Jay Landesman, suggested would be cheerfully received. (Landesman: 'Take her some-thing to drink. She's a person who gives too much. People take advantage of Elizabeth's hospitality. Tell her I'm still waiting for her to get her head together enough to publish Elizabeth Smart's scrapbook. A great idea.') I also proffer a bottle of dry cider from my home county. She pours it for me, mumbles 'Thank you but I'll stick to vodka', with a hint of disappointment in her eyes, a certain sizing up that she'll be whiling away the next few hours with a non-serious drinker. We clink glasses. The frying-pan sizzles. Smart says: 'I thought you were going to be a man. "Val" is often a man's name ... anyhow, forgive the mess in the sink. Something's amiss. Drain's blocked. I'll have to get my son to see to it. Or the Vicar. He calls here regularly hoping to make a non-believer see the light. It's prudent to be polite because I have my eye on an eventual plot in his churchyard. I've introduced him to the works of Yeats whom he persists in calling "Yeets".'

We are sitting at the kitchen table. Smart remarks that she's slightly decrepit these days, like her house, but what the hell. I have the impression that her warm, welcoming, cosy home is often a refuge to writer and poet friends who arrive, out of the blue, no doubt drawn as much by Smart's

well-thumbed, dog-eared poetry collection (many first editions, signed) as by Smart's extraordinary kindness.

At 66 Smart is making a literary comeback. Her prose
masterpiece and cult novel *By Grand Central Station I Sat
Down and Wept* (1945), one of the most rapturous chronicles
of a love-affair ever written, has been recently adapted for
radio, a film is planned, and, as Smart points out, royalties
from the book's fourth reprint keep her in typewriter
ribbons. Her resurgence, or what she calls 'My resurrection'
has left her bemused. 'Suddenly after 40 years they want to
know me which is terrific for one's self-esteem. Posthumous
recognition is decidedly unsatisfactory for a writer . . . But
it's extremely mysterious to me how *Grand Central Station* is
so much more appreciated in the 1980s. I think it must have
something to do with women's liberation and the way
women are now writing and expressing their most profound
feelings.'   •

By Grand Central Station was an exorcism, of sorts, of a
great love affair. As a young woman Smart read a collection
of George Barker's poems, fell in love with him through
them, pursued him, seduced him, and later wove some
aspects of their relationship into a novel which many critics
initially derided. Brigid Brophy alone recognized its worth.
In her introduction to the paperback edition (Panther 1966)
she wrote: 'I doubt if there are more than half a dozen
masterpieces of poetic prose in the world. One of them, I am
convinced, is Elizabeth's Smart's *By Grand Central Station I
Sat Down and Wept* . . . the entire book is a wound, even
when its rhythm expresses the throb of pleasure, the pleasure is so ardent that it lays waste to the personality that
experiences it . . . it is one of the most shelled, skinned,
nerve-exposed books ever written.'

Smart recalls how: 'They somehow sneered at feminine
emotion in 1945, they dismissed my subject-matter as trivial,' and absent-mindedly she turns onions with the fish-
slice, flinging a handful of parsley into the pan and topping
up her glass. 'If they said such things today they'd be
lynched. My mother didn't like the book either. She was
convinced that it was about her in some way, had it banned
from Canada where I was born and raised, bought all the
copies she could lay her hands on and burned them.'

Smart confesses that it's 'distinctly boring' to be continually raking the embers of a book which first blazed 40 years ago. A couple of months back when the film people arrived to discuss adaptations and screen-play all she really wanted to discuss was the poetry she now writes and the way she has plucked up the nerve to perform live at various poetry venues. 'The film people didn't want to hear about my poetry. But they were very charming. They even painted the kitchen while they were here, pulled out all the rusty drawing pins, took down the posters, the newspaper cuttings, little poems, erased everything with their virginal white emulsion paint . . . it didn't seem kind to explain that I actually like dust and a few friendly little cobwebs about the place.'

Smart's struggle after the war to raise Barker's four children 'more or less single-handedly' (he never married her but set up his own menage) is recounted in *The Assumption of Rogues and Rascles* (Panther 1980) about which a *Times* critic raved: 'Miss Smart writes like an angel' and a *Sunday Times* critic welcomed 'her ability to encompass the whole modern female reaction to the male-ordered world'.

Smart remembers that this novel was written during a time of despair: 'Sometimes I felt so *alone* with the children that I would have kissed Stephen Spender's toe had he crossed the threshold, I was so desperate . . . I was nearly arrested once in Soho for being drunk in charge of a pram. The book was launched at a wild party in the Round House. One hundred glasses got broken, the place was lit up with thousands of candles, but I found it hard to enjoy myself because I had been made ill by a reviewer who composed such a vile attack on me that for days I felt as if I'd been mugged on the streets.'

Smart pours a copious quantity of red wine into the frying-pan, tips the contents into a casserole dish, and puts it in the oven. We move from the draughty, stone-flagged kitchen to armchairs in front of the fire. Smart remarks that the only thing her mother ever taught her was how to be a good hostess. It's ingrained, she says, as natural to her as breathing. 'It's a very curious thing this hold our mothers have over us. I still wake up screaming at night after dreams about mine. I've always been deeply suspicious of Colette's euphoric, passionate writings about her mother. She didn't actually live with her for long, did she? Moved out pretty damn quick and only saw her once every few years . . .' She puffs heavily on a French cigarette. Drains her glass. Levers off her wellington boots and asks whether I could face listening to her reading some of her poems. 'Since I've become a "performing poet" I've been gadding about like a demented ant's nest, up to Edinburgh, down to London. Edinburgh was my debut. I had previously bribed yawning friends, as I'm bribing you now, with drinks at my home to hear me rehearsing aloud. Oh my! Live readings could very well be the death of me. I've never been an actress, you see, or president of the WI, or captain of the debating society, so getting up on stage, reading my work and being the focus of attention is hell for me, utterly terrifying. George (Barker) was there at Edinburgh offering encouragement, he told me it wouldn't matter if I read any old junk that came into my head because poetry audiences are notoriously well-behaved and far too polite to protest.' Leaning forward to shovel more coals on the fire she adds, 'George always looks so amazingly cool on the platform. I can still make George laugh, you know, and that's a real draw . . .'

Opening *Bonus* (Polyantric Press) at random she reads aloud. For half an hour I sit spellbound, scarcely able to believe my good fortune. It is the first time a poet has ever read work aloud to me. She then reads aloud from her own notebook 'This old woman/waddles towards love/Becomes human/But the Muse does not approve . . .' Smart has a graceful Canadian-accented voice which conveys sustained wonderment and passion. She writes about plants, animals, and the desolation of growing up: 'Growing up is the strange death/In life that nobody mourns/The forgotten babies that/filled the whole world/When they were first born.' She writes too about writing: 'To be in a very unfeminine/Very unloving state/Is the desperate need of/anyone trying to write.' Occasionally she sounds a surprisingly cynical note: 'Don't telephone anyone/Write it all down/Maybe someone will/understand you better/After you're gone.'

Between poems she sips vodka, chain-smokes, quips that she was encouraged to write poetry, in a manner of speaking, by the poet George Macbeth:

'After attending several of his readings I had to admit that his genius was completely lost on me. I thought: "Goddam it, I can do better than *that*." I truly believe that when the Muse visited Macbeth she whizzed past him in a Daimler gently waving like the Queen Mum . . .' Occasionally she gets angry with herself for spending too little time writing. She puts off the dreaded moment of picking up her pen by gardening, or tinkering with her mo-ped which, she says, is handy for burning off across the gravel-pits to the shops and railway station.

We sit in silence for five minutes or so. Then Smart says: 'Will you do something for me? There'a a magical short poem on the flyleaf of Scott Fitzgerald's *The Great Gatsby* which has intrigued me for years. It's by Thomas Parke d'Invilliers, but I have a suspicion it's really by Fitzgerald himself. I have never been able to discover anything else written by D'Invilliers. Will you check him out for me? She recites these lines from memory:

'Then wear the gold hat, if it will move her;
If you can bounce high, bounce for her too,
Till she cry, "Lover, gold-hatted, high-bouncing lover,
I must have you!"'

Smart then scribbles them onto the back of an envelope and hands it to me. I know that I will keep the scribble always.

Smart explains how, in winter, she fixes a blanket over the kitchen door, stokes up the stove and writes at the kitchen table. Nothing, she says, is more daunting than the terrible whiteness of the blank page. I tell her that I think I could die happy if I'd written just one particular line of hers. 'Which one?' she wonders. I quote, from *By Grand Central Station*, a line which never fails to make the little hairs on the back of my neck stand up: 'Under the waterfall he gave me what I could no more refuse than the earth can refuse rain . . .'

Suddenly Smart reached out to take hold of my hand. She has the most compassionate eyes that brim unexpectedly. 'My dear,' she says, so very generously to someone who is merely a hack with a page to fill and a features editor who thinks all poets are mad and who really wants to drag up some gossip on George Barker, 'when some young writer tracks you down when you're an old crumbly and tells you that she could die happy having written a particular line – it's only *then* that you can die happy . . .' I have never felt so honoured, so grateful, so certain that I am in the presence of a writer, a *real* writer, one who is slightly burnished with the shimmer of genius.

Elizabeth Smart was born in 1913 and died in 1987. This interview took place in 1981.

By Grand Central Station I Sat Down and Wept (Panther Books, 1966).

ERICA JONG

THE WORST PART IS WHEN THE
SHMUCKS WHO ONCE CARPED NOW
CLAIM THAT MY BOOKS ARE CLASSICS
– IT MAKES ME *CRAZY*.

You feel very conspicuous in the Palm Court of the Ritz Hotel if you're not wearing mink. I was waiting there for Erica Jong and ploughing through her latest novel when I reached page 237 and nearly choked on my jam scone and clotted cream. Talk about disgusting! 'He dived into her muff with great exuberance, parted it, found her white string that dangled chastely there and pulled her Tampax triumphantly out with his teeth. "Aha! A string!" he said between clenched teeth. He chewed on the Tampax lightly, savouring its taste . . .' I tell you, I nearly threw up in the Palm Court's echelon marble fountain. It quite put me off my Choice of Finest Pastries. It also put me off meeting Jong, even though she's hailed as the 'dazzling virtuoso of post-feminist prose'.

Jong's novel *Parachutes and Kisses*, described by Hermione Lee in *The Observer* as 'an epic of silliness, self-advertisement and execrable writing', is a consistently embarrassing read. Isadora Wing, the self-absorbed heroine of *Fear of Flying*, is back again ten years older and just as daft. She owns a silver turbo-diesel Mercedes whose personalized number plates spell QUIM. She's become rich, divorced, world-famous and the sexual fantasy of a million male readers. By the end of the book the priapic Tampax-eater is satisfying her rapacious needs. At the ripe old age of 39 she has acquired such world-shattering insights as: 'Whenever a man said "I worship pussy" – the odds were excellent that he didn't. Those who can, do; those who can't talk about it.' and 'The intimacy of genitals in each other's mouths does ease the pain of divorce . . . I blow, therefore I am'; and 'In the '50s, the women couldn't come; in the '80s – Goddess help us – it's the men!'

Isadora Wing has abandoned her habit of writing 'juicily erotic poems' to her third husband's fabled organ in its various stages of tumescence and detumescence. Instead she 'fucks her brains out' with any available wimp, and struggles to raise her child with only a stream of nannies, domestics, secretaries, and a fridge full of champagne to ease the burden of single parenthood.

As I drank tea in the Palm Court amidst a throng of surly Arabs I began to ask myself, all things considered, whether I

ERICA JONG

could actually *face* an interview with the writer whose
'cheerful sexual frankness brings a new flavour to female
prose' (John Updike). To be honest, if *Parachutes and Kisses*
had been written by a man, I would denounce it as tacky,
tacky, tacky! and fling it in the trash bin.

I had just decided to sneak away when a punctual PR
person arrived and whisked me up to the Ritz suite (£380 a
day) where Jong and a callow-looker called 'Chip' (who, it
later transpired, enjoys a 'very monogamous relationship'
with America's most controversial novelist) were installed
for a week of book-plugging.

Chip was a Tampax chewer if ever I saw one. Definitely.
You could almost detect a vampirish rim round the edge of
his teeth. Jong, in the flesh, didn't look quite as Dallas-like
as her book jacket photo would have you believe. The
Barbie-doll blonde curls are not quite as blonde, the bland
features are rather less bland and the wide-eyed gaze not
altogether as candid. It was somewhat bloodshot in fact, but
this could have been due to her contact lenses.

'I'm having a problem with my lenses,' drawled Jong,
throwing back her head and squirting antiseptic solution
into her eyes. 'I've got some glop on one of them. Excuse
me.' Then it was straight down to business. Jong began to
dictate. 'A book is a kind of hand grenade, my novels set up
chain reactions all over the world which I can't control . . .'

Chip padded across the carpet in pallid bare feet demand-
ing camomile tea. I asked him whether he was Jong's son, or
manager, or secretary, or something. He replied, 'You can
say I'm her manager, her boss, her PR, and the guy who
writes her books.' Jong chuckled full-throatedly, insisted
that Chip was joking, and offered him a strawberry puff.
Chip declined and retired morosely to the bedroom. Forget
about strawberry puffs. He was obviously dying to get his
teeth into a Tampax. 'Everybody asks me whether the
insatiable Isadora Wing is really me,' continued Jong, 'and
everybody accuses me of being evasive when I reply that 66
per cent of her *could* be me or *none* of her . . . it is important
not to confuse writers with their books.'

Jong declared that she's only too aware that writing about
sex is suddenly no longer fashionable. 'In the '70s, post-
Portnoy, you couldn't pick up a novel without getting sperm
on your hands; today all the poetry of the penis, the sweet

sexuality that peeked out of the fly of the Brooks' Brothers' pants for a brief decade, is in danger of being covered up again. The Puritans love that, of course. "Let's have High Literature without sex is *their* cry." However, I believe we shouldn't leave sex to the crap writers, or to the 42nd Street porno guys.

'And I consider myself a good writer. Much better than most of the people who criticize and carp about my books. None of them could write *Fanny*. Or *Fear of Flying* which, incidentally, became a world-bestseller, is still in print, is the subject of doctoral dissertations and has even been translated into Serbo-Croat

Everybody asks me whether the insatiable Isadora Wing is really me, and everybody accuses me of being evasive when I reply that 66 per cent of her *could* be me or *none* of her . . .

and Macedonian.' 'No Kidding?' 'No Kidding', she chuckled, and bewailed the fact that lavish praise alternating with vicious attacks had been heaped upon her throughout her career: 'The worst part is when the shmucks who once carped now claim that my books are classics – it makes me *crazy* . . . I was called a "mammoth pudenda" by an insulting person called Paul Theroux. He, in case you haven't heard of him, is an intellectual hack writer who churns out books for money. And "pudenda" in Theroux's context is not even grammatically correct, it should be "pudendum" – but getting accustomed to bitchiness is all part of being a veteran writer. If you write *honestly*, and no-one writes more honestly than I do about what a woman goes through, the literary critics all start screaming, "this is *trash*, not literature, Jong should be burnt as a witch or stoned" – thank goodness I wasn't born in the 1600s, I *would* have been burnt as a witch. Hostile reaction to my books simply reveals how misogynistic our society is . . .'

Between a strawberry puff and a cup of tea I confess that I tend to go along with Paul Theroux, particularly after having read the Tampax sequence. Jong looked astounded. 'But that scene is playful, funny and very Rabelaisian, Didn't you find it funny?' No, I said, I found it repulsive. 'That's sad. That's interesting. Hmm. Maybe you have negative feelings about menstruation?' replied Jong, 'maybe you haven't confronted the reality of being a woman? Obviously this scene has struck a nerve, a lot of people have tremendous problems with the taboo topic of menstruation, you can't reason these things, they go beyond intellectual argument, and far be it for me to rationalize . . .'

Funny she should say that about 'confronting the reality of being a woman', I was thinking. Personally I believe it takes more than getting your lover to eat your tampon. I believe it takes more than advocating indiscriminate prom-iscuity, and countenancing haphazard use of drugs to in-crease sexual gratification, and generally displaying a fierce contempt for the vulnerabilities of men. Breaking into Jong's searing psycho-analysis session I ask: As a 'mature' writer and a mother, isn't it somehow, well *silly* of you to glorify the bourgeois, hedonistic lifestyle without drawing the reader's attention to certain potential drawbacks like herpes and drug addiction?

'I'm not writing a *sermon*,' replied Jong, 'I'm writing a satirical novel. Anyway, people don't want to read about herpes, despair and drug addiction. Incidentally, I'm very against drugs but one thing that teaches you how bad drugs are is to do them . . . In fact the comments you are making about my book are totally different to any reaction I've had so far. I'm kind of surprised. My book is a tremendous satire of casual sex. It seems to me that you are taking it the wrong way. And that's sad. Isadora Wing is a model of how to get along with the opposite sex. There's a lot in my book about motherhood, how a mother conveys the reality of being a woman to her daughter. Isadora is a model, I hope, of great courage. I am trying to chronicle where women are in the 1980s, what it's like being a single parent, dating, having a career, infiltrating the male power structure, having it all . . .'

Jong added that she was amazed, yes *amazed*, at my suggestion that her book is anti-feminist. The passage on page 7 where she writes: 'Isadora's old buddies, the femin-ists, are passing out leaflets on street corners protesting about pornography and in general doing their best to blur the distinction between sex and rage . . . Of course feminists don't mean to come out on the same side as the Moral Majority when they denounce pornography, but alas they do. And sweet sex is dragged in the gutter again' – is of course highly satirical. And while we were on the subject

Jong continued: 'I do think that the whole glorification of lesbian love is a lot of rubbish. It was a very silly period in feminist history, lesbianism is not *the* answer to life's problems and as a woman writer I've attempted to satirize the women's movement in the same way that men do. The fringe feminists now realize that they cannot pretend to be a bunch of hippies forever, the reality of politics is that you must have a leader, otherwise nothing gets done. In realizing this they've come a long way.'

Our time was nearly up. I reached into my bag and brought out a new Penguin paperback I'd been reading called *Last Ferry to Manley*, by Jill Neville, which lacks all the sales advantages originated by the Jong hype machine. Coincidentally, Neville and Jong are the same age (early 40s), both are writers of shimmering poetry, and both choose as their novel's theme the middle-aged, autonomous divorcee confronting the reality and responsibility of being grown up. Compare their different attitudes to a woman's love affair with a much younger man:

Neville: 'He is at an age when not enough happens, and he can give his all to her. They are two waves colliding. Hers going down. His coming up. They meet in foam.'

Jong: 'You have a great cock, Roland,' said Isadora . . . "you have a great cock" is not exactly a line she hasn't used before, though Isadora reserves the compliment for special cocks – not the common-or-garden variety zucchini. Roland is exceptionally well-endowed; indeed it is his chief charm other than his hypertrophied brain . . . 'she takes it in her mouth, twirling and tonguing it . . . How delicious for a woman of 39 to have a 26-year-old lover. The delights of playing mentor, the ego trip of being wanted by youth itself.'

Neville's stunning and brilliantly crafted novel suggests that a woman alone can be strong, can survive to dispense old-fashioned gifts like love, caring, friendship, tenderness, wisdom and responsibility. Jong's novel suggests that a woman alone is a frenzied blot on the patriarchal landscape.

I do think that the whole glorification of lesbian love is a lot of rubbish. It was a very silly period in feminist history, lesbianism is not *the* answer to life's problems . . .

'You'd be interested to read Jill Neville's novel', I suggested to Jong, 'it might teach you a thing or two.' She laughed hugely.

Chip reappeared. Jong made a whinnying sound. They smooched. Jong came up for air to deliver the final panegyric: 'We live in a society of instant journalist digestion. Everybody's got to have their little rubric. Raquel-Welch-Sex-Symbol, Philip-Roth-Masturbation-With-Liver. Erica-Jong-Zipless-Fuck, it drives me crazy . . . All I'm trying to do in my novel is tell the truth through the eyes of a main character who mirrors present-day society . . . My advice to writers is to ignore the labels, never sit nursing yourself after the critics attack, just go forward, as I have, and stick to your vision . . . '

Parachutes and Kisses (Grenada, 1984).

One does the Booker because of a fellow-feeling with other writers. After all, reading is almost more important than living.

Fay Weldon

There are those of us who tuned in to this year's televised Booker Awards simply because Fay Weldon was the first woman to chair the judges' panel. And there are those of us who fell off our settees in shock when Weldon, the feminist's friend and guru, loomed on to the small screen in sequins, lip gloss, dangling diamond earrings and gold-mesh, stiletto-heeled dance shoes.

'People were to a certain extent, shocked,' agrees Weldon, whose Booker gear could well have brought the mighty wrath of the Women's Movement tumbling about her perfumed ears, 'but frankly I didn't feel sexist or daft – not a bit, with platinum highlights in my hair and a sexy skirt I felt wonderful. I'm all for artifice and to hell with all this reality . . . I'm so hooked on fiction that I've promised myself five years and then I'm off to Los Angeles to locate a top plastic surgeon who can turn me into a glamorous fictional character . . .'

Is she kidding? I think the fat, dishevelled Weldon that we all love and presumed we *knew* is having her little joke. The joke continues in her latest novel in which the ghastly heroine achieves triumph of an agonizing sort by under-going years of gruesome cosmetic surgery in order to turn herself into the sex object of her husband's fantasies.

'I knew that women in the Women's Movement are astonishingly horrified by the notion of cosmetic surgery and the emphasis on youthfulness and all the rest of it,' says Weldon, who on the day of our meeting was wearing reassuringly concertina'd tights and a cardigan flecked with dog hairs, 'but when so many women base their entire happiness on the admiration of men, it is perfectly reason-able to accept that instead of *discarding* their looks, as some feminists seem to insist, they want to concentrate on not losing them. Wouldn't you agree?' Well, no and yes. And despite Weldon pretending she'd succumbed to the ubi-quitous Joan Collins/Jane Fonda brainwash, her new book is a ferocious, sabre-rattling diatribe about women as victims, not only of men but of themselves. *The Lives and Loves of a She-Devil* is a novel about revenge; a cautionary tale which will give you goose pimples and tickle your ribs, concerning the nature of love and the nature of power. Ruth, dutiful wife and clumsy, lumbering six-footer with sprouting moles on her chin, yearns for 'power over the hearts and pockets of men'. Instead she gets ditched by a wimpish husband who moves in with a blonde, petite and childless million-airess.

... women who write are given some importance for themselves, you see, and not as adjuncts to men.

'A man cannot be expected to remain faithful to a wonderful mother and a good wife – such concepts lack the compulsion of the erotic,' groans poor old Ruth, echoing the message hammered and hammered relentlessly home by all Western mass media which persistently deny sympathy, status and sexuality to women past the age of 35. 'I want to give hate its head,' mutters Ruth through clenched, horsey teeth, then proceeds to burn down her delightful suburban home, murder the guinea pig, abandon her two children to her husband's mistress, and storms back into the world to wreak her terrible vengeance.

Fuelled by *envy*, she rebels against the whole business of putting up with fate.

As Weldon explains: 'In Ruth I have spotlighted the woman we all fear to be, the sexually unattractive loser who is expected to opt out – instead she opts back in, joins the enemy and triumphs by behaving badly . . . it is not an anti-feminist book, it takes courage to burn down one's house and give away one's children – the feminists will certainly approve of that bit . . .'

It also takes courage to stand up at the Booker McConnell prize dinner and lambast the staid assembly of publishers for their wily capitalist dealings with authors. 'Writers are in a fair state of indignation,' raged Weldon, making herself as popular as a British football fan in Luxembourg. 'The writer dislikes your paternalism. The writer dislikes the way you say, "Aren't you *lucky*? We're going to publish your book, actually publish your book." It's wearing very thin . . .' and so on until the PA system mysteriously conked out.

Weldon says she was 'a trifle amazed' at the repercussions of her invective. For her 'the Booker is to be taken extremely seriously . . . the actual judging is crucially important, the prize and ceremony being a necessary sacrifice that writers must make for the sake of literature and it's best that it remains as dignified as it possibly can ... one does the Booker because of a fellow-feeling with other writers. After all, reading is almost more important than living ...'

Weldon is renowned for her availability. Journalists traipse freely round her two spacious houses (in London and Somerset) noting kids, clutter, au pairs and the sticky fingermarks on the stripped pine. She's been interviewed by Melvyn Bragg, she's been on 'Pebble Mill' and 'Afternoon Plus'. She dashes about the country giving lectures, presiding at workshops, planning community plays and supervizing writing courses. 'These days', she says, 'they only have to put the words "Women and writing" on the course programme to ensure a maximum attendance ... I believe this is because women feel that an explanation is owing to them and that only other women can explain the curious nature of their lives ... women who write are given some importance for themselves, you see, and not as adjuncts to men.

'There are two levels of women's writing,' she continues, 'the élitist literary novel and something completely *new* in female communication, women writing *for* women, which takes a literary form and is very genuine. Often it may lack literary grace, it is almost on the broadsheet principle, but it is enormously important because it takes literature out of the universities and back to the people.

'I have enormous respect for women story-writers and poets who often do badly in literary terms and may be *despised* or even laughed at by the literary élite. But what they do in human terms is admirable – they are women speaking women's language by them, for them, to them ... I tend to be able to bridge the two worlds, and I believe that one of the most important achievements of the Women's Movement is the writing workshops that have sprung up, on housing estates, in high-rise flats, in community centres, enabling women to reach wider horizons.'

Her massive self-promotional work is undertaken, she explains, *not* merely to sell her books but because she's gregarious and likes to mingle. 'Also because of a female thing with me of not knowing how to say "No" – I was indoctrinated with being a woman: to respond to people's needs whether they are my husband's, children, publishers, TV producers ... I grit my teeth and off I go, my audience needs me to give an account of myself . . .'

But in fact, she avoids giving an account of herself at all. She gives a lively account of Weldon the writer, but Weldon the woman is slippery, elusive, very private and as impenetrable as a windsurfer's wetsuit. For example, when she lets slip that she underwent psycho-analysis for several years, a certain laser-like look from her very blue eyes totally stalls further questions. A slight chink in the formidable Weldon armour is apparent in occasional inconsistencies. At the Booker she congratulated John Fuller's *Flying To Nowhere*, describing it as 'a truly wonderful novel'. This is not at all how she described Fuller's flight of charnel-house fancy to me off the record . . .

Personal questions are deflected with enormous charm. 'No, I'm not exactly starving in a garret, but one is never free from money worries and I've always spent more than I earn . . .' and 'a lot of people find it hard to believe that writers

I have enormous respect for women story-writers and poets who often do badly in literary terms and may be *despised* or even laughed at by the literary élite. But what they do in human terms is admirable – they are women speaking women's language by them, for them, to them . . .

actually make things up . . . luckily my husband doesn't take my books personally at all, but others take them personally on his behalf and look at him in rather a peculiar way.'

Although I am itching to meet this elusive husband Ron, who can be glimpsed through the window building a barbed wire fence to keep the sheep from straying, he refuses to come indoors, even when he's called for lunch (twice). 'We've adapted to variances in our lives . . . he's now more of a feminist than I am – he does most of the parenting and the cooking these days,' says Weldon. I can't help suspecting that Ron, in the flesh, might blow the gaff. He might come in, kick his wellies off, shout 'Eh up, Fay, girl, get your knickers off' and slap her across the bum. But I'm only guessing.

What is beyond dispute is Weldon's brilliant ear for authentic female grievance. 'Women don't have lots of time

– unlike men,' she notes crisply, adding 'dumped, that's what happens to the plain and virtuous. They get dumped.' Like she-devil Ruth, who with red-rimmed eyes and hooked nose dripping with tears, stands in the matrimonial bedroom reciting *The Litany of the Good Wife*, which goes: 'I must pretend to be happy when I am not, for everyone's sake' and 'I must build up my husband's sexual confidence, must not express any sexual interest in other men, in private or in public. I must ignore his way of diminishing me by publicly praising women younger, prettier and more successful than me, and sleeping with them in private if he can, for everyone's sake.'

Weldon points out that although we are 20 years into the Women's Movement, female discontent has not diminished in Western culture. As she says, in her astringent, unputdownable novel: 'Someone to love, something to do – it's all any of us want.' If only it really *was* that simple.

The Lives and Loves of a She-Devil (Hodder & Stoughton, 1984).

FIONA
PITT-KETHLEY

I CALL A SPADE A SPADE; A PENIS A PENIS.

'A poet is a nightingale who sits in darkness and sings to cheer its own solitude with sweet sounds.' Percy Bysshe Shelley wrote that. I wonder what Shelley would have thought of Fiona Pitt-Kethley. She calls herself a poet. She has published two hugely successful slim volumes, *Sky Ray Lolly* and *Private Parts*, and fans flock to her readings. But 'nightingale' is certainly not a word that springs to mind in connection with Pitt-Kethley. Nor 'sweet sounds'. I first saw her reading her poems on Waterloo station as part of a Poetry Live event where she was castigated by commuters for using bad language. A few weeks later I heard her read at the Chelsea Arts Club literary evening. She read a poem called *Bums* (about having been reprimanded as a child for writing the word 'bum' on her school desk), and one called *Girlie Mags* ('I do not care a toss if blokes must look/at glossy big-boobed photos of bad girls . . .') and one called *Penis Envy* ('it seems a strange adornment for a crutch,/like sets of giblets from a butcher's shop,/two kidneys with a chicken neck on top . . .'). Each poem elicited a few sniggers and a great deal of coughing. On the whole the audience seemed stunned. 'Smut!' exploded one couple, storming from the dining room, 'Utter filth!' I personally couldn't keep a straight face. Pitt-Kethley may not be in the same league as Elizabeth Barrett Browning, say, or John Betjeman, but as popular poets go she's beginning to make quite a splash.

Her raunchy travel book, *Journeys to the Underworld*, made a splash too. Described as 'the year's most controversial travel book' and as 'Subtle as two fingers up your nose', it is Pitt-Kethley's record of travels to Italy where the basilicas, grottos, amphitheatres and art galleries are incidental to her efforts to get laid. 'The English on holiday are a more carefree lot than at home. Booze and casual sex are a must for both men and women . . .' she observes in her introduction; 'most women on package tours pick up the waiters in the hotel, I'm more into picking up the guides and archeologists working on sites and in museums.' Even as you find yourself wondering what *else* she picks up you will probably agree that such sentiments hardly belong to a lady. But why not? Why can't a lady, in these post-feminist days of sex-equality, think like the guys? Or, indeed, act like the guys have been acting for centuries?

It was this question I planned to thrash out with the poet as I made my way to her home in St Leonards-on-Sea. And boy, was I nervous. Pitt-Kethley had warned me on the phone that some people, a lot of people, apply such labels as 'tramp', 'slag' or 'cheap' to her type of woman. 'I don't care a toss, but I'm not cheap, I'm free. There's a world of difference,' she'd explained somewhat aggressively in quite a posh voice, and what with her being a poet, and all, I didn't know whether she was using the word free as in liberty or as in money. 'Of course my attitude means passing most of my life without a regular boyfriend and in many people's view being without a boyfriend is a kind of disability. I think this idea dehumanizes women . . .'

So there I was, anxiously climbing the steps to a front door behind which I feared an encounter with some kinky, depraved, sex-sodden nymphomaniac. Seagulls screamed round the chimneys of Pitt-Kethley's vast, crumbling Gothic villa. It had a turret. It looked like the motel house in *Psycho*. It gave me the creeps. As I rang the bell I wouldn't have been surprised if Tony Perkins had opened the door smiling insanely and saying 'Come in, Val, mother's resting right now in the basement'. Instead Pitt-Kethley, frosted pink lips, green eyeshadow, hair all frizzed and wearing a taffeta cocktail dress, opened the door and said 'Come in, Val, mother's resting right now in the basement'. I nearly dropped dead.

In I went, into a sepulchral hallway full of frescos, gold cherubs, twirly plaster swags and dominated by a monumental Italian marble staircase. It was like *Brideshead Revisited* but without the servants. There was a smell of mildrew. And cats. Through various open doors I glimpsed huge dilapidated rooms with paper peeling from walls, fly-blown gilt mirrors, and ladders precariously propped. 'It's a full-time job trying to make this house habitable,' said Pitt-Kethley ushering me into a dank, panelled back room looking out over what I took to be a small, tangled vacant lot

> **I had 86 rejections before I got one poem published in a non-paying magazine.**

but was the back garden – 'It was built in 1815 by an eccentric Italian millionaire. Today I've been using nail-varnish remover to lift some lime green paint covering a fresco . . . the kitchen is very squalid. Rain drips in, there are buckets to catch it everywhere, there's a very rusty fridge, we haven't had a proper roof since the hurricane.'

Pitt-Kethley opened a bottle of sherry and we sat in musty armchairs. I experienced a sudden attack of sneezing and terrible interviewer's block. She didn't look like a tramp or a slag. She didn't look like a person who writes rude poems. She looked like, and I hope she'll forgive me saying this, a rather prim, pop-eyed, spinsterish sort of a certain age who is glad of the chance of a chat. I asked her whether I could see the kitchen. 'Oh no,' she replied with a gutteral chuckle, 'my mother would kill me. She'd never get over it. It's too dark in the basement. The strip lighting hasn't worked in ages. Or the cooker. That's why we live on sandwiches and Cup-o-Soup.'

What was down in the basement? I could almost hear the *Psycho* theme tune. Hear Tony Perkins putting on his wig. Despite the freezing temperature I broke out into a hot sweat. I asked Pitt-Kethley to talk about being a poet. 'Yes, well, I've been writing full-time for 8 years, subsisting on cash from casual jobs or the dole . . . At first it was awful. I had 86 rejections before I got one poem published in a non-paying magazine. I've written at least a thousand poems. It's a fair estimate to say I had 500 rejections before I got paid for a poem. When my first collection was published it meant I was booked at last to do paid readings. Incidentally Andrew Motion at Chatto takes all the credit for "discovering" me but that's not entirely true. He rejected my work at first, then it went to and fro several times. I had a very good, crowded book launch at Bernard Stone's Turrett Bookshop and I kept off the booze until afterwards. I disgraced myself at my second launch, fortunately most people had left when I started being sick, not in the shop I'll add. Cheap wine has that effect occasionally. The second time I threw up was at a Poetry Society reading. I'm banned from reading there now, but they're such a snooty lot what can you expect, I've heard that they object to my subject matter . . .'

How would she describe her subject matter? 'Sex

and satire I suppose. But only half of it's about sex, though the critics think it all is. One or two critics accuse me of making it all up but if I say I've done something I have. When I pick someone up and they say "your place or mine?", it's always theirs, I'm afraid, it wouldn't be at all erotic here what with the damp and mum around. People faint with the cold

The second time I threw up was at a Poetry Society reading. I'm banned from reading there now ...

here. My life has mainly been a series of pickups. I'm into instant lust and no involvement, so far anyway. If I happen to run into somebody on a train or in the street I quite like one-afternoon stands, no unpleasant morning after . . .'

My thoughts were whirling. Was mother creeping about the basement with a meat cleaver? Was Tony Perkins? Was this interview going to be suitable for *You* magazine? Was this Pitt-Kethley person having me on? 'Are you having me on?' I asked her, noticing that she had strange, vampirish-shaped eye-teeth and a lot of books on the occult scattered about. 'Of course not. Some old-fashioned women talk about "needing a man" well I don't *need* a man. I fancy one, though, from time to time like I fancy chocolate or ice cream . . . I like to think I'm a sort of gay bachelor, Don Juan or Casanova. I believe in honesty. My poem *Respect* ends with the lines: "I want respect of quite another sort/for men to see my feelings are as strong/as theirs, my aims the same." Yes. I'm a feminist. I'm hoping with my work to persuade people that a woman shouldn't be treated differently by society.'

She poured more sherry and explained how her work attracts many fan letters. Mostly from OAPs and retired vicars. 'I have just had a gem from an 84-year-old vicar who suggested I go on a cleansing fibre diet and then ended with a kinky proposition. I get a lot of invitations from wierdos, absolute nutters, a spate of old gents. I'm sick of it to be honest. Even the *Independent* newspaper assumes I'm only interested in sex. It has commissioned me to write about Page 3 girls and female masseuses and stripogram people and I keep trying to tell it I have another serious, literary side . . .'

She paused and the house seemed ominously silent. Gulls screeched above the turret. Wind whistled through gaps in the windows. I asked whether I could see Pitt-Kethley's mother. As she nodded and stood at the top of a flight of basement steps calling 'Mother would you care to join us?' my insides just about turned to water. Was that the *Psycho* shriek I was hearing? Was that the light gleaming on Tony Perkin's meat cleaver?

You could have knocked me down with a plastic shower-cap when a robust, cheery mother appeared, hand outstretched, saying 'Hallo, dear,' and declined a drop of sherry. 'Mum's my unpaid proof-reader,' said Pitt-Kethley, fussing round Mum and turning up the gas fire, 'she's got a good sense of humour. She cares more for truth than about my being a randy so-and-so. She's got her priorities right.' I asked Mum whether this was so. 'Certainly. I may be an old geyser of 75 but I'm fairly broad-minded. I was brought up by Plymouth Brethren, jolly nice but far too strict and saintly. It's my view that girls have always been at it on the quiet. They just kept quiet about it. Fiona's more honest than most. Her pickups and all the rest of it don't bother me. I value honesty much more than chastity. Silly old-fashioned word. I admire the way Fiona fights against prejudice and injustice . . .' Pitt-Kethley chipped in: 'I call a spade a spade, a penis a penis'. Mum nodded.

Pitt-Kethley, whose work has been described as 'a colossal tease', 'ultimately banal' and 'irrepressibly ribald', is currently working on 4 books and a new collection of poetry. In the space between house restoration, cruising and writing she does bodybuilding classes to trim down her, frankly, chunky legs. They don't look appropriate in the sheer seamed stockings and gold high-heels she favours. Laurie Lee told her she's the best-looking poet since Rupert Brooke. A *Guardian* critic told her she makes too much of a song-and-dance about being filthy-minded *and* female. An American critic told her she sounds like a demure schoolmistress with a stuffed up nose. I told her I thought she was taking me for a ride. She flashed the vampire teeth, blinked her protuberant eyes and she and Mum gave way to genteel chuckles.

Journeys to the Underworld (Chatto & Windus, 1988).

Fiona Richmond

People think writing about sex is a doddle, but
when you're writing about the same subject all the
time it gets harder, and harder, if you'll forgive the pun.

'*M*y little cottage is the pink one with the thatched roof,' Fiona Richmond had explained to me on the phone, in a slightly bossy, cut-glass voice not unlike Mrs Thatcher's. Picking my way through the rural pot holes in the lane leading to the fabled Sexpert's front gate, I was feeling nervous. I mean, it's not every day I meet a living legend. Would the famed yellow E-type Jag, number plate FU2, be parked in the drive? Would the star of *Come Into My Bed, Let's Get Laid* and *Yes We Have No Pyjamas* perhaps be dashing about the kitchen bare-bummed in thigh-boots and suspenders? Would Britain's 'Sizzling Sex-pot', once arrested for riding naked on a horse in Piccadilly, offer me a cup of coffee?

You could have knocked me down with a goatskin tickler when the self-styled 'Egon Ronay of the bedroom' herself, pasty faced, bare-footed and hung-over looking, peered round the door hugging her shortie kimono to her bony chest. 'Some sort of stomach bug,' she said, 'so don't be surprised if I keep running . . .'

Suddenly I was up to my ankles in shagpile carpet, peering at the indoor swimming-pool, noting the bamboo kitchen units, sinking into a puffy armchair and wishing Fiona would sit still for five minutes and relax. Fiona, in the flesh, minus the make-up, glycerined lips, lashes, rouged nipples and fluorescent pubic hair, is a bit of an anti-climax. Taut, pale, pretty with mousey hair and a girlish smile that never quite reaches her eyes, she looks more like the Young Conservative sort, organizer of whist drives and church raffles than the person famed for winning the *Men Only*'s Limp Dick Award (this, you probably won't recall, was awarded for her smutty magazine articles purporting to spill the bedroom beans about men).

'Naturally you're here to talk about my new novel *In Depth*,' says Fiona, throwing back her head, laughing, running her fingers through her hair. 'I've written seven best-sellers so far and *In Depth* is my wildest one to date . . . it's about a girl journalist's first-hand investigation into jet-set sex . . .' head back, laugh, running fingers, '. . . sub-titled *Around The World In Eighty Lays*.' She adds that we can take it from her, in her capacity as frequent feature writer for various publications, including *The Sunday Telegraph, Evening Standard* and *Punch*, that Fleet Street throngs with brainless, nubile girls *exactly* like her new heroine Georgie, who sleep with lecherous editors in order to advance their careers. 'Not that I've ever slept around to get on,' declares Fiona. 'I'd rather achieve success on the merits of my own talent than sleep with some horrible old beer-bellied boss . . .'

> I'd rather achieve success on the merits of my own talent than sleep with some horrible old beer-bellied boss . . .

Fiona experiences 'total terror' each time she signs the contract for a new novel, which might take anything from 12 days to nine weeks to write. 'People think writing about sex is a doddle, but when you're dealing with the same subject all the time it gets harder, and harder . . . if you'll forgive the pun . . .' head back, laugh, running fingers '. . . vocabulary is the main problem – it's difficult not to repeat yourself. It is not simple to write about the sex act many times, many ways. Fortunately my ideas come easily, it's all straight-forward sex stuff, nothing kinky. And, after all, let's face it, I've already done the research – you don't drive a car without taking lessons first, do you?' She thinks of herself as 'Barbara Cartland with knobs on' and reckons 'a writer can get away with murder' so long as the rudeness is funny. 'I dictate each chapter to a gay manfriend of mine, and if we're both paralytic with giggles as I go along, I know I'm on the right track.'

She's well aware, she says, that she'll never win the Booker Prize or the W.H. Smith Fiction Award or see her work reviewed on the literary pages of quality newspapers, but nevertheless, her autobiography, called *Fiona*, sold well over a million and *From Here to Virginity* went into several editions.

Thin on plot, her book *In Depth* describes the acrobatic, contortionist minglings of various 'joy sticks', 'poles', 'swollen stalks' and 'wrinkled willies' with assorted 'hot spots', 'passionate portals', 'honey pots' and 'fluid fannies'. Bone-shaking climaxes burst like boils; hot undulating pitches of sensuality, not to mention heaving pantings of frenzied desire, happen on alternating pages. Typical of the Fiona Richmond prose style are such sentences as: 'Georgie heard the whip of a zip and the bong of a dong' or 'Acapulco had taken Georgie's breath and her knicker elastic away in one . . . it was way beyond her wettest dreams.' You get the flavour? Can't wait to buy a copy?

'Of course it's all fantasy,' trills Fiona. 'People, particularly men, don't want to read about sexual failure, they want raunchy escapism, superstuds, multi-orgasmic girls.' Doesn't she feel slightly daft – shamefaced, even – at the age of 36, to be churning out material which, to anyone with the slightest respect for the printed word, reads like schoolkid smut?

Fiona flings me a glance with a spike in it. 'I don't claim to write works of art,' she snaps, forgetting the toss, laugh and running fingers. 'I'm well aware that in certain quarters my books are beyond the pale, but just bear in mind that each first print run is a hundred thousand copies and few of our so-called quality writers can claim that. The more this country sinks into economic depression the more demand there will be for happy, titillating novels like mine.'

Throwing me another sharp look, she adds that 'women's libbers' get somewhat up her nose. When she stood for the rectorship of Dundee University in 1977 against Clement Freud (and incidentally pulled 545 votes), a crowd of raging feminists heckled her, shouted, screamed, yelled, accused her of exploiting the female form, of perpetuating the notion that women are simply sex objects, of demeaning female sexuality. 'You could say they were knocking me because of my knockers,' smiles Fiona. 'I told the women's libbers that they ought to be *proud* of me because far from being exploited myself I am exploiting men who buy my books and pay a lot of money to gaze at the nude revues.'

It was the same at Wimbledon in 1979, on the opening night of *Yes We Have No Pyjamas*. The Mother's Union was out in 'frantic force', waving banners and handing her a petition signed with 4,000 signatures, saying: 'What you are doing is debasing womanhood and undermining the sanctity of marriage.' Fiona, the vicar's daughter made bad, can't understand what all the fuss is about and throws back head, laughs and runs fingers through hair for several minutes: 'I probably spend a lot less time thinking about sex and more time doing it than the protesters. Certainly – and note that I'm not afraid to admit the fact – my parents had some reservations about my chosen career after I gave up a secretarial course to be a Bunny Girl and then a Penthouse Pet . . . my job wasn't exactly what Daddy would have chosen for me – he was a professional footballer, you know, before he took the cloth – but both Mummy and Daddy (before he died) came to see everything I did on the stage.'

After *Come Into My Bed*, however, about which one critic wrote that the performances were so wooden that the entire cast ought to be investigated for dry rot, poor loyal Mummy confessed to a newspaper reporter: 'Absolutely repulsive . . . we were terribly shocked. I mean, to think it was our own daughter up there doing these things. We love her dearly, but honestly, we really don't love what she is doing.'

Nevertheless, Fiona certainly loved

. . . just bear in mind that each first print run is a hundred thousand copies and few of our so-called quality writers can claim that. The more this country sinks into economic depression the more demand there will be for happy, titillating novels like mine.

what she was doing. She was also making a fair bob or two and the tidal wave of royalties from sales of her books now subsidizes the sumptuous renovation of her thatched cottage and maintains a bijou London *pied-à-terre*. But the sex symbol who once owned a £50,000 yacht called *Veste Demente* (the Latin for Get 'em Off), who had herself photographed wearing only boots and panties with the Crystal Palace football team during a training session, has recently decided to hang up her sequin-spangled G-string, retire from strip revues and settle down to her steady boyfriend and a typewriter.

'I've had a good innings', she says, 'and I'm quitting while I'm still in good shape. The reporters still comment that I'm "in magnificent condition" and I can assure you that I've never had to resort to silicone implants or buttock lifts . . .'

She has what she calls 'a faithful relationship' with someone called James; he isn't in the least freaked out by her nude cavortings on stage. 'I'm delighted with the man I've got, and I'm totally turned off these days by the very thought of one-night stands. I've also traded in the yellow Jag for a

Lancia because it made me so *conspicuous* when I was whizzing around . . .'

'Of course, there have been a lot of men in my life, but dozens and dozens rather than hundreds. I like good, straightforward, normal sex. I'm not into anything kinky.'

Fiona's most recent stageshow, *Space In My Pyjamas*, was, she confesses, something of a flop. 'We had dire reviews as usual, with the exception of Aberdeen and Lincoln which had sold out before we arrived . . . acting can be so unpredictable.' Fiona laughs in the sunny room where pink satin curtains rustle, lamps glow and bamboo, cane and wickerwork gleam. Pot plants thrive, teddy-bears, dolls and fluffy toy animals are heaped artistically upon an enormous sofa and *Hold my hand, I'm a stranger in Paradise* tinkles softly on the radio.

'I'll be off then,' I say, with my copy of *In Depth* under my arm. 'Cheerio.' She gives me several pounds of cooking apples because her lawn is knee deep in them and they tend to attract wasps. She's looking pensive. Doubtless she'll have knocked off another money-spinning novel in the time it takes me to write this piece. I can almost hear her mind revving up: 'He thrust her liquid, satin body against the sink in the aeroplane loo, blood pounded in his ears, musky perfume arose from her taut nipples, his frenzied, throbbing, pulsating etc, etc, etc . . . ' Many times. Many ways.

In Depth (Arrow Books, 1984).

I've always hankered after being a writer. I knew I had a book in me after I had been doing the stripper circuit and had jotted down a huge collection of true anecdotes.

FRANK
JAKEMAN

Frank Jakeman is a man with a chip on his shoulder and a boil on his backside. I first encountered him at the *Sour Grapes* bar in Ruislip where I was a reporter and he was the star attraction at a rumbustious hen night. 'Meet fabulous Frankie, Britain's number one sex stripper, the man putting the sex into Middlesex!' roared the compere, as Jakeman, strobe-stippled and perspiring, shimmied through the bead curtain and out amongst the swirling cigarette smoke and gin fumes to the theme music from *Fame*.

'We want winkle! We want winkle!' chanted the frenzied fans with wet-look lips and hot-look fingernails. Jiggling his eyebrows and jutting his jaw, Jakeman let fall his sequin-embroidered cloak. (Screams). A flying beer mat smacked against the giant eagle tattoo spanning his massive chest.

Off came his trousers. (Gasps!)

Off came his boxer-shorts. (Roars!)

Naked but for black wrestling boots and orange posing pouch, he squirted baby oil on his eagle, wriggled his pelvis and winked. (Pandemonium).

Fake-tanned and flawless but for the boil on his buttock he assumed a double biceps pose and winked again. Someone hurled a pickled onion. Jakeman gyrated slowly, baring his teeth and rolling his eyes. He looked like King Kong on Largactyl. Hoarse hen-nighters hooted: 'Get it off! Get it off!' The theme music from *Fame* reached a crescendo. Jakeman, pulling out all the stops, slipped off the pouch and whirled it furiously above his head to guffaws, chuckles, the odd cry of 'Spotty bum!' and the click of a hundred polaroids. 'Seen more meat on a butcher's apron,' shrieked one hen-nighter.

Laugh? We split our sides.

But there is more to Jakeman than meets the raucous hen-nighter's eye. I witnessed his serious side at the time of publication of his hugely successful autobiography *Being Frank* for which he received the sort of exorbitant advance that must make Booker prize contenders feel like banging their heads against brick walls. We met in a London beer garden where, even in mufti, he was recognized by sniggering by-standers and a barmaid who squealed 'Oo-er, it's *Fabulous Frankie*' behind the beer pumps.

'I'm used to fans making it hard for me', Jakeman explained, nudging me in the ribs, jiggling his eyebrows suggestively, and fidgeting with the zip of his black leather bomber jacket. 'No. Joking apart, it bugs me that people don't take my stripper work seriously. It's an *art*, you know. Okay, everyone knows me as the guy whose appearance on *EastEnders* broke all TV viewing records since

My book is not a kiss-and-tell smutty item of rubbish. The punters won't be expected to fork out money for old grope . . .

Charles and Di's wedding, but I'm well aware that people don't respect a bloke who gets paid to go on stage and flash his winkle.'

Maybe they don't. Maybe they would, Jakeman reckons, if they could only begin to understand the skills involved, the stamina required, the humiliation that has to be endured. Heartbreak, hardship, ridicule, 31-year old Jakeman has known them all. His marriage collapsed ('My wife said "You're no Rambo, you silly berk, for God's sake pull yourself together and get a proper job".') He lived in five bedsits in two years. He sold his record collection to pay his rent. He sank into despair. *EastEnders* was his big break and turning point.

He maintains that few men could survive the nightly ordeal of exposing themselves (often in draughty rooms) to hyped-up, hysterical hen-nighters.

'In that situation you can't just stand with your bum to the audience until your backing tape runs out. No way. You have to take deep breaths, turn round and try not to drop dead.' Here he paused to unzip his bomber jacket, casually exposing the giant eagle tattoo and making the barmaid gasp. He recalled how during the early days he was often immobilized with stage fright:

'It was even worse after *EastEnders*. Before I went on stage I'd start shaking like a leaf when I heard the compere's patter start up: "Here it is, girls, the little bit 21-million viewers didn't see, ta-ra-ra, meet and greet **Fabulous Frankie** . . ." I was terrified of the big build-up, felt that I didn't have enough to offer . . .'

He can say that again. In fact he did. And he jiggled his eyebrows again. However, as he explained, inside the stripper there was always the thinker fighting to get out.

There was the gnawing longing to become a successful author, to take the world of books by storm. Jakeman recalled his first stirrings of literary ambition.

'I used to be a zoo keeper. I became one after reading every one of Gerald Durrell's books. That guy is my hero. I even sent him an inscribed copy of *Being Frank*. I've always hankered after being a writer. I knew I had a book in me after I'd been doing the stripper circuit and had jotted down a huge collection of true anecdotes.'

His favourite anecdotes concern an ignominious stripper rival (and ex-plumber) called The Flaming Foreskin. His act started with a spectacular entrance to the *Spartacus* theme music. He wore a full-length fur cloak, steel breast-plate and viking helmet with horns three foot high full of lighter fuel.

'Foreskin was an impossible act to follow,' sighed Jakeman, 'he would walk on, there'd be a drum roll, he'd throw open the fur cloak, let out a blood-curdling howl like a crazed wolf and huge flames would jet up from his horns. It brought the house down.

'I once did a gig with him at an office party. The drums rolled, cymbals crashed, Foreskin's flames shot up, all the typists screamed, and I suddenly felt a splash on my head. I looked up. Water was pouring from the ceiling. Foreskin had set off the sprinklers. Firebells rang. Jets of water gushed everywhere. Photocopiers and typewriters were ruined. The damage ran into thousands.'

Frank said he was keen to make one thing clear. *Being Frank* is serious stuff. The whole of human life is there. He had only agreed to give me an interview because he didn't want some 'thick, sensation-seeking git from the tabloids' writing up sleaze publicity. No way. 'My mum's a Sunday School teacher, right? My book is not a kiss-and-tell smutty item of rubbish. The punters won't be expected to fork out money for old grope . . .' More eyebrow jiggling, another massive nudge in the ribs. Then he suddenly offered to 'bounce his pecs' and make the eagle's wings flap. Flap, flap they went, in the afternoon sunlight, just like *The Flight of the Condor*.

Fascinated bystanders gawped. The barmaid swooned. I sat, bemused, watching Jakeman's pecs flexing in the sunshine and wondered whether British literature is truly ready for *Being Frank*. Will it oust out the heavyweights in the bestseller list? Who can predict in the fickle world of publishing? Speaking as someone who once interviewed crusty old Kingsley Amis I must admit that things would have livened up a bit if *he* had had pecs to flex and a giant eagle tattoo. Jakeman is certainly something of a novelty.

Zipping up the chunky bomber jacket, he said he had to be going as he was doing a private hen-night in a stately home. The posh ones were the worst, he added, like animals. He said that now he's a writer he can hold his head up high. He has four more books in the pipeline. He has no place to go but up. 'I tell you this, there's a really heavy side to *Fabulous Frankie*,' he insisted, tapping his nose with a beefy forefinger. I'm in Greenpeace. I campaign for Save the Whale. If anyone wants to discuss the fact that a rain forest the size of Wales dies every week in the Amazon basin due to slash and burn methods of agriculture, then I can talk for hours and get really heavy. I always rattle Greenpeace collecting boxes round the audience after my gigs. That's before the girls go on the rampage, of course. They always do. Like armies of soldier ants, stripping any man that crosses their path.'

> I'm in Greenpeace. I campaign for Save the Whale. If anyone wants to discuss the fact that a rain forest the size of Wales dies every week in the Amazon basin due to slash and burn methods of agriculture, then I can talk for hours and get really heavy.

Being Frank (Headline Books, 1987).

Germaine

Greer

I'd like to postulate my theory which is that men in the '80s are *faking orgasm* – they groan, roll their eyes, jerk their feet and so forth, but it's all a *sham*.

Germaine Greer is so famous, such a celebrity, such a big-timer these days that when one of her books appears, her publisher hires a PR team to handle publicity and a classy hotel to handle the world's press beating an avid path to the 'Goddess of the Sexual Revolution'. Why can't I interview her *at home*? I asked the PR person. Max Bygraves, Debbie Harry, Fay Weldon, . . . I've interviewed them all at home; Fay Weldon even cooked me a curry. The PR person tut-tutted, gushed, and insisted that it must not be assumed *for one moment* that Greer is in any way a prima donna, but she is so *frightfully* in demand, inundated with interview requests, whizzing off to America, Canada, Italy, signing books, opening supermarkets, doing TV – in fact I must think myself *very lucky indeed* to be squeezed in between two literary luncheons and the man from *Over 21*.

Which is how I came to be waiting in the queue in the bar at Brown's Hotel as the world's hacks went in and out, in and out like gynaecologists' specula, with Bill the hack from the Bin-liner reading selected juicy bits from Greer's *Sex and Destiny* aloud to while away the wait.

'Get this!' Bill bawled, slapping his thighs, 'on page 132, in a bit about "condom-related sex play", she says "It is now vitally important that we find a way of making the condom a cult object of youth . . . we need to see the Fonz dropping a packet on the floor now and then" – wa-ha-ha, and how about this, on page 202? "Where once men were troubled by unwanted tumescence, they are now troubled by inconvenient and intractable detumescence. None of their advisers will say that they ought to stop peering into their underpants and get on with some other activity. Instead they will be treated for dysfuntion" – ya-ha-ha. Tumescence? Detumescence? Sounds like steam trains. Why can't the old windbag call a hard-on a hard-on?'

Then, catching sight of the Amazonian six-footer herself thundering through Brown's vestibule in plum-tinted tights and thick-knit two-piece, Bill chortles: 'Blimey, not much fear of any unwanted tumescence with that around if you ask me . . .' No-one is, in fact, asking him. Belt up, Bill, belt up, stop knocking one of my heroines, I want to shriek, except you don't use words like 'knocking' to boys from the Bin-liner.

'Anyway,' says Bill, the old female Enoch (sic) would be the first to start belly-aching if some Masai warrior got her up against his mud hut, after a tribal pig-kill, brandishing his female circumcision knife. No, joking apart, if you ask me Germaine's a crazy, two-faced cow telling all these women's libbers to rush out and fuck themselves stupid one minute, then telling them they should all be born-again virgins the next.'

Apparently Bill's Missus laughed herself daft at Greer's description of the tribulations of a diaphragm wearer, which Bill insists on reading aloud to the quivering fascination of Brown's bar staff: 'Here we go, folks. Page 133: "The loaded diaphragm is likely to shoot out of the wearer's grasp and fly through the air, splattering glop in all directions. The spermicide is cold, dense with a slithery consistency, it is meant to coat the cervix, but succeeds in coating everything else as well with chilly sludge . . . oro-genital contact is definitely counter-indicated, especially as spermicides are as toxic as if sperm are mice . . . if toothpaste tasted as disgusting as spermicide, the teeth of the nation would have fallen out years ago." '

Bill roars. 'Teeth of the nation, teeth of the nation! Cor, they didn't put that bit in *The Sunday Times* serialization!'

And then it is my turn to interview Germaine Greer. Into the tea-lounge I scurry, where tea-cups tinkle and people nibble with little moist sounds at cucumber sandwiches. I am extremely out of my depth. *Sex and Destiny* (the politics of human fertility) is one of those bulky, ponderous tomes scattered with words like 'ecdysiasm', 'sequelae', 'paraphilia', 'egregious' and 'blastocyst'. It is exactly the sort of book befitting someone educated at the Universities of Melbourne, Sydney and Cambridge. It is so brilliant, polemical and didactic that I've only managed to plough through and intellectually grasp the two chapters entitled 'Chastity is a form of birth control' and 'Changing concepts of sexuality'. I've even consulted a North London Poly lecturer as to what might be an intelligent first question. He suggested: 'Does your book indicate a paradigm shift?'

So, hoping to God I pronounce 'paradigm' correctly, I whip out my reporter's notebook and ask 'Does your book indicate a paradigm shift?', thinking to myself that if Greer simply replies 'Yes', I'm scuppered. Greer replies 'Yes'. I'm scuppered. A tense silence ensues. Greer suddenly hisses: 'Jeezus, is that Lynda Lee-Potter from the Fascist *Daily Mail* sitting over there stuffing her face with scones? Did you *read* what that bitch wrote about me screaming for champagne, chucking my skirts over my head to prove I wear no knickers, and tearing my hair out in desperation for a man? If it *is* her I'll tip the contents of the bloody cake stand in her lap, or a cup of coffee would be more fun . . .'

Disappointingly, it isn't Lynda Lee-Potter. Greer simmers down. 'Does your book indicate a paradigm shift?' I repeat tentatively. 'If it does, it's a shift of emphasis only,' replies Greer enviably articulate, enviably at ease. 'You see, people have been rewriting history, they've now decided I ran the sexual revolution by sitting at home issuing directives to the troops when, of course, I spearheaded the whole caboodle. I've always been a maverick, even in the days we were extolling the universal tongue bath and the ecstatic happiness which could be got from sexual congress *I* was actually saying it will all end in tears – like the great nanny I am . . . I think they got me mixed up with Hugh Heffner who sold eight million copies of *Playboy* a month, each copy reputedly read by five people, while I sold a mere million copies of *Female Eunuch* . . .

'So *I'm* not responsible for the sexual revolution, I don't think it actually happened, and I said so repeatedly, but I did believe it *could* happen, which is why I attended the Wet Dream Festival and edited *SUCK* and all those other pioneering activities. But I was never talking about the same things as the Wet Dreamers, I've *always* objected to sadistic material, to boring Swedish technicolour masterpieces showing slippery dicks the size of armchairs and women stuffing bottles up themselves, and the mass fixation with *genitality*.

'It was as a *campaigner* that I let them publish the famous,

> It was as a *campaigner* that I let them publish the famous erotic photo of me, which no one dares reprint under the British obsenity laws unless they stick a bunch of daffs up my arsehole . . .

erotic photo of me, which no one dares reprint under the British obscenity laws unless they stick a bunch of daffs up my arsehole . . . Yes, I shudder mildly about that photo now, but I've no regrets . . .' She pauses for breath and offers me a cucumber sandwich. 'Orgasmism', she continues, 'is a Western neurosis, but I say once you've had one, you've had them all . . .' Well, that may be *her* experience, I'm thinking, eyeing a plate of jam tarts. Better keep quiet though, in case she accuses me of being orgasmist.

Instead, I try my second question. 'In *Sex and Destiny* you appear to advocate chastity and celibacy – will this notion catch on in the West?' Greer sips her Perrier. 'What I'm saying is that restraint is an intrinsic part of sexuality – men think they must jump on and plug away like maniacs. I'm advocating restraint, also coitus interruptus, oral sex, a higher degree of perversion, if you like, sexual *alternatives*. I've re-evaluated the '50s, which were magical times . . . ten years of foreplay in the back seat of a Pontiac . . . Christ, remember the eroticism of the hot breath in your ear, knicker elastic, the panting, the snuffling . . . I must say I'd go a long way to hear a good pant.

'Fear of pregnancy is an excellent reason for refusing to fuck. It may also result in forms of love-making which women find more pleasant and gratifying than the missionary position – why not teach oral sex as a wonderful contraceptive method, for God's sake? Incidentally, I'd like to postulate my own theory, which is that men in the '80s are *faking orgasm* – they groan, roll their eyes, jerk their feet and so forth, but it's all a *sham* . . .'

A man sitting on Greer's left chokes on his buttered muffins. He is conspicuously and unwantedly tumescent. Everyone in Brown's tea lounge has gone quiet. All ears are flapping, Greer has an authoritative, resonant, voice. 'Every youth who reads his manual of sexual etiquette now knows that he must•belabour the tiny clitoris with his well-meaning intentions . . . a technique, incidentally, which effectively disguises any ineptitude in the phallic department.'

I ask her whether she lives in a state of celibacy herself. She pauses, reflectively picking her teeth. 'I was just about to say I haven't had it for six months,' replies Greer, the man on her left spreading his linen napkin furtively across his groin area, 'but that's not quite accurate, but I have had long spells of total sexual inactivity, six weeks here and there; it's about time that we accepted total celibates are no more deranged, inefficient, unhappy or unhealthy than any other segment of the population . . .

'Certainly my sexual partners are too numerous to count, I often can't remember whether I *did* or *didn't* when I see men grinning familiarly across rooms or at parties, but then I say to myself that if I *did* and I can't remember then it couldn't have been a very big deal, I don't hold it against them. I've

. . . it's about time that we accepted total celibates are no more deranged, inefficient, unhappy or unhealthy than any other segment of the population.

never been totally indiscriminate, occasionally I have been known to leap out of strange beds and hop on the 49 bus in the middle of the action when things have proved insipid . . .

'Look, it took Warren Beatty *a year* to get me into bed, he's irresistible, wonderful . . .!' Her eyes roll. I'm beginning to forget that this is *the* Germaine Greer I'm interviewing. She's suddenly turned all chatty, rapping on like one of the girls . . . Warren Beatty's not really *my* sort, I interrupt, spilling some tea down my boiler-suit. She flings up her hands and with ribald cackles, exclaims: 'No woman can resist him, physically he is practically *flawless*, I'm telling you Warren Beatty is irresistible.' I tell her that I'll just have to take her word for it. She bets me that I'd be putty in his hands. (If you are reading this, Warren, Greer and I have a tenner both ways so just drop me your address c/o the small ads.) Greer confides that Warren has a certain physical attribute only revealed in bed which she's not prepared to divulge but of which only his lovers have knowledge. Those that say they have slept with Warren and don't know about his certain attribute are lying. It separates the sheep from the goats.

My time is nearly up. There's bin-liner Bill champing at the bit, not to mention the *Irish Press, City Limits, Liverpool Echo, Glasgow Herald,* and *Birmingham Post.* Greer announces: 'I've begun to feel uncomfortable in my tum', and says that as she's never got any money can she have 20p to tip the lavatory lady? I give her 20p. While she disappears I tuck wildly into sandwiches and cream slices because all I had for lunch was a cheese roll while Greer worked her way (with Terry Coleman from *The Guardian*) through Brown's luncheon menu (minimum £17.20) which includes items like 'fresh crab soup infused with black truffle top-hatted with puff pastry' and 'mosaic lobster, salmon, sole and scallop infused with fresh herbs in a sea of vermouth jelly' and bottles of Chateau d'Yquem ('69) at £62.

I also dip into the book again, a book which will put everyone off what Greer terms 'genital dabbling', off the IUD ('a permanent abortionist's tool that transforms the womb into a poisonous abbatoir') and off the Pill ('steriods to be munched daily encouraging fungal infections and destruction of natural vaginal defence mechanisms which increase the risk of exposure to the cervix of carcinogens'). I quickly gen up on Greer's study of the most abstemious society in the world, the Dani of Indonesia, who abstain for stretches of six years with no signs of stress. I read about the anthropologist who lived with the Xinguanos without once seeing an erection in 25 years, about the Yam Growers of New Guinea who abstain during the yam-ripening season and the Yoruba who practise cliterodictomy. Ouch, I think.

Then Greer returns looking all het up and continues: 'Why the fuck *should* women be sexually accessible to men at all times – that's what women should be asking themselves? Why should we erect the model of recreational sex in the public places of the world? Nowadays the young woman who displays clitoris, labia minora, and vaginal introitus in a double spread in a girlie mag suffers less injury thereby than she would if her telephone was tapped. This is Western Society's way, but most societies have not brought the despiritualization of the body to anything approaching such a level – in ignoring or flouting the fear and reverence which other people feel for the body and its sacred orifices we inflict a socially ruinous kind of stress ... even now, after years of punctilious revolution, no woman likes to be thought *cheap*. Serious personality disorders can result from haphazard sexual experimentation.' Serious personality disorders? Is she telling me something about *herself*?

I decide to fire my last two questions. We're a similar age, I say – I chose marriage and two kids, you chose to sleep around and abort. Whose choice was most difficult? And, when you theorize about family life and motherhood, don't you think that you put yourself in the position of the big game hunter who has never caught any big game? (Apart from Warren Beatty.) Greer replies that she'd have gone insane tying herself down in her youth to one man and kids. Ok she does, to a certain extent, regret not having a child. And she's not afraid to say so. 'The reason that I never had a child is that my innards are all messed up. I'm a casualty of so-called permissiveness maybe . . . at 25 I got a low-grade infection, bled all the time . . . discharges, fibroids . . . one abortion . . . surgery . . . I was opened up, my womb was a mess, it had to be reconstructed . . . certainly, I'd cherish a child, I'd still have one if it happened, but at 45 the chances grow less . . .'

A journalist from the Irish Press hovers nearby with tape recorder. It's time for me to go. In the bar Bin-liner Bill decides he can't hang around for the 'Sexual Revolutionary' any longer as he's got to meet his kids from school. 'I'll phone Germaine's PR lady and say I had to pull out at the last minute . . . get it?' says Bill. I get it. Look, buy Greer's book. Make your own mind up about it. Between the bullshit it's brilliant. It's dazzling.

Sex and Destiny (Secker & Warburg, 1984).

Guy Playfair

THESE MEDIA PEOPLE ARE CUNNING. THEY LEAVE US AUTHORS ALONE
IN THEIR HOSPITALITY ROOM WHERE THE FRIDGE IS BULGING SAYING
'MAKE YOURSELF AT HOME', WHICH WE DO OF COURSE.

Hats off to Guy Playfair. He may not be a household name, he may not appear on best-seller lists, or on *Book at Bedtime*, or do sign-ins at W.H. Smith's, but for years he had been banging away assiduously on his Olivetti portable and knocking out compulsive books with titles like *The Flying Cow* ('75), *The Indefinite Boundary* ('78) and *This House is Haunted* ('80), to name but three, which sell in their tens of thousands. Playfair is as addictive as Brian Inglis, say, or Doris Stokes or Colin Wilson.

His most recent book, *If This Be Magic*, was inspired by a youth known as the Fishskin Boy (from East Grinstead) whose body was covered in a vile, black, malodorous substance bearing no resemblance to human skin. But more about Fishskin Boy anon ... The first time I encountered Playfair was in 1980 when he had just finished a 14-month poltergeist investigation at the Enfield council house of Mrs Peggy Hodgson. Along with several TV crews, news reporters, vicars, exorcists, a dry-rot man, spiritualists, Dyno-Rod, and diverse psychiatric social workers Playfair (Cheltenham and Cambridge educated) witnessed flying saucepans, spinning chairs, levitating tables, flapping curtains and the sudden ghastly manifestations of pools of foul-smelling liquid. While the long-suffering Mrs Hodgson and her three children went about their normal daily routine, Playfair installed himself and his sleeping bag on the landing and pottered about with tape-recorder and remote control video capturing paranormal happenings.

As soon as he entered the house inexplicable rapping sounds began. He got whacked around the head by a flying kettle. The puzzling words 'I AM FRED' and 'GET ME A TEABAG' materialized on the bathroom door. A young Hodgson levitated in full view of a lollypop lady on duty outside the house. The budgie died. So did the goldfish. And when Playfair produced his book *This House Is Haunted*, many people fell about laughing. They said that Playfair was off his head. They insisted that the young Hodgson had pulled a fast one. They sneered that 'The Creepy Crusader', as they nicknamed Playfair, had been hoodwinked good and proper. Not that Playfair lost any sleep; he never does. His book still sold all over the world and went into paperback.

He simply developed a thick skin (shades, here, of Fishskin Boy) and ignored the cynics.

'Quite honestly, the flak doesn't bother me,' he explained, as we ate lunch in a wine bar with other people's cigarette smoke be-fouling our three-bean salad and crunchy croutons, 'people believe what they want to believe. They also reject out of hand anything that doesn't fit in with their view of the world. In the ordinary course of events you can't make settees turn over without touching them, or things go through walls, or excrement appear from nowhere ... so when these things happen most people refuse to believe them. They also reject the power of hypnosis and the fact that one person can heal another without drugs.'

Paranormal healing phenomena are the subject of Playfair's latest book, *If This Be Magic*, and here we return to the Fishskin Boy of East Grinstead, whose amazing cure by hypnosis made medical history and was reported in *The British Medical Journal* in 1952. As Playfair explained: 'The Fishskin Boy was a horrible sight with large, warty excrescences 5 mm wide all over his legs and feet while his hands were enveloped in a rigid horny casing from which blood-stained serum oozed ...' At this point several wine-bar patrons put down their knives and forks. ('Do you mind. Some people are trying to *eat*.') But Playfair masticated in a melancholy manner and carried on regardless: 'Plastic surgeons could do nothing for him. He was declared incurable. Then a skilled hypnotist, experienced at removing warts by suggestion, cleared first the boy's right arm, then much of the rest of his body. There are many well-documented cases of such cures in recent years and my book is an appeal for the much wider use of hypnosis by the medical profession.'

I must say I was beginning to understand why Playfair had not been on *A Book At Bedtime* or done *A Life In The Day Of* and so forth. My abandoned crunchy croutons congealed on the plate while he described his extensive research. It was he who turned up the 1897 experiments of a Professor Delboeuf whose obliging servant, Mademoiselle J, volunteered to lay her bare arms on the table so that Delboeuf might place a red-hot bar across them while suggesting she would feel pain in her left arm only.

More recently (1975) a Dr Chertok also demonstrated that

wounds can not only be healed by suggestion, but *caused* by it. He produced a blister on a patient's arm by placing a cold coin on it and suggesting it was red hot. 'Such experiments offer irrefutable proof', argued Playfair, removing a shred of watercress trapped between his front teeth, 'of the influence of mind on physiological processes.

'Oh yes,' he added, sorting out his slices of tomato and pushing them to the side of his plate, 'hypnotic suggestion is already a powerful force in people's lives.' Whenever he is out distributing Liberal Party leaflets in the Earls Court area where he lives, he observes, through their grimy windows, the hypnotized masses slouched in front of their TV sets and he concludes that TV is one way to mesmerize the nation on a massive scale.

It is perfectly plausible, of course, that TV, or the Liberal Party come to that, could be agents of mass hypnosis . . . But perhaps, by now, you are beginning to sense that Playfair in the flesh is somewhat heavy-going. Certainly, he is not exactly a bundle of laughs. And try as I might I couldn't persuade him to swallow more than half a glass of house red. He explained that it was his intention to remain stone cold sober because he was en route to the John Dunn Programme at Broadcasting House. The last time he was there, he confessed darkly, he was not his usual lucid self. 'It's rather a recondite point, as a matter of fact. These media people are cunning. They leave us authors alone for an hour in their hospitality room where the fridge is bulging and the ice bucket crammed, saying "Make yourself at home", which we do, of course, being nervous and apprehensive. I once went on the air with a hostile interviewer, not mentioning any names, not *drunk*, I might add, but having supped several lukewarm beers on an empty stomach, and I certainly didn't do justice to my topic.'

Here he flashed a sepulchral smile, and apropos of the Fishskin Boy, I suppose, I suddenly found myself blurting out: 'As a matter of fact I have this patch of eczema. I'm not in the same league as the Fishskin Boy, of course, but . . .' 'Ah, Eczema . . .' he began, nodding his head, eyes ablaze. The winebar cleared. It occurred to me that no other author I've ever interviewed possessed the force to elicit such a confidence.

If This Be Magic (Jonathan Cape, 1985).

~ Heather Hay ~

*If you have read in newspapers
of saga authors getting £40,000
advances my dear, forget it.*

*H*eather Hay has just had her first novel published. Before that she kept pigs, goats and chickens, made jam and fudge to sell to the National Trust, and game-pies and pasties to sell to tourists who visit the stately home of Lord de Lisle, Penshurst Place. Heather Hay is very keen on stately homes. Her novel, *Heritage*, described as 'the first volume of an enchanting new saga, set in the lushlands of England', is set in a stately home called Pencombe Hall where Lord Montford's family gather round their snooker table brooding about England. *Heritage*'s heroine, Isabella ('pale and pensive') has dreams that range far beyond the hazy hush of Pencombe and the click of ivory balls on green baize ... *Heritage*, like all sagas, is clamorous with the sound of ripping bodices, and packed with purple passages such as 'With her head bent back she felt herself part of the warm night, a creature of abandon. Deeper she slipped into the waking dream, deeper into an ocean of sensation . . .' and 'His kiss was brutal, his mouth hard. She heard the ripping of muslin before she felt her dress tear . . .'

Crass stuff, you might be thinking. Or absolute tripe. But, as sagas go, *Heritage* has made history. What makes it 'unique' and different from the countless indistinguishable pulp sagas foisted upon the saga-loving public each year is its author's willingness to fork out £200,000 to host her own book launch. Enterprising Hay devised her own promotion party before she'd even finished the last line ('They walked out of the room together, away from the snooker table, out into the starlit night and into their future'). This was terrific news for her publisher, Grafton, who, like most publishers, tend to launch first novels with trepidation, peanuts and a few cheap bottles of plonk.

Heather Hay's bash for 600 guests was the Rolls Royce of book launches. A coach packed with freeloading publishers and book critics drove from London with everyone wearing evening dress and drinking sparkling wine and eating smoked salmon sandwiches all the way to Leeds Castle in Kent. Well, not exactly at Leeds Castle but in a draughty marquee in the grounds of Leeds Castle where a biting east wind whistled round the female guests' bare shoulders and where Kentish soil clogged up their stiletto-heeled party shoes. There was free pink champagne. There was dancing. There was curly endive in walnut vinaigrette, baby roast poussin and nougatine brittle. There was a message from the author inside everybody's menu which read: 'Thank you for being with me this evening. When I wrote the climax of *Heritage* I imagined a glorious party – beautiful people, magical setting, delicious food and above all an exhilarating sense of drama.' There was a televised snooker contest between snooker aces Steve Davis and Jimmy White, the prize a £50,000 white gold, diamond and topaz necklace. And there was Heather Hay herself (largely ignored by the beautiful people) distributing complimentary copies of *Heritage* (autographed) and posing for photographers, and whirling about waving her pen as if she was as big as Anita Brookner, say, or Barbara Cartland.

Flushed with the triumph of it all she flashed euphoric smiles (Hallo Steve! Hallo there Jimmy! Oh look there's Gerald Harper, Hallo Gerald! Isn't it all absolutely thrilling. I've just spent half an hour doing my eyes for the photographs . . .') and gazed upon her personal notion of beautiful people, magical setting, delicious food and an exhilarating sense of drama.

'Who does she think she is, daft bitch,' bitched one of her guests scraping mud from her sling-backs, 'and who *are* all these freeloading creeps anyway?' Well she was one, I was one, and Page Three girl Samantha Fox was another. 'What do you think of this book, Samantha?' I inquired as we queued for the outdoor portaloos. 'Wot book?' replied Samantha Fox. 'The book called *Heritage* which we have all been invited here to celebrate at the author's own expense.' 'I don't know nuffink about a book. I'm here for the snooker – I love snooker,' snapped Samantha Fox above a cacophony of abortive flushes and a chorus of anguished voices crying 'Chain won't work. Chain won't work'. In fact Samantha Fox's love of snooker led her to volunteer to lie on her back on the snooker table, her famed big boobs pancaking-out over the sides of her strapless ballgown, while the 'beautiful people' crowded close shouting 'Wohr! Good old Sam!' With her head back, she surely, in Heather Hay's words, 'felt herself part of the night, a creature of abandon'. 'I've always said this game's a load of balls,' she riposted, as a snooker ace placed a ball in her glossy mouth and knocked it with the cue across the green baize. 'Cor, I fink I'll go back to topless modlin, it's much safer.'

Meanwhile Heather Hay beamed and twinkled and waved at her unheeding guests. Never mind that no-one congratulated her upon her first book. Never mind that 600 complimentary copies had been ground into the mud by the end of the bash. Between sips of pink champagne she joined me on the party periphery to discuss *Heritage*. 'It took a year to write. I had to fit it round my other commercial interest, catering. I'm busy most of the time helping my husband organise clay pigeon shooting at stately homes and so on. I am utterly delighted with *Heritage*. When it first came back from the publisher in paperback form I took it up to bed. I know this sounds a hoot but when I'd finished it I had to admit that I'd enjoyed it very much. It's wonderful. I hope it will establish me as a saga writer of some repute.'

I am utterly delighted with *Heritage*. When it first came back from the publisher in paperback form I took it up to bed. I know this sounds a hoot but when I'd finished it I had to admit that I'd enjoyed it very much.

How much had this party cost her? 'Not very much. I can't be precise about figures. The secret is sponsorship. When I'd almost finished *Heritage* I began to plan a fabulous launch. I worked out how to get sponsorship from the snooker world, and from Ratners jewellers who provided the £50,000 snooker prize necklace as well as a second £50,000 necklace which I'm offering as a readers' prize. The competition form is on the last page of the book. It was my idea to have stickers on the front cover announcing "Win the £50,000 Heritage necklace".'

How much advance did she earn? 'Oh dear, I was hoping you wouldn't ask me that. If you have read in newspapers of saga authors getting £40,000 advances my dear, forget it. My agent said "Don't be ridiculous" when I mentioned that sum. Very few writers get that, and they write books which are usually rewritten by a vast team . . .' Yes, but how much *did* she get? 'Well, I'd hate to upset Grafton, I don't want to suggest they're stingy. Oh all right. £4,000.'

And great news for saga fans. *Heritage* part 2 is already in the word processor. The launch party is already planned. As Heather Hay explains: 'It came much quicker this time. Seeing your first novel in print is a terrific boost. I'm negotiating a better advance this time. Motor racing is the

> I hope it will establish me as a saga writer of some repute.

theme and I'm planning a lavish launch at Brands Hatch. Thanks to the publicity engendered by this launch I've just done a deal with Penguin. They've paid £30,000 for a book about the snooker scene called *The Business* which I'm writing with snooker promoter Barry Hearn.' Yes but can she *write*? Don't ask silly questions. Who cares when she's game enough to do free promotions.

In the Leeds Castle marquee there was no-one who had actually read *Heritage*. Even the people from Grafton looked shifty when asked for their opinion of the 'enchanting saga set in the lushlands of Kent'. I tackled snooker ace Steve Davis, winner of the £50,000 necklace. 'What do you think of Heather Hay's book, Steve?' 'Can't say I've got round to reading it. It's not a men's book.' Snooker ace Jimmy White looking disgruntled and aggressively adjusted his bow tie: 'Did you enjoy the book, Jimmy?' 'He don't read, know what I mean,' quips Jimmy's wife. Snooker manager Barry Hearn dislodged fragments of poussin from his teeth and admitted he hadn't read *Heritage* either, adding: 'But here's a fact that will amaze you. In 1927 Joe Davis won the first ever world snooker championships for a prize of £6 and ten shillings. He had to give half the prize money back to pay for the trophy.' Amazing. And Heather Hay stood by beaming, twinkling, waving, and lapping up the click of ivory balls on green baize while the band played on and the freeloaders walked out of the marquee, away from the snooker table, out into the starlit night and into their future.

Heritage (Grafton Books, 1988).

HENRY ROOT

Scoop Root has documented the successful man's need to be involved in a scandal as per my friends Archer and Sir Halpern.

enry Root, man of letters. Is he a poseur or polymath? What makes the wet-fish entrepreneur tick? Such are my thoughts as, circumnavigating a cat crouched over a rotting kipper, I climb three flights of stairs and ring the bell of 139 Elm Park Mansions. From somewhere inside a Bee Gees record is replaced by *Hits From Rigoletto*. The front door is flung open by a human blancmange redolent of 'Brut' and over-active armpits. A large framed photograph of Margaret Thatcher hangs on the wall. Root is wearing voluminous jog-pants, and a Burton leather-look bomber jacket, its velcro fastening half open to reveal foxy chest hair into which dangles a gold ingot medallion.

'Ah, it's the Potter woman. Been in a fight, have you? Come in . . .' he bellows, ushering me along a passage (Potter? What's the fat fool talking about?) and into an office full of filing cabinets. In and Out trays, a shredder, an Olivetti portable, a prodigeous number of Tipp-Ex bottles, bulging Filofaxes and one pair of rusty chest-expanders.

'. . . I know your boss, Sir English. I used to be the "Voice of Reason" in the *Mail on Sunday*, the man who said what others hardly dared to think. Scoop Root. Sir English fired me when I asked for my own desk and 'phone . . .'

In vain I try to interject, in vain I try to explain that I am not Lynda Lee-Potter from the *Daily Mail*, but Root booms on regardless. 'Listen, Mrs Potter, Madam, I'm a busy man. Don't usually grant interviews to newspaper chappies. I've already dispatched two down the liftshaft. Max Hastings, and Bernard Levin wittering on about *La Condition Humaine*. Don't tell me . . .'

He steers me towards an *Observer* offer sofabed brandishing his new book *The Soap Letters*, an epistolary history of how Root conceived, launched and financed a TV soap opera. 'I've sold it to Grade', he continues, flashing daunting dentures and kicking the chest-expanders behind a portable fax machine.

'I outbid him. During our negotiations he wore reflector shades and I wore reflector shades myself *vis-a-vis*. Grade, staring into the shades, found himself negotiating with himself and thus gave in to his own demands. *Crack Up*, by

Henry Root starring the Duchess of Argyll, Lord Weymouth, Cecil Parkinson, Archer, Quant, Ingrams, the Marquis of Blandford and various other disgusting people we are putting back to square one in front of an audience of millions . . .'

As he pontificates I glance round his office. A photo of Henry Root junior, in make-up and bunny costume, stands beside a larger one of Tina Small 'the girl with the 54-inch boobs' from *Sunday Sport*, and a larger one still of the Queen. Root's bookshelf is packed with Jilly Cooper books. Intercepting my glance he remarks:

Amis? Kingsley's boy? . . . sad business. Three foot three inches tall, wears a wig and goes swimming at midnight in Hampstead Pond with Hermione Lee.

'I only read Jilly Cooper. No time for anybody else. Thighs like nutcrackers. If she gets them round a man's neck he'll know all about it. Not a word to Leo, mind, personal friend of mine . . .' Here he taps his bulbous nose with a podgy forefinger and suggests a little snorter. 'This'll take the balls off a rhino, get this inside you,' he roars, uncorking a bottle of Mrs Root's rhubarb wine, and taking a large swig.

Seizing this opportunity to get a word in, I steer the conversation back to *The Soap Letters*, my pen and notepad poised as he begins:

'I've turned down Wogan, talks too much. Likes to do all the talking himself. I prefer a turkey like Aspel. Nothing to say for himself. I shall be signing copies in Hatchards, the Queen's bookshop. Her Majesty may be present. Sir Burnett will be doing something on *News At Ten*, personal friend of mine, hope for the best, kill the Irish . . .'

Suddenly with an animal howl Root lunges and flings himself upon me gasping: 'You'll do, Potter. Over you go. On your back. Cash on the table I imagine. Haven't done this in a long time.'

I scream. I struggle. I put up a heroic fight. I fall on to the Habitat Flokati rug with Root floundering on top of me as if I'm a waterbed. Not since I interviewed Christopher Logue has anything so horrible occurred. We thrash about with Root grunting 'Margaret! Margaret!', his hands like pudgy flippers up the legs of my 'Next' Bruxelles-lace-trimmed Cami-knickers (Pink).

'This didn't happen when I interviewed Martin Amis,' I gasp, trying cerebral shock tactics to bring the flabby fiend to his senses in the way Andrea Dworkin suggested in her anti-rape handbook *Intercourse*.

'Amis? Kingsley's boy?' pants Root through lust-bloated lips, track suit round his ankles, buttocks, in orange boxer shorts, like Belisha beacons winking wildly, 'sad business. Three foot three inches tall, wears a wig and goes swimming at midnight in Hampstead Pond with Hermione Lee. Don't tell me . . .' He flings back his head affording a ghastly glimpse up his tangled nostrils. A spider plant crashes on to his bald spot. *Hits From Rigoletto* and Root's slobbering gasps pound in my ears.

I dread to think what might have happened had not Mrs Root arrived home unexpectedly and popped her *en bouffant* head round the office door. Root springs up exclaiming: 'Just checking the Potter woman for wiring, Mrs Root. Bugging devices. I read the *Bonfire* book by that wispy-looking American chappie. Wears white suits. Taking no chances. Chap can't be too careful. Doesn't want to be misquoted.'

I stand up, straightening my 'Bymail' hip-skimming cotton jersey mini-skirt.

'Beg pardon, Mr Root,' apologizes Mrs Root. 'Kitchen calls. Cake in the oven. Kippers cooking. Will Mrs Potter be staying for tea?'

As I retrieve my Ravel ankle-strap stiletto-heeled shoes, Root brushes spider plant from his bomber jacket and blusters:

'Tried looking for wiring the other night in the Garrick Club. Tipped some woman on her back, turned out to be Geoffrey Wheatcroft. My mistake, madam, I said. Fellow's now in a clinic, with a saucepan on his head, walking into the walls, lost his sense of spatial relation . . .'

Root is breathing heavily, snorting almost, causing a foreign body which blocks his left nostril to descend and disappear as if emphasizing his words. With every inhalation it retreats, with every exhalation it drops.

'Right. Got that off my chest. Straighten up, Root. Back to business. Now then, where were we, Potter? . . .' (Down drops the foreign body.) 'O'Mara publisher? Yes, I like them. They have a rubbish list, Royal books and Sir Burnett, make a fortune. They begged me to join to bring in a bit of literary ballast . . .' (Foreign body soars up.) 'I suggested to Michael O'Mara how about *The Royal Avalanche Pop-Up Book*. He went on his knees for me to join. He's very quick on his feet. I thought, why not? Lord Weidenfeld let me down. I took Princess Michael to his Christmas do and was stopped in the porch. Flunkey wouldn't let me in. Said "It's a fat man with a girl from Chelsea Escorts Ltd". Flunkey went head first into a bollard . . .' (Now you see it.) 'The Princess and I went in, hardly an Everest for social climbers, I think you'll agree. Ha . . .' (Now you don't.) 'Room full of plagiarists and men in velvet slippers. As we were dancing together I overheard Geoffrey Wheatcroft say we looked like Abbott and Costello, so he went headfirst into the bowl of punch . . .'

> I suggested to Michael O'Mara how about *The Royal Avalanche Pop-Up Book*. He went on his knees . . .

Enough is enough. Picking Flokati rug hairs from my 'Bymail' body-hugging short-sleeved sweatshirt I tell Root that he's a randy old ratbag and that I'm not Lynda Lee-Potter.

'You mean you're not writing this for *The Daily Mail*? he explodes, lips hanging off his face like Roy Hattersley's.

When I explain that I'm writing it for *The Literary Review*, he kicks his Kaleidoscope pump-action exercise bike across the room. 'What's that? Don't know that one. Russian, is it? Left of centre? Get out of here. I don't know. In the early afternoon. Woman comes into my home saying she's Potter . . .' He manhandles me towards the door shouting in-coherencies about Joan Ruddock, Commie agitators ('Here's a hanky, dear,' says Mrs Root, scampering out of the kitchen and back again), Anne Diamond and Melvyn Bragg.

'Here's the point of my book, my good woman,' he roars, pushing me on to the narrow landing. 'Scoop Root has documented the successful man's need to be involved in a scandal as per my friends Archer and Sir Halpern. Who had heard of Halpern until he was caught in his half hose with a topless bimbo? Front page news. Boots shares go up. I sought his advice and he explained how these days a fat man with a charge card can impress the girls. Bring on the bimbos says I. Problem is, once caught it's three years in the wilderness as per Jack Profumo. Charity work in the East End and a fragrant boot-faced wife standing by. Is it worth getting your feet a bit muddy if that's the price you pay . . .?'

High heels clacking on concrete, I flee from Elm Park Mansions with Mrs Root leaning from an upper window shouting 'Yoo-hoo, Mrs Potter, shall Mr Root walk you to the Underground?'

Walk? Not bloody likely. I'm going in a taxi.

Letter from Henry Root to the *Literary Review* following interview.

Sir,

Imagine this – you're sitting in your lounge-room in the early afternoon – legs outstretched, a tumbler of port from Boots to hand, from the tape-deck the swell of fat ballooning ballads with a patriotic underthump – when a woman of a certain age, purporting to be a bubble-skirted punk reporter from *The Daily Mail* (Lee-Potter at a guess) drives through your front door with her hormones in an uproar and her thighs akimbo. When the 'interview' appears (not, I may say, in *The Daily Mail* but in your magazine), does a literary man, with back-list credibility and oeuvres forthcoming, in the general run of things riposte? As a rule, I'd say not – but in the piece by Potter/Hennessy/Whoever in your last edition about my important new book, *The Soap Letters* by Henry Root (Michael O'Mara Books, £9.95), I'd like to put the record straight. The joke, such as it is, is on the Potter/Hennessy Whoever woman, and not for the first time, I imagine. The piece was accurate in every detail, I'll say that for it, except in one respect. The plain fact is that the man she wrestled on the floor and quizzed while prone wasn't me, but Kingsley Amis.

Here was the way of it. That day I'd lunched substantially at the Garrick, as is my custom, had sat at the buffers' table in the centre with my friends Sir Elton, Paul Johnson and Amis père. We pull well, together, the four of us, we're peas in a pod, sharing a sense of humour – none of us having one. We're cutlet men, we like a cutlet underdone with port and racontage to follow. Amis does faces, often Welsh, with a comic voice to match, likes to shock literary types adjacent by pretending to have heard of no one. 'Borges?' he says.

'Who's he? I've never heard of him!' and he pulls a face, no doubt Welsh, whereat Sir Elton, Johnson and I roar with laughter, though we're not sure why. Plus at the mention of women, Russians, young people we turn plum-red with indignation, we suffer intestinal over-stretch, we inflate suddenly like rubber dinghies – it's happened many times.

On this day at the end of lunch, Sir Elton and Johnson took off to discipline their dogs, bark orders at their women-folk etc, while Amis and I decided to walk off our general indignation, to return on foot to my duplex maisonette in Fulham, where to discuss declining standards with a bottle handy. Finding myself clean out of port, I told Amis to sit tight in his woolly waistcoat, to answer the door to no-one, to listen to *Hits From Rigoletto* (Our Price, £4.99) – the Potter/Hennessy woman got that right at least – while I repair to Oddbins locally. I was absent for twenty minutes at the most, returning to find Amis in a state of shock, his face as white as herring-roe, moaning to himself and staring at the wall.

'Good God, Amis!' I cried, 'You look as though you've just been interviewed by a woman from *The Daily Mail*.' I tried to cheer him up, to bring his colour back. 'Nabokov!' I said. 'Who's he? Ha! Ha!' and pulled a face – Welsh, I hoped – but he didn't laugh. When he could speak at last, he told me what had happened. In my absence, there'd been such a banging at my door that, fearing for the safety of the block, he'd gone to answer it, whereupon a mad woman, growling like a starved lioness, wrestled him upside down – and the rest was as you printed it.

Yours for a Bill of Rights against invasion in the afternoon.

Henry Root
139 Elm Park Mansion
Park Walk
London SW10

The Soap Letters (Michael O'Mara, 1988).

Hilary Norman

I suppose my motivation was
wanting to write the sort of book I
enjoy reading when I'm on a long
plane journey.

'The padded on bare feet to the open window and gazed out over her dark garden. The soft Normandy breeze, laden with fragrance, fondled her long, black hair and slipped past her to ruffle the letter on her desk . . .' Thus, on page nine of Hilary Norman's novel *In Love And Friendship* we are introduced in cringe-making, schmaltzy prose to the heroine Alexandra. This is Miss Norman's first novel. It is described on the dust-jacket as 'a beautiful, affecting story of endearing love and friendship'. It has already earned its author a quarter of a million pounds. And it is, not to put too fine a point on it, absolute drivel.

These days publishers go mad about drivel. They froth at the mouth for it. Drivel sells, see? Drivel makes no intellectual demands upon its reader. Drivel can be banged out in no time at all, and can be hyped, marketed, paperbacked and sold at railway stations, petrol pumps and airports. It can be profitably turned into trashy TV movies, particularly in America where drivel-lovers are prepared to fork out very big bucks. So, who are the entrepreneurs eager to give us our daily drivel: Let us consider the attitudes of Hilary Norman's publishing consultant, Brian Levy, an exuberant man in heavy horn-rims who insisted on being present when I went along to interview his protégée. In fact he hogged the interview to such an extent that Hilary Norman hardly said a word.

'This book is a feast of a novel, an absolute feast,' raved Brian, while 37-year-old Hilary sat, smiling modestly beside him and passing round potato crisps. 'It is really storytelling at its very best. It came to us at Hodder and Stoughton as an unsolicited manuscript; we were just about to chuck it in the "slush pile" along with all the hundreds of other unsolicited manuscripts we receive every day, but no, we took a close look and we all said, "Wait a minute. Hang on. This is not bad, not bad at all!" I sat there reading through this huge bundle of 600 sheets and I couldn't stop. I was totally riveted. At the end I poured myself a long drink and shouted, "This book has got something, boys, it has definitely got something!" '

But what exactly has it got? Apart from a lot of sex and

violence and a vile scene where a nymphomaniac called Rosa ('She grabbed at his hand, her skin scalding, pulled him close and stroked him through his trousers . . .') comes to a Harold Robbins-ish end? I put this question to Hilary who was about to reply but Brian got in first: 'I'll tell you what it's got, it's got that elusive page-turning quality that old hands in the publishing game, like me, get an instinct for. Oh yes. Old hands like me develop a nose for what makes a thumping good read. I haven't been in the business for 15 years without acquiring a sixth sense . . . And the book is totally *sincere*. The sincerity shines through blah-blah . . .' For crying out loud, Brian, shut up and let Hilary get a word in . . .

Hilary laughed. Okay, she agreed, she's certainly no Charlotte Bronte but she's sure made a great deal more cash banging it out than poor old Charlotte ever did. She was 'utterly amazed' when Brian bought her manuscript. 'I'd never wanted to be a writer. I work at the BBC. I woke up one morning and started to write out of the blue. I've always been a great reader. I like Judith Krantz, Sidney Sheldon, Jackie Collins . . . I suppose my motivation was wanting to write the sort of book I enjoy reading when I'm going on a long plane journey.'

She nibbled a crisp. 'I can't believe I've hit the jackpot with my first attempt.'

Here Brian exploded into ecstatic monologue pointing out that Hilary's is the sort of winning-the-pools success story that writers dream about. 'Everyone we've shown this book to has fallen over themselves. At the Frankfurt book fair we sold the Italian, Finnish and Norwegian rights. Then the Americans got interested. Six publishers were bidding for it and we got a quarter of a million dollars. Film rights and foreign rights will eventually clock it up to half a million quid. They can't *all* be wrong, can they?'

Well, that's an interesting point, Brian. What do *you* say, Hilary? 'I was shaking like a leaf, stunned, when Brian phoned from Frankfurt and mentioned a quarter of a million dollars. I poured myself a stiff drink and I straight away packed up my job to become a full-time writer.'

Did she think that *In Love and Friendship* makes a valuable contribution to British Literature and that the sincerity really does shine through the steamy adventures of Alexandra, 'a modern American heroine, beautiful, talented but desperately wanting something'? Before she could open her mouth Brian had the last word: 'It's a nice piece of writing, make no mistake about that, but, let's be honest, it's not going to be on the A-level syllabus in ten years' time.'

Too right, Brian. Sadly these are meretricious times when money-making motivates publishers rather than a desire to promote literary excellence. This month Hilary's book is being hyped in America, plugged with the publicity slogan: 'Buy the book, if you don't agree it's sensational we'll give you your money back.'

One can imagine Hilary padding on bare feet to the open window, gazing out over her Golders Green garden and, with the soft London breeze laden with diesel exhaust fondling her thick curly hair, laughing herself legless.

In Love and Friendship (Hodder & Stoughton, 1986).

Howard Jacobson

I sometimes get the impression there are
only five people and a parrot writing
novels in Britain, the way the same
names hog the literary pages.

*T*wo chortles, one snigger and a full-throated chuckle by page 4 can't be bad! I laughed so long and hard reading Howard Jacobson's *Peeping Tom* that I gave myself an asthma attack. 'Long and hard?' queries Jacobson with a certain ribald hooding of the eyelids and a Benny-Hill-ish flare of the right nostril, 'that's what a man likes to hear. Hmm.'

We are discussing his new novel *Peeping Tom* at his Clapham flat and I've decided that no sexist smut or lewdness is going to be allowed to creep into this interview. Jacobson is an academic, right? He's already told me that he thought twice about being interviewed by someone who hasn't distinguished herself as a novelist, and that he dreads his words being trivialized. Keeping things serious is going to be tricky. Mainly because Jacobson's novel is about sex. It's the funniest book about sex ever written. Robert Nye raved about it in The *Guardian* calling it 'a glorious whirl of sex and scholarship', and fumed that it was 'disgusting that this brilliant book was not in the running for the Booker prize'.

As well as being a glorious whirl, *Peeping Tom* is a side-splitting character assassination of Thomas Hardy. Jacobson's hero, Barney Fugleman, describes Hardy as 'a prurient little Victorian ratbag' and 'a morbid, superstitious rustic who confused high peevishness with tragedy, niggardliness with humour, and mean-naturedness with melancholy'. Why was he like this? Because, according to Fugleman (and, we must suppose, Jacobson), 'he couldn't get his end away'.

Fugleman learns, under hypnosis, that he is a reincarnation of Thomas Hardy. It transpires that the acclaimed author was sexually turned on by ogling hanged female miscreants and by pursuing mindless milkmaids. Without doubt, stodgy academic critics will swarm, like flies to a dog turd, upon Jacobson's erudite carnage. Thomas Hardy enthusiasts will rise up and rage. The Hardy Society will call for the book to be burnt. Robert Gittings will blow a blood vessel. John Fowles will jump off the Lyme Regis Cobb. 'Oh let 'em, let the pompous humourless buggers scream and shout . . .,' says Jacobson whose sensual lower lip lurks beneath a droopy, moist moustache in much the same manner as Hardy's lurked in the later photographs, 'anyway I'm not very keen to discuss Hardy'.

Critics? Don't mention critics to Jacobson. They make him sick. He says he's been tempted to throw himself under a tube train during the past few weeks what with opening his newspaper and reading Angela Carter on J.G. Ballard. And Ian McEwen on Angela Carter. And Martin Amis on J.G. Ballard, talking about Angela Carter. And Ian McEwen, not to mention Julian Barnes, enthusing about Martin Amis's piece on J.G. Ballard. 'Christ', shrieks Jacobson, nostrils opening and closing with emotion, 'I sometimes get the impression that in Britain there are only five people and a parrot writing novels, the way the same names hog the literary pages . . .'

Jacobson has the most mobile nostrils ever seen. They have a life of their own. I find my eyes boring into them as I steer him away from the topic of literary critics and towards his feelings about Thomas Hardy: 'Very well. If you insist. One of my characters, Camilla, points out that what lay behind all that female craving for submission in Hardy's work, all his fear about women wanting nothing so much as to be tamed, was his own pathological certainty that he didn't have what it takes to tame them. In other words, Hardy used his novels to have the women he loved, real or imaginary, violated by proxy.

'It struck me that Roman Polanski's wholly boring film of *Tess* was extremely faithful to the original because the director shared an identical fondness for dewy-lipped virgins, and an identical aesthetic interest in watching them defiled. Polanski, for his pains, is exiled. Hardy is buried, without his heart, in Westminster Abbey. If the kinky little sod were around today he'd probably be up on a paedophile charge . . . incidentally, I just don't understand why any man would want to lay a finger on a woman under thirty. Let alone man-handle her in print, which is more serious.'

Which brings us to the second significant theme marching through Jacobson's work, the allure of the autonomous, intelligent, raunchy, wholly self-confident new woman. Jacobson's female characters are wonderful, articulate getters-of-the-upper-hand. They have a powerful sense of their own rights, and of their moral and intellectual superiority. And they are not particularly young. As Jacobson explains: 'I'm one of that increasing number of men who believe that women don't start looking really nice until they possess a few life lines around the face. Older women are so much more interesting and animated than young girls because of their life experience.'

Hardy is buried, without his heart, in Westminster Abbey. If the kinky little sod were around today he'd probably be up on a paedophile charge . . .

Here I gasp involuntarily. My gasp is still probably echoing round the twentieth century. Older women are actually *desirable*? This is *exciting*. This is a revelatory concept at a time when the mass media has convinced every woman with spreading hips and crowsfeet that she'd be doing the world a favour by sticking her head in the gas oven. Let me quote Barney Fugleman on the attractions of older women: 'Rabika Flatman must be getting on for 50 now . . . I have never shared Hardy's horror of ageing beauty. I suppose there must come a time when women's looks stop improving, but I can't trust a man who thinks that that time is around their eighteenth birthday . . .' Fugleman also says: 'I'm not certain, either, that women ought to be victims of the lunatic vagaries, the precariousness and the fragility of male romanticism.'

Meanwhile Jacobson, pacing ruminatively between kitchen and sitting-room, continues: 'I think that breasts look nice when they sag a bit: perfect breasts are wholly tedious. Eyes look best when they crinkle, I *like* bags. I love droop lines round the mouth. As a boy I used to be *mad* about Jeanne Moreau. Mind you, she always had droop lines, even when she was 18. Hmmm. All this talk about sagging breasts, lines and droop . . . phew . . . I'll have to have a drink . . .' He pours himself a beer. He makes me a cup of tea. I'm about to remark that I like his pink cups but find, silly subjective me, that my thoughts have flown to my own underwired pink cups (34B). I start wondering whether perfect breasts are really wholly tedious. Whether my own slight sag is irresistible? Stop being trivial, I remind myself, and focus attention upon Jacobson who continues: 'I'm very anti the body fetish, all those skinny women killing themselves at aerobic classes. I'm also against the pursuit of tragedy. That, of course, is what Hardy was up against. Every woman he found beautiful went and wrinkled up on him, so he moved onto the next in the full knowledge that she'd inevitably do the same. Guys who do that, who go from one 18-year-old to the next, do so because they like, they actually *enjoy*, the pain.'

Pain, Jacobson adds, is another of his novel's important themes. *Peeping Tom* is about *sex* first and foremost because he sees himself as a 'little crusader'. He attacks the manner in which comic writing about sex has hitherto focused in a banal way on 'clumsy couplings, on women with fat bodies, on tits that bounce, on limp dicks . . .' Here I interrupt to point out that he does, in fact, use 'limp dicks' himself to raise several laughs, particularly on page 153 where the self-possessed Melpomene, from Swansea (whose buttocks gleam like aubergines), issues such precise and detailed instructions to Fugleman about how she likes to be spanked that he is rendered impotent. Fugleman snivels: 'It wasn't just Melpomene who could no longer feel it throbbing against her belly. I myself couldn't locate it anywhere. It was, to all intents and purposes, gone. Some evolutionary process – nature shedding what it had no further use for – had speeded up in me . . .' As Melpomene raps out orders poor old Fugleman can only rummage for his detumescent member, delighting morosely in the delicious smell of bacon wafting up the stairs.

'Point taken,' says Jacobson, 'but that scene is certainly not meant to be funny because a bloke can't give a girl what we all know a girl wants to have – that scene confronts the absurdity of the whole sado-masochistic vocabulary. My hero finally realizes that he is not philosophically serious enough to be a good sadist. But to return to *pain*, my novel investigates the pleasure of jealousy. It causes us immense agony and we *love* it. We wallow in it. One of the reasons why men are so violent in their jealousies is because they can't bear the pleasure they are getting from it.'

Jacobson hopes that his novel might go some way towards shifting certain entrenched male attitudes towards female sexuality. He believes that all men are frightened by women, and especially by confident, sexually assertive women. 'Being a man sexually is exceedingly difficult. There's a mythology about male supremacy, about the male impulses to fight and rape. I think the current jokes men make about feminists and lesbians are fed by fear and jealousy. Men are *fascinated* by lesbians. When they imagine lesbians making love they fantasize about being in the middle, or on one side watching. I tell you this, however much those soldiers at Green-

I'm very anti the body fetish, all those skinny women killing themselves at aerobic classes.

ham Common jeer and show their bums out of charabanc windows to the Peace women, the images they have of the lesbians embracing on the other side of the perimeter fence must be highly erotic. If I was one of those guys I couldn't sleep at night, and believe me my wakefulness would have nothing to do with being stuck with the most terrible weapons in the world.' He taps his nose and adds, with the hooded eyelids and the right nostril flaring with innuendo, that it's the Cruise missile he's referring to, of course.

Of course, I say, and now let's discuss your novel's controversial ending which I found very rude and offensive and thought might cause ructions amongst feminists. This, the ultimate Hardy spoof, takes place on the sacrificial altar stone at Stonehenge where, splayed out with two young studs amongst the trilithons, and flaming sun stones, Fugleman's wife heaves and twists 'careless of discomfort, druidical decorum, or her marriage vows, her legs thrown wider apart than Barney Fugleman had ever seen them thrown'. In the sarsen circle she is violated by proxy (and choice) as Fugleman looks on, Hardylike, with his motor engine revving.

This set piece is wickedly interwoven with Hardy-esque metaphor and authentic quotes from *Tess of the d'Urbervilles*. Never will one be able to read the pages of *Tess* again without a giggle. Never, never incidentally will one be able to read John Fowles's acclaimed *The Enigma of Stonehenge* without seeing Fugleman in the bawdy mind's eye. Jacobson chuckles. He downs an entire pint of beer in one gulp. 'I want to defend the Stonehenge sequence. It is not intended to shock or outrage, but to help readers perceive that every woman is sexually her own person. Not a fantasy object. Not a possession. Not someone to be manipulated for male pleasure or pain ... and, of course, after this scene the woman triumphs because she has polished Fugleman off for ever.'

Before I leave Jacobson's flat he takes me to the windows and points across the road. He looks haggard round the jowels, his eyes gleam with diabolical spleen. 'You see that house over there? That's where Angela Carter lives. Don't mention that name to me. You don't know what it's like to have a Booker Prize contender opposite, to have her type-writer tapping in the small hours, to have to bump into her when you're going to buy your newspaper. These days I only go out after dark . . .'

Peeping Tom (Chatto & Windus, 1984).

■ Let's face it, I can't ever imagine being compared with Byron or Wordsworth or anyone like that.

IVOR CUTLER

When I met Glaswegian poet Ivor Cutler I was reminded of Nietzsche's observation: 'The spirit of the poet craves spectators – even if only buffaloes.' In Cutler's case the spectators tend to be fish. Or rhinos. On chilly days Cutler does his writing in the thermostat-controlled fug of the Aquarium at Regent's Park Zoo. His illuminated, battery-operated pen darts like a neon tetra in the gloom. On balmier days he chooses to work sitting on a wooden seat up-wind of the rhino enclosure.

It is at the rhino enclosure that we arrange to meet. Cutler, wearing Harris-tweed knickbockers, whizzes up on his bike. The autumn sun winks on his NHS spectacle lenses and glints off the vast assortment of badges (Save the Whales, CND, Butterfly Preservation Society) pinned on his cap and kitbag. A frisky-looking rhino glowers malevolently in Cutler's direction, then thunders round its enclosure breaking wind as Cutler observes, in his soft Glaswegian lilt: 'I believe that rhinos are bad tempered because God put their heads on upside down. Their eyes are full of malice because they know that everyone is thinking how funny they look.'

Not only funny. Bloody lethal. This one keeps charging in our direction and defecating prodigously while the poet remarks that scarcely a day goes by when he doesn't pause, pen poised, to marvel at the thinness of the wire round the rhino enclosure. 'I used to come to this zoo with my descant recorder to play soothing tunes to the various inmates,' he says, waving a stubby, reproving finger at the rhino; 'most were appreciative. I played Arabic melodies to the camel hoping to get the odd tear out of his eye as he remembered the old days of taking tourists round the pyramids.

'I played God Save the Queen to the lion who roared with approval. But play as gently as I like the expression in the rhino's eye always said "If I could get out I'd ram that recorder right up the old fart's nose".'

There are some people who think that 66-year old Cutler is slightly unhinged. In the past 20 years he has acquired a cult following. His quirky prose and poems are greeted either with enthusiasm or derision. Critics have described him as 'one of the most original writers of our time' and as 'a total headcase churning out unmitigated crap'. He writes on such topics as the romantic passion between a halibut and an albatross, the market stall that sells second-hand cups of tea, and how to teach bats to play jazz piano by ear. At live readings he performs with such staggering, po-faced eccentricity that fans often fall off their seats, even writhe on the ground gasping and punching the air. 'Actually that one was meant to be serious,' Cutler will announce with melancholy resignation, peering past the footlights at people stuffing handkerchiefs into their mouths. This year his short stories *Gruts* ('cult listening on Radio Four') are published by Methuen. His book of poems *Fresh Carpet* is published by Arc. At the Edinburgh Festival his one-man show sold out every night despite the inclusion of what he considers a 'socially provocative line'. 'I took a chance with Episode 3 of my poem *Glasgow Dreamer* and read aloud the line: "And we could smell the fecund Edinburgh middens/Forty miles away . . ." I am glad to say that for two weeks I read that contentious line and didn't get my nose punched once. Instead I got a lot of laughter. I couldn't tell whether it was Edinburgh laughter or non-Edinburgh laughter. Of course it grieves me to point out that actually this particular line is meant to be very serious.'

Ask him why he does all his writing in Regents Park Zoo and he replies 'Because I've got a season ticket'.

Ask him whether the stares and chortles of day trippers and zoo-visiting schoolchildren disturb the creative process and he barks a sudden staccatto laugh 'Heh. Heh. Heh.' which makes the rhino stop in its tracks. 'Heh. Heh. Heh. Yes. It stuns the creative process. Cripples it. I loathe the strident clamour of children. My ears always hurt. Any raucous noise makes me feel ill. I no longer go to the cinema because of the volume of sound. I've come to the conclusion that these days all cinema projectionists are half deaf because they listened to too much Heavy Metal music in their youth. Builders' transistors are the worst noise pollution in the world. I am a campaigning member of the Noise Abatement Society, I carry its special, exclusive brand of ear-plugs with me all the time.' Here he rummages through his ruck-sack to produce a box of them. They are squishy, yellow and, he tells me, more malleable than the wax variety. He gives me one to take home and try out next time the gasboard is drilling the road. He also gives me a homeopathic pill (Bach's Flower Remedy) for stress, explaining how two dissolved under his tongue had proved efficacious after a violent nightmare during the early hours. 'What's good enough for HRH Prince Charles and the Queen Mum is good enough for me,' he says.

I confess that the subtlety of Cutler's work is rather lost on me. With Cutler I find it easier to talk about ear plugs and homeopathy than literary endeavour, the dynamics of creation and so forth. But I battle gamely on. How would he describe his poetry? 'Ah ha. Well I'd call myself a *craftsperson* not a poet. Let's see if I can talk about it. Difficult. It's the kind of writing that some people would say wasn't poetry. Heh. Heh. Heh. Let's face it I can't ever imagine being compared with Byron or Wordsworth or anyone like that. What a laugh! My poetry doesn't have a rhythm and doesn't rhyme. Except for fun now and then. Just occasionally I let a rhyme surface.

'My ear listens for hidden rhythms. For years I've been interested in bongos, and African drums . . .' He is suddenly interrupted by a statuesque blonde woman wearing a green boiler-suit who flings her arms round him (knocking off the be-badged cap) exclaiming 'Ivor! How are you? You gorgeous beast.' Her name is Frances. She is the Regents Park Zoo vet. She informs us that the flatulent rhino is off his food. Cutler suggests that what it needs is a few Bach's Flower Remedy pills. He delves into the kitbag and Frances dashes off, brow crinkled in concern, towards the rhino enclosure. Cutler shakes his head and continues: 'I started writing poetry at the age of 42 but wasn't any good until I was 48. One of my early poems advised women that if their breasts are too big they will fall over unless they wear a haversack on their back. That one was written before I became a feminist. I am not proud of it. I try very hard to be a feminist but I've got a long way to go. I keep getting caught out in so far as I still take for granted the things men always took for granted before feminism became an issue. Things like men being superior. And women doing the washing up. For me some of the conflict is caused by women themselves. If I see a woman wearing high-heels she goes down a couple of notches in my estimation.' (He glares at my feet.) 'Sorry, but there it is. A woman wearing high-heels is playing a man's game. High-heels aren't feminist.'

Has Cutler got a girlfriend? He pauses. He coughs. He pleats his lips and snaps peevishly: 'Really! What sort of question is that? It's the sort of question I'd expect from *Woman's Weekly*. Hmmm. On second thoughts are you by any chance making me an offer? I could easily disregard your high heels. Heh. Heh. Heh. Only joking. No, I've been living alone since my marriage broke up in '64.

'An instinct told me not to get hooked again. But I have enjoyed the love of women. I have recently ended a long affair with a woman who had a lot of marvellous negative virtues. She didn't blab. She had a capacity for not being too tidy. She was much more intelligent than I am which isn't saying much. The break up was a great relief to both parties.'

A brisk autumnal wind has begun to whistle up our legs so we decide to take a stroll to the Gorilla house. As we walk, Cutler wheeling his bike, my high-heels clacking on tarmac, he explains that it is very difficult to distinguish between the white rhino and the black. Apparently they are both grey and always covered with mud and dust. 'You live and learn,' I remark, wishing I was interviewing Seamus Heaney, say, or Kathleen Raine. Some *real* poet who doesn't witter on about rhinos, or use the Regents Park Zoo for their work room. 'Black rhinos have pointed lips and feed on bushes. White rhinos have square lips adapted to feeding on grass –' says Cutler, waving at Frances who is in the distance examining rhino droppings. 'Talking of square lips makes me think of Ted Hughes. I think he's doing a grand job. I have no really strong views on the subject of the position of Poet Laureate although I was flattered that someone suggested me for the job.' Bending to adjust his cycle clips he adds 'Even though it'd be hard to write poems in order. I would have accepted if Her Majesty and I had been able to agree to mutually convenient terms. I would have negotiated for cash in preference to crates of champagne . . .' As he pedals briskly off into the sun setting over his Tufnell Park bedsit I remind myself of some lines from his poem *Creamy Pumpkins*: 'The world needs dreamers/Heads like creamy pumpkins/Quiet skin, eyes that swivel round like smoke/Like turquoise, like bulby grapes/Seeing where others face an empty wall.'

Fresh Carpet (poems) (Arc Publications, 1987).

JAMES HERBERT

I AM WELL AWARE
THAT IN CERTAIN
QUARTERS MY
BOOKS ARE NOT
CONSIDERED GREAT
LITERATURE.

Be warned: this is no fairy tale. James Herbert, 43, son of East End market traders, one-time dishwasher and office boy in an advertising agency, is now recognized as Britain's leading writer of horror fiction. Spinechiller after spinechiller flows from Herbert's fast felt-tip, hideous tales of creeping evil with titles like *The Rats*, *The Fog*, *The Dark*, and *The Spear* which raise goose pimples, not to mention huge profits for their author.

For someone so wrapped up in the occult, and the gruesome and hideous consequences of mutation, Herbert in the flesh is a let-down. He looks rather *pleasant*. He has a boyish grin. He has none of that dank-handed creepiness you might expect from an expert in nightmares. He certainly doesn't make your nervous knees knock or your blood run cold.

In fact, when he met my train at the small Sussex station near his home and sprang from his gleaming Jag XJS in his stressed-leather bomber jacket and tight blue jeans shouting, 'Hallo there, lovely day', I was slightly disappointed.

Was this the man who launched a thousand rats into London's Underground at rush-hour; the man whose prose is so shot through with ghastliness that I couldn't get beyond chapter six of *The Fog*?

It was, but as we sped along the Sussex lanes with Herbert admiring clumps of primroses and daffodils and the bursting buds of horse chestnut trees and grumbling about income tax and accountants, I found it increasingly difficult to associate the man with the author famed as 'the Edgar Allan Poe of our time'.

His latest book, *The Magic Cottage*, is as sinister a story of mystery and magic as any horror-fiction fan could want. It tells the story of a young city couple who move to a quaint cottage in the woods but – yes, you've guessed – nothing is quite as it seems.

Supernatural manifestations and Herbert happenings horrendous beyond belief occur, making your hair stand on end and putting you off woodland dream cottages for life.

'I must admit it's my favourite novel so far,' enthused its author as we climbed out of the Jag he calls The Beast. 'Some people are saying it's Herbert gone soft, but it's more me than any book I've written. The main character is a bit of a cynic and through him I'm having a go at the conventions of horror fiction.'

Into Herbert's beautiful country house we went and entered a spacious sitting-room where we stood ankle-deep in white shag-pile carpet, admiring Herbert's lush acres of land. He's certainly come a long way from the East End fruit stall and the bomb-blasted boyhood home condemned under a post-war slum clearance scheme.

'Sure, I have,' he agreed, bouncing his two-year old daughter on his knee, 'but I try to avoid falling into the old ego trip of rags-to-riches, cockney sparrow made good.

'I had a great time as a kid. I didn't notice any poverty; everyone was in the same boat. Of course I've gone up in the world, thanks mainly to the 11-plus exam and getting to a grammar school, but it's not entirely due to my books. I had a very successful lucrative career in an advertising agency before I decided to try my hand at writing at the age of 28.'

The initial run of 100,000 copies of his first book, *The Rats*, sold out within three weeks of publication. There have since been 21 reprints, worldwide sales and a film.

The book critics' reactions taught Herbert a valuable lesson. 'A reviewer in *The Observer* described *The Rats* as rubbish and said it should be tossed into the dustbin. That crushed me somewhat and I seriously believed there was no point in becoming a writer.

'Then the following week *The Sunday Times* said it was brilliant. I realized that neither reviewer was entirely right, though I kind of leaned towards *The Sunday Times* of course . . . Everyone's entitled to their opinion. I decided to carry on.'

And carry on he did. Shutting himself away in his study each day at 10 and emerging at 1 ,for his 'daily fix' of television news, newspapers and post. Back into the study after a lunchtime snack ('I often nod off with my head on the desk') and by about 3 he is in full flow, scribbling frenetically till about 7.

'I work a five-day week, I reserve Saturdays to reply personally to all my fan mail, business letters and pay my bills. On Sundays I take a break so that I can be with my wife and three daughters. I am very much a family man and my marriage is of great importance to me.'

Herbert gets annoyed when critics label him macabre and grotesque. 'They stick this false reputation on me. If only they read my work properly they'd see that each of my books has a high moral content.

I suppose my ambition is to be accepted by the critics as a fine writer.

'I think I'm a cynical idealist, and of course there's my Catholic background I have to contend with. As I get older I'm more firm in my Catholicism than ever. Yet I'm not very orthodox in my beliefs; I'm one of those guys who hates to obey all the rules of a club yet also refuses to leave.'

His books always contain a sex scene which, he hopes, represents an ideal of mutual enjoyment and affection. 'I reckon if I can describe horror scenes, then I shouldn't balk at love scenes.'

Herbert admitted to a certain amount of apprehension about his forthcoming massive promotion campaign. He will appear on *Wogan*, on radio, at bookshop signings and at the Cambridge University Literary Society.

'I find the Cambridge invite very scary. I'll be talking to really clever people there. I don't know, as yet, what I'm going to say.

'I must admit that I find publicity and promotion a bit of a hassle. All I want to do is sit down and tell good stories.

'And I have to admit that the critics can be daunting. I'm well aware that in certain quarters my books are not considered great literature. But I consider them to be literary works and I do the best that I can. I suppose my ambition is to be accepted by the critics as a fine writer. My books take far too much sweat for me to treat them like jokes. I put a hell of a lot of effort into each one. Speaking as an ex-East End yob, I must admit that I find my success very funny . . .'

Herbert's current preoccupation is fitness. He explained that he keeps feeling that he ought to be doing something to counteract all those hours spent sitting behind a desk. 'When I moved to Sussex I bought a tracksuit and ran round the garden three times. On the third day it rained and I thought "sod this for a lark" and gave the tracksuit to Oxfam. I hope I wasn't tempting malevolent fate . . .'

For the first time in the conversation the Unknown intruded. Herbert laughed a strangled little laugh. You half expected thunder to crash, a rook to fall down the chimney, or a giant crow to flap down and bang its beak against the window.

It didn't, of course, As I said at the start, this is no fairy tale.

My books take far too much sweat for me to treat them like jokes. I put a hell of a lot of effort into each one.

The Magic Cottage (Hodder & Stoughton, 1986).

JEFFREY ARCHER

BELIEVE ME, IF I HAD A MAGIC WAND, I'D BE UP ALL NIGHT,
OR ALL DAY RATHER, WAVING IT.

*M*eeting the whiz-kid, best-selling author, Deputy Chairman of the Conservative Party, Jeffrey Archer, is like having a walk-on part in *Dynasty*. Boy is this guy *rich*. You enter his penthouse 'pied-à-terre' over-looking the Thames and sink into one of his half-dozen plushy, cream upholstered sofas. As you balance your drink (tea) on a smoked-glass coffee-table (vast enough to display a nonchalant scattering of 100 hardbacks with titles like *Everest The Unconquered Ridge* and *The Conservative Party From Peel To Thatcher*) you begin to feel oppressed by the picture windows. They surround you on all sides. One glance out of the panoramic views across London and your head starts spinning.

Jeffrey Archer's penthouse (and he also owns Rupert Brook's old house in Granchester) is the sort of sumptuous setting that cries out for shoulder-pads, slinky skirts, a sun-bed tan, a facelift, a slash of lipstick, sex, intrigue . . . in fact I feel a bit of a berk sitting there in my NHS specs and last year's mac. I had planned to interview Archer the bestselling author. I had planned to chat about his latest book, ask him the secret of his literary success, beg for a few tips on how to write a blockbuster. But suddenly as I sit there sipping my tea watching Archer flapping about his desk, and briefing his secretary, inside my head I hear the voice of my friend Beryl. 'Put the cocky little squirt on the spot, Val. Grab the opportunity to have a go at him about that remark he made about young people being unwilling to get jobs.' In that instant, as Archer, tanned, alert, fingers forming a point under his chin, paces towards me exuding smugness, I decide to abandon the literary interview and concentrate instead on Margaret Thatcher's controversial strategy on youth unemployment. Archer wears conker-bright Gucci shoes, a gleaming Longines watch and trouser creases sharp enough to draw blood.

'Do call me Jeffrey,' he says, with a boyish grin, a boyish toss of the head. He likes to be called 'Jeffrey'. Mrs Thatcher calls him 'Jeffrey'. No-one has ever called him 'Jeff'. Absolutely not. According to his headquarters hand-outs he is 'deeply committed to fostering in others, especially the young, the idea that you can achieve what you aim for if you are prepared to work hard and not be frightened to seek your fortune in other than your own backyard'. Which is exactly the point I am going to raise once Archer has dismissed a stroppy, mysteriously-hovering cab driver, and settled his taut, muscular, squash-player's buttocks onto a sofa.

'Haven't a clue who the cab-driver fellow is . . .' says Archer, who has the sort of face that springs to mind whenever you see the sign SMART BOY WANTED in a grocer shop window, 'Now where were we. Ah yes. I've just sold options on serialization rights of my book *Not A Penny More Not A Penny Less* to the BBC for exactly £58. Now why did I do that for a mere £58? Guess?' Because he doesn't need any more money? Archer chuckles. 'No, no, no. Oh dear me no, I sold it, rather appropriately, for the price of a television licence!' He beams. I try to beam back. The autumn sun beams cruelly through the picture windows illuminating the deep laughter lines etched round Jeffrey's shrewd eyes.

And then it's down to business. Beryl would be proud of me. 'Right Mr Archer, er "Jeffrey",' I begin, in a burst of spontaneous outrage, 'thousands of parents were appalled by your recent prononcement that youngsters are unwilling to go out to work. I was appalled myself, as it happens. My own 19-year-old son with six O-levels and a City and Guilds qualification has been looking for work for a year. He exists on £22.50 weekly dole. There are thousands of parents whose unemployed youngsters have A-levels, university degrees, professional qualifications . . . these parents represent the "middle class", the traditional bastion of Tory support, the advocators of the work ethic. They are all bloody cheesed off. They want to know what the Government is doing to enhance the life-chances of their kids.'

It is like slamming my foot down forcefully on the accelerator. Archer revs up and delivers: 'First let me say that the remark of mine you refer to was, I regret, taken out of context. I've had so much trouble since – hundreds of angry letters; I have been up every night replying to each one personally – and I honestly do not want to discuss the matter further. I had assumed we were going to discuss my next book . . . I am naturally very sorry about your son, about all the unemployed sons. However, it must be realized that there are 13 million unemployed people in Europe so this is not only a British problem. This Government has, since 1983, created 620,000 jobs compared with 200,000 in the rest of Europe put together . . .'

Archer breaks off and calls across the room to his young, red-eared, furiously typing personal assistant. 'David, pass me a blue sheet. You know how touchy I am at the moment on the unemployment topic. Let's get these figures right.'

David, about the same age as my son and, as Archer explains: 'very bright, just down from Oxford, and hoping to become an MP,' smartly hands over a blue sheet of paper. Consulting it Archer declares: 'This Government has provided £2 billion to help one million schoolchildren. Since April 1983 we provided up to a year's work-based training for over 700,000 school-leavers, two-thirds of whom have gone into a job, further education, or training.'

Handing back the blue sheet he adds: 'These figures show clearly our deep concern. Lord Young spelt out at Blackpool exactly what we hope to achieve for young people.' What was that exactly? 'We know it is no easy task. It angers me when I hear the Labour Party say that we lack compassion, while I watch a minister like Lord Young doing absolutely everything, repeat *absolutely everything*, in his power to solve a seemingly insoluble problem.'

'I was at a school this morning . . .' Which one? 'Which school was it, David? Pass me my sheet. Near Gosport, Alverstoke . . . where a highly articulate 16-year-old boy made a great impression on me. His well-informed list of questions included: "Why don't the Conservatives have a massive Government spending programme to solve unemployment" and "Why not give teachers bigger pay packets in recognition of their important work?" I offered him the old trick – no "trick" is the wrong word, put "truth" – I offered him the old truth and said: "Where does the money come from? There's no such thing as Government money." I asked him "What does your father do?" The lad replied "boat building". His father also pays tax. Right, I said, tax is *real* money. That's what the Government gathers from all people to pay for the unemployed, teachers, hospitals . . .'

'Hang on a minute, Mr Archer, er "Jeffrey". If you'd asked "what does your father do?" in Merseyside, say, or Dorset the children might have replied "nothing" or even "I haven't got a father". How then would you explain the link between father's income-tax and government money?' Beads of perspiration glint on Archer's brow in the sunlight streaming through the picture windows. He hurls me a glance with a kick in it and continues:

'In Britain 87 per cent of the population are earning. Never exaggerate the unemployment figures. At the end of the day there *has* to be an economic strategy. Labour's policy has always been to spend, spend, spend, and then to borrow, borrow, borrow. The Conservative Party has always believed in earn, earn, earn, and then pay with real money. Don't think I'm not worried unemployment. Believe me, if I had a magic wand I'd be up all night, or all day, rather, waving it.'

The Conservative Party has always believed in earn, earn, earn, and then pay with real money. Don't think I'm not worried about unemployment.

Believe me I feel very tempted at this point to tell him that I hate his novels. That the only time I've ever seen anyone reading one of them was on a cruise I was writing about for the *Daily Mail* where the average age of cruiser was 72. The Promenade Deck was always knee-deep in Jeffrey Archer novels.

Archer admits to fretting occasionally about his own young sons, and yes, he would be *horrified* if they wound up with UB40 forms and £22.50 dole money a week. 'One would hope', begins Jeffrey, looking horrified enough at the prospect of two sons on the dole to dive through the picture windows, 'that one had created in them an attitude that made them search for work very widely before giving up. Parental teaching and the idea of the work ethic should go on continuously over the years. I don't believe in half measures.'

He sips his tea. He says: 'Phew! My goodness me!' He remarks that this interview is more 'hard-hitting' than he'd anticipated, and we'd certainly strayed a long way from his career as a writer. Mustn't grumble, he says. Someone in his position must be prepared to take the knocks. *No*, he refuses point blank to discuss whether Mrs Thatcher castigated him after his recent tactless off-the-cuff utterances about youth employment. Absolutely not. A mental image of Mrs Thatcher thundering: 'If you shoot your mouth off again,

Jeffrey, I'll smack your legs' flashes before my eyes as Archer says: 'You *may*, however, ask me whether I've been gagged.' 'Have you been gagged Mr Archer, er Jeffrey?' 'Of course I haven't. What rubbish. I wouldn't be sitting here talking so freely if I had.'

Gesturing towards David he adds: 'The way the media has knocked me of late might very well have caused this excellent young man to lose heart. All that hostility is enough to make him say "to hell with politics" and become a banker. Twice the pay, half the hours. And yet . . . you enter a hall where 450 voters have turned out to cheer you on and you realize it's all so wonderfully worthwhile. The good work goes on.'

Yes, but what about answering the question. What *did* Lord Young spell out at Blackpool? 'He spelt out that we are determined to create real jobs, jobs that will last, and not invented jobs that have no real substance.'

Archer is unable to say what sort of jobs. I remark that Lord Young's job creation plans certainly won't offer immediate hope to all those disenchanted youngsters roaming round our inner-cities whinging 'No Future' as they eke out their baked beans in dingy bedsits subsidized by the DHSS. Youngsters, incidentally, who feel woefully ignored by politicians. Archer snaps that the Conservative Party has never ignored the young. Neither, he sneers, has it stooped to street level to capture the youth vote. It has no intention of going to Neil Kinnock's gimmicky extremes of twanging guitars and making trendy pop videos. Absolutely not. Neil Kinnock has worked it all out very cleverly but the young aren't fooled.

Archer shakes his head, then nods it solemnly when I suggest that it will take considerably more than twanging guitars to politicize an indifferent, disillusioned, economically disenfranchized generation. Returning to Jeffrey's now infamous phrase about the young being unwilling to quit their own backyards in search of work I remind him that 'the young' are not all self confident, dynamic, resourceful types. Most of them are vulnerable and insecure, and want to stay near their families and friends. 'I realize that now,' Jeffrey confesses darkly, 'I realize that *now*. But I *do* listen to what youngsters say.' David (of the red flapping ears) chips in to say: 'What about that splendid Youth Training Scheme thing in Fulham, Jeffrey, remember? The kids were superb. So pleased to see you, Jeffrey. So grateful for your personal interest. It was very moving.' Did the kids mention that the YTS is being used by unscrupulous employers as a source of cheap labour? 'No', snaps Jeffrey, 'They did not.'

Someone in my position must be prepared to take the knocks.

His eyes slide towards a book on the coffee table. Edited by Mary Wilson, it is an anthology of celebrities' favourite poems. All royalties go to the Leukaemia Trust. His choice is included. He has chosen *One Thousandth Man*, by Rudyard Kipling, because, he explains, it sums up everything required of a true friend. Here he quotes: 'One man in a thousand, Solomon says will stick more close than a brother.' 'Goodness me, What a line! When I collapsed, when I was left with debts of £427,727 and was on the verge of bankruptcy at the age of 34, I then learnt which people were indeed my true friends . . .'

From unemployment, to poetry . . . and now on to Mrs Thatcher . . . I inquire how post-gaff relations are between Archer and the Prime Minister. 'Whenever I see her I am very respectful, I think carefully about what I'm going to say so that I don't waste her time. I so often find that she has considered constituency matters in great depth even before I present my reports.'

I put away my notebook feeling brave because I hadn't asked him any of the questions I was supposed to ask him about his books. I linger to admire his two solid silver cigarette boxes, lifesized reproductions of his two bestsellers inscribed 'Presented to Jeffrey Archer to celebrate 1,000,000 copies sold by Coronet paperbacks'. He accompanies me to the lift. 'The tide is turning,' he remarks cheerfully. 'The knockers have had their day.'

Not a Penny More, Not a Penny Less (Hodder & Stoughton, 1981).

Jeffrey Bernard

I'm not talking about my bloody book. They mess you about, soddin' publishers.

Being the start of the flat-racing season and me being partial to a little flutter I was thrilled to receive an advance copy of Jeffrey Bernard's entertaining fragment of autobiography *Talking Horses*. It came with a somewhat muted (for a publicity person's letter) suggestion that Jeffrey Bernard might make an interesting subject for an interview. 'Don't mention that bloody man to me, the obnoxious swine ... only *please* don't quote me,' shrilled a publicity person from 'Fourth Estate' with uncharacteristic lack of savoir-faire when I phoned, 'getting Bernard's book together has been a nightmare. A nightmare ...'

Bernard, a man of volatile charm, who was once described by *Racing Post* as 'racing's tormented, vodka-swilling literary genius', decided to celebrate publication of *Talking Horses* with a rave-up at Lingfield Park race track to which I was invited. It turned out to be one of the worst days of my life. I waited, as instructed by the publicity person , at Victoria Station's platform 19 for the 10.35. The 10.35 departed. No sign of Bernard or the publicity person. I stood there shivering and recalling the last time I'd encountered racing's tormented, vodka-swilling literary genius. It was at the Chelsea Art Club where I was enjoying lunch at a trestle table in the garden and Bernard happened to be sitting at the other end of the table. Imagine a pleasant buzz of conversation, the chink of glasses, the clink of cutlery, butter melting in the sun, one or two elderly artists dozing with their heads in their soup plates, and Bernard's articulate tones silencing the general conversation: 'I had an erection last week,' he announced, helping himself to some broad beans sprinkled with parsley, 'I was so amazed I took a photo of it.' Afterwards he and I had an argument about money which ended with him hurling a glass at me and knocking over a chair.

Standing at the ticket barrier I was just deciding that I must have come on the wrong day when I caught sight of Bernard, the harassed-looking publicity person and a motley rabble of drunks (mostly men) with their tongues hanging out stumbling out of the Victoria pub, singing songs, waving bottles above their heads and flapping copies of

Sporting Life in the faces of passers-by. They lurched towards platform 19, sweeping me with them onto the train.

Champagne corks popped, plastic cups frothed, filthy fag fumes filled the air, copies of *Talking Horses* were distributed (Bernard: 'It's a bloody awful book, terrible, rubbish . . .') and hiccupping men – and one woman – with strawberry noses engaged in slurred altercations about the favourite in the 2.45. Two people, giggling and holding each other up, got off the train at the stop before Lingfield. It turned out that they weren't Bernard's guests, just two innocent commuters who happened to be on the train. 'Maybe British Rail is shelebrating shome annivershary . . .' said one to the other as they stumbled along the platform through the mist.

At Lingfield Station we were off – sprinting along a footpath (dew-spangled, bunny-burrowed, fern-fringed) through turnstiles, into a pavilion (Bernard leading by a neck) and straight to the bar. There was much clinking of glasses, chinking of ice, 'glug-glug-glug' noises, intense staring at video screens, and a great deal of yelling 'Come on, Token Dancer you bugger, come on!' and so forth. These yells were followed by doomed wails of 'I've lost fifty quid' which were punctuated by the gurgling-sound of sorrows being drowned by liquid.

The harassed publicity person from 'Fourth Estate' told me: '*Talking Horses* is a witty, wonderful collection of racing reminiscences, a *must* for anyone in thrall to the pungent allure of the race track . . .' She then rushed off to stop a brawl which had broken out among several of Bernard's guests. A woman who had won £150 was almost lynched. 'Oh dear, oh *dear*, my *God*,' muttered the publicity person, perspiring and in shock, 'where *is* Jeff for heaven's sake. It's his *do* and he keeps wandering off. I almost can't *cope* . . .'

We all searched for 'Jeff' who was outside in thrall to the pungent allure of a bottle of vodka. I tried to tackle him for a few quotes seeing as how this was meant to be an interview. 'I'm not talking about my bloody book. They mess you about, soddin' publishers, boss you around, put everything in the wrong order,' said Jeff, 'anyway if one thing gets right up my nose it's the way you women freelances earn five times as much as I do . . .'

Then lunch. Popping corks, everyone going glug-glug-glug again and falling upon cold meats. The conversation turned to Bernard's appearance the previous day on break-fast television. 'I kept farting,' said lugubrious Bernard, coleslaw trailing from the corners of his mouth, 'every time they asked me a question, I farted. I suppose it's one of the drawbacks of going on breakfast telly. Most people tend to fart a lot first thing in the morning. Anne Diamond must get used to it, I suppose, one of the drawbacks of the job.' A fierce guest called Marsh, suddenly slammed down her knife and fork and snapped, 'For Christ's sake. I really don't find this topic amusing over a meal.' 'Wa-ha-ha,' roared one of Jeff's guests, a crapulous man with bloodshot eyes called Norman, 'wo-ho-ho, tee-hee-hee,' and slithered off his chair and disappeared under the table. Jeff continued: 'The worst thing is getting an attack in a crowded lift, and suddenly you start going off like a Howitzer, with a captive audience, everyone hoping that no-one thinks it's *them*, all staring at the ceiling . . .'

After lunch, more drinks, more betting, more punch-ups. At 2.15 a few stalwarts, including me, stumbled outside to watch the *Jeffrey Bernard Handicap Stakes*. Bloodshot Norman whined that the horses were galloping much too fast ('You get a better view and see more of the horses on telly, Jeff').

Bernard presented the winning horse's owner with a signed copy of *Talking Horses* and a cut-glass bowl full of vodka. Overawed the owner shook Bernard's hand effusive-ly, exclaiming: 'Mr Bernard, I have been a fan of yours all my life, this is a proud occasion for me . . . what shall I do with the vodka?' Jeff suggested he could always pour it back in the bottle. 'Wa-ha-ha,' roared bloodshot Norman. Drinks all round.

A friend of Bernard's whose teeth were clogged up with potato salad began telling me he was into spanking. I made my excuses and departed, just after the 3.45, leaving them all blubbering and beating each other over the head with their copies of *Talking Horses*. It is a highly enjoyable book. It sheds a great deal of light on the world of racing enthusiasts whom Bernard describes in his introduction as 'mostly lunatics and nutcases who live in a world of their own'. He said it.

Talking Horses (Fourth Estate, 1987).

Jeremy Reed

A MAN SHOULD CULTIVATE HIS CREATIVE, FEMININE SIDE,
THE SIDE THAT UNDERSTANDS WOMEN.

'Oh God, not *that* effete little pseud,' groaned Andrew Motion, literary editor for Chatto & Windus, choking on his champagne at a literary party where I had just remarked that I think Jeremy Reed is one of Britain's best young poets, '. . . Most of us think of Reed as the David Bowie of the poetry circuit, and have you heard him *read*? Well, don't. He sounds like a fish under water, he's too camp, too excruciatingly awful for words . . .'

Talk about fire my curiosity. I was banging on Jeremy Reed's front door before you could say *Penguin Book of Contemporary Poetry*. I had just read his collection *By The Fisheries* (Cape) which a *Guardian* critic described as 'The best book of poetry since Ted Hughes's *The hawk and the Rain*' ('58). Reed's poetry is that rare thing, the sort you can understand and thrill to, which is more than you can say for much of the poetry published these days. I've tried Craig Raine's, for example, and Christopher Reed's and, as a matter of fact, Andrew Motion's and finding them more or less unreadable I've given up.

'Hi there' says Reed in his strange whispering voice, ushering me into a West End bedsit no bigger than a wardrobe. He is deathly pale and is wearing black leather trousers, black leather bomber jacket and black nail-varnish. 'Actually this isn't my place. It belongs to a very dear, kind friend. I have no home, I have no money. People who believe in and recognize the value of my work have been very kind to me. It is by their kindness that I survive.' He puts the kettle on and makes us both a cup of tea. As he talks he sort of writhes. Occasionally he smiles a ghastly, primrose-coloured smile and runs the black finger-nails through floppy, straw-coloured hair. He looks as if he's walked straight out of a Vampire movie, or *The Cabinet of Dr Caligari*. I have to keep reminding myself that this is the man described by Kathleen Raine as 'without question the most imaginatively gifted poet since Dylan Thomas'. I'm sure she's right. But the nail-varnish and teeth are a bit off-putting.

'I've had a total commitment to poetry since the age of nine which has led me to sacrifice a career, security, relationships and personal possessions . . .' he continues, 'apart, that is from a few thousand books and a comprehensive collection of Lou Reed bootlegs . . . I'm one of the circle of people throughout Europe who tape his every concert. Of all pop musicians, his use of words comes closer to poetry reading than any other's.'

Twenty-eight-year-old Reed (no relation to Lou) writes poems that snow goose-pimples onto your flesh. Like John Clare (the subject of the best poem in this collection) he plucks his images from nature; an ivy-leaf is 'a diamond-lit frog's back', autumn blazes with 'the bee-hung flame on the gorse flower' and sunlight makes 'a star on the shards of a broken gin bottle'. Reed is pained by people who imagine that poetry writing is a part-time occupation, that you're supposed to be a civil servant for five days a week and a poet for two. So much for T.S. Eliot and Philip Larkin . . . 'This attitude', he says, lying back upon a divan and applying more black nail-varnish, 'fosters grey, spineless commentary-type poems like those of Larkin and his disciples.'

He walks two paces to the kitchenette, refills the kettle and explains that his childhood in Jersey was a solitary 'dark-sided' one. He turned to landscapes, nature, even fish for company and has always felt an outsider, 'in the sense that being a poet isolates a person in life . . . I have a profound compassion for people who are outlawed for psychological problems, speech impediments, homosexuality, hare-lips, kleptomania . . .'

Such sympathy inspired his forthcoming, partly autobiographical novel *The Lipstick Boys*, which he describes as 'a voyage to the other end of the night, a disturbing and harrowing study of sexual outsiders . . .' It took him a year, he adds, to write the first 20 pages. His friends have been 'deeply moved' by it. I wasn't exactly deeply moved myself, found it a bit turgid in fact, but there is no denying that Reed uses words in the way that sixties painters used paint, piling them on, layer upon layer of great hypnotic splodges. You feel that the novel is *special*, but you somehow fail to connect. It is however, worth noting that Kathleen Raine, in a solemn introduction to *The Lipstick Boys*, tells us how Reed 'early discovered that in appearing in public places in his poet's androgynous mask he aroused contempt, violence, vile abuse of a kind easy to imagine from virile gangs of mods, rockers, and their kind'. She also describes the novel as being ' "the life-blood of a master-spirit" as we used to be told great books were in days before it became too embarrassing to the literary world to be reminded of values of that enduring kind.'

I have no home, I have no money. People who believe in and recognize the value of my work have been very kind to me.

Outside the window we hear the roar of pneumatic drills and the wail of a police siren. We sip our tea and I say something like 'I bet you don't hear noises like that in Jersey'. Reed makes no reply but starts fixing his eyeliner. I decide to brush my hair. Reed combs his. I ask him whether he is gay. He flashes the primrose smile, and replies a trifle evasively: 'The whole subject of gender is a complex one . . . Man should cultivate his creative, feminine side, the side that understands women . . . I find the isolated sterility of the extreme gay movement loathsome; to exclude the opposite sex to such a degree can only lead to negation in terms of creativity, human life, and far more importantly, human compassion.'

Yes, but is he *gay*? '. . . For instance, I've always enjoyed wearing cosmetics in the way Egyptian priests wore cosmetics. It heightens my creative powers and divides me from my audience so that I can transmute my material into something magical and ritualistic . . .' A skilful question-dodger is Reed. He puts his bottle of nail-varnish away, fidgets with his mystic magic-eye ring and changes topic by revealing how, when he was 12, he received his first visitation from a phantom with violet eyes.

'This hermaphroditic figure is my creative source. I am always very conscious of my psychic protectors being with me . . .'

A longish silence ensues. The conversation seems to be taking an unforeseen turn. I'm definitely feeling out of my depth. The thought crosses my mind that Reed is on something. Tripping perhaps. 'Are your psychic protectors with you *now*?' I inquire, peering nervously round the bedsit. 'They are always with me, as yours are with you. Shelley, Yeats, Byron and Blake were all visited by their guardians.' 'Is Andrew Motion visited by his? Craig Raine?

Christopher Reed? Reed (again no relation) ignores the question. 'Sadly, those
people out of sympathy with such phenomena dismiss them and now if you'll
excuse me I have a reading at Bernard
Stone's bookshop which I must get dressed for.'

A few days after this interview he sent
me a poem which I've framed and which
is hanging on the wall in my bedroom. I
treasure it greatly. Thanks Jeremy. Here
is the first verse:

SNOWDROPS FOR VAL HENNESSY
The skyline's heather-pink banded
    by green.
First stirrings and a pheasant whirrs
its molten oils clear of the hedge
    and lifts
with clumsy reverberant ricochets
towards a stand of pine. Circling
    rooks drift
as damp earth draws me, sniffing out
    green shoots,
sure by my instinct that the first
    are there,
and are, crotchets with bell heads,
    reading lamps
fixtured above the violet's tiny roots.

...I find the
isolated sterility
of the extreme
gay movement
loathsome; to
exclude the
opposite sex to
such a degree
can only lead to
negation in
terms of
creativity, human
life, and far
more
importantly,
human
compassion.

The Lipstick Boys (Enitharmon Press, 1984).

Jill Tweedie

People don't want to wade through a load of descriptive garbage; we are living in 1984, time's running out, writers should be writing about 1984 issues.

*L*et's start with a bang, and guess the author: 'A pink nipple brushed his face. Galvanized, he bent down, pulled off his boots and grey jodhpurs. Then he stood, his heavily muscled legs smooth and bare, his penis rising purple from the paler scrotum. He took two steps towards her, put his hands, dark against her wet white skin, on her waist, turned her towards the bath and bent her over. Then, as she gave a small groan, he spread her buttocks and drove into her. Stumbling, trembling, she hung on to the bath's edge, her hair streaming down into the water. Six times he went into her, fast and then he paused, his penis just inside her, its bulbous head wet in her wet lips . . .'

So, who wrote it? Jackie Collins? Harold Robbins? Fiona Richmond? Wrong. The author is no less a distinguished pen-person than Jill Tweedie – *the* Jill Tweedie – the *Guardian* goddess, feminist, polemicist, bloody fine journalist and now novelist.

Tweedie's pacy new book *Bliss*, which snipes away at the stinking rich, Fleet Street, Valium, radical feminists, Robin Day, pornographers and the wholesale destruction of the Amazonian jungle, is not, in my view, likely to win the W.H. Smith Literary Award, but it is likely to get very much up the Wimmin's noses. Already they are crashing about Islington, wringing their boiler-suits and raging over 'Turncoat' Tweedie's heterosexual bias and bewailing her perfidious use of 'juicy bits' to pep things up when the plot starts flagging.

To make matters worse, Tweedie's blonde, big-breasted heroine Claire gets off on masochistic sex and *enjoys* being pseudo-raped by her ghastly husband or, as the book puts it: 'Claire heard a litany of abuse from her husband's lips . . . she was shameless and insatiable and could not rest until each orifice was gorged with male flesh. It was grotesque . . . with now familiar self-disgust she felt heat flicker along her thighs and a pulse begin to beat between her legs. It was a physical betrayal beyond her control, the treachery of a quisling body.'

Phew! Heck! Tweedie sure knows how to hit things on the head. And maybe it's all of those treacherous quisling bodies that are to blame for the halting impetus of the Women's Movement.

I was very aware that the sexy bits might be controversial.

So, is there life for a feminist writer after being blackballed from the shelves of Sisterwrite? I ask Tweedie as we share a Bird's Eye haddock lattice pie round her kitchen table. 'I was very aware that the sexy bits might be controversial,' replies Tweedie, who is much more beautiful, one might almost say *gorgeous*, in the flesh than that familiar *Guardian* picture might suggest, 'but I *loved* writing them. I've never written stuff like that in my life. I had to keep slapping my hand down, saying "That's enough, Jill" – it was a revelation to myself.

'I'll admit that several times I wondered whether certain passages were strictly speaking necessary, but the sex thing with Claire is vital, she is a woman who despises herself for being aroused by masochistic sex but nevertheless she *is* aroused, some women *are*, and much as we'd like to pretend otherwise, it is *so* – all women who have that tendency feel guilty, and hate the men who exploit it. Masochism is indigenous to men and women and I wanted to show that when it exists it is disastrous to a relationship.'

Thoughtfully, chewing her haddock lattice pie, Tweedie admits that she's long been a target for feminist fury. They'll carp about *Bliss*, she says, like they've been carping about her writing ever since 14 years ago she became the first journalist to champion the Women's Movement: 'The bitterest blows I get are from feminists; in my experience they hate any woman who actually achieves anything on her own without the support of her sisters. I once watched Kate Millett address a meeting at a London's Women's Centre and I could feel in my bones that she was about to be attacked . . . Suddenly a woman shouted: "You've made a lot of money so you're not a *real* feminist, you've lost touch with the grass roots", and I wanted to weep, it's such an unforgiving, unsupportive attitude – it's the slave syndrome, the acrimony of the oppressed (i.e., women) when one of their number gets above her station . . .

'I spent years *devoted* to feminism, angry all the time, hating men, then I slowly emerged and had to decide whether to go on constantly erupting like a geyser or whether to cool down . . . what amazes me about feminism

is how it *began* to break away from the rules and conditioning that men put upon women. Now we've got a new
situation where women like me who've felt deeply about
feminism are having another battle to break away from that
frightening conditioning that *feminism* has put on women!

'When I wrote *In the Name of Love* some heavy feminists
banned it on the grounds that I'd once written an article
about lesbians in which I admitted that I felt uncomfortable
about being with women sexually . . . I'm telling you, somewhere out there are women who will not let the anger go.
They can kill you. No joking.'

Tweedie puffs on a cigarette. Teenage son lurches about
with a frying-pan. No, he doesn't want haddock lattice pie,
he'll have fried eggs. And some frozen crispy pancakes.
Tweedie hands him the fish-slice and explains how she sees
fiction-writing as an escape from the constraints of journalism. 'Journalists cannot always write The Truth because of
writs, upsetting the advertisers, or offending readers.' She
says that she plucked up the nerve to quit journalism after
reading *Black Tickets* by Jayne Ann Phillips. 'She is *miraculous*, the way she writes is beautiful but it struck me that like
all the stunning women's fiction I've read over the past few
years, her work is about feelings and not about what runs
the world and makes it the place it is . . .

'It seems to me that the pressure of what's happening out
there is so terrifying that I've got no time any more for mere
literary works of art, I'm not saying they are trivia, but what
the hell good do they do? I had the idea of writing a novel
with an underlying message, i.e. conservation – a work that
might reach out to people and hopefully make them aware of
how we are destroying our planet.'

Tweedie says she's the first one to admit she's no Salman
Rushdie. Combining high literature with a message is
perhaps not her forte but she wrote *Bliss* as 'stylishly as I
possibly could. I re-wrote it three times, nearly killing
myself, and I *know* it's not half as good or polished as my
1,000-word *Guardian* articles – but if 200 people read it and
think "There are valuable medicinal plants to be saved in
the Amazon, we must *do* something," I shall have achieved
something worthwhile. Look, I *could* write describing my
kitchen table like a table's never been described before so
that your literary types might say *"wonderful* writing", but

who gives a fuck about kitchen tables? People don't want to wade through a load of descriptive garbage; we are living in 1984, time's running out, writers should be writing about 1984 issues.'

She was pissed off, yes, *pissed off*, when she met academic novelist David Lodge on the platform of the Birmingham Writers' Festival and he inquired whether *Bliss* came in the 'commercial' or 'literary' genre of novels. She bets no-one asked Dickens, Bronte or Trollope such a daft question. 'Sorry,' she told Lodge, 'I didn't know they divided novels into categories like that.' Snooty bastard.

There was a time, she adds, when she might have been cowed by these oh-so-superior academic types who imagine they know everything. They mostly learn about life from books. She learnt about life by *living*. She can remember her first big journalistic assignment, a trip to Munich with the then-unknown Rolling Stones. She was stuck in a huge, mucky hotel room with them and Mick Jagger was lying on the floor, nose in a book, raving 'Wow, man, this book is really cool, it's by Dostoevsky,' while Tweedie, bored witless, yawned and snapped back, 'I've read it, so what?' and paced the room wondering why life was passing her by.

'The point of this story', she says, 'is that I was so insecure and wrapped up with impressing people with the books I'd read that I didn't recognize Real Life (i.e. Mick Jagger) slap in front of my eyes. I look back to that assignment as the high spot of my career – I'd never come across anyone as famous since, and I blew it.'

A sudden feline shriek indicates that teenage son has sat on the cat. It springs, limping, across the floor. Tweedie undislocates its leg and offers it the last of the haddock lattice pie. Teenage son mutters 'sorry' and carries on eating his fried egg. Tweedie rages that something is terribly wrong with the world at the moment. 'If all human beings are shit, then men are more so than women. I couldn't survive in a world full of men. I feel they are dangerous, there's something very retarded about most men, something atrophied.' Teenage son smirks, yawns and switches on children's telly.

Obviously there can't be anything retarded or atrophied about Tweedie's third husband, Alan Brien. When he first walked Tweedie's way, a thousand violins began to play and they've been a loving couple ever since. 'Yes, I'm absolutely happy now,' insists Tweedie, 'I believe companionship, friendship and sex with one person is paramount. I do sometimes ask myself why it was my fate to get lumbered first with a Dracula figure and then with a dopehead, both men making me feel a complete failure with no gift for human relationships . . . I always thought life should be more loving; had the men I married not been so *mad* I would have been perfectly all right.'

Tweedie points out that after 14 years of writing about women every week, reading everything published about women, meeting everyone who's been anyone in the Women's Movement, she's reached a stage where she says to herself, 'Jill, you can trust yourself – you're a woman – and if you can't sort things out for yourself, no one can.' So she looked round, waxed indignant at the male destruction of the Amazon rain forest, declared 'I'm not fucking having that' and dived in the deep end with an ambitious and entertaining first novel.

As for the aforementioned rampaging feminist mafia, Tweedie reckons they refuse persistently to see an obvious truth, that *every* book, poem, painting, piece of music, newspaper article done by an individual woman is also collective because no one lives in a vacuum. As she says: 'The Women's Movement itself coined the phrase "The personal is political" yet they sneer at the personal unless it reflects some collective view hammered out at endless dreary meetings and translated into a jargon that makes your teeth ache to read.'

You can take it from me that Tweedie's *Bliss*, one helluva rattling good yarn, is refreshingly jargon-free, and it certainly won't be your teeth that ache when you read it.

Bliss (Heinemann, 1984).

Chloe is ambitious, romantic, spirited and rather nice, just like me. I intended her to be the best fictional creation since Scarlett O'Hara

JOAN COLLINS

Squaring her shoulder-pads and smiling through clenched, exquisitely-capped teeth, she braced herself to face the throng of people she thought of as 'slimy Fleet Street reptiles' and 'vile paparazzi'. The same people whose prying lenses and vitriolic pens were the price she had to pay for being Joan Collins, superstar, envied and adored by every woman, and many men, her life illuminated by the merciless glare of fame.

Joan Collins, the woman whose life has been played out against the glittering world of money, sex, power and glamour that is television today (if you don't count Channel 4), flicked an invisible speck of dust from her Gianni Versace cream silk blouse and black silk neck bow, held high her seductive, luscious-lipped, exotic head and prayed that the Press would recognize that inside the fabled actress a stunning novelist had at last clawed her way out.

'I know this hung-over pack of wolves is hoping my eyelashes will fall off, my face crack, my underwired padded bra snap' she thought anxiously, as a hack with acne snatched a surprise shot in the corridor. She caught sight of the female reporter she dreaded above all others, 'The Barracuda of Fleet Street,' invisible venom dripping from her ballpoint, and prayed: 'Oh, please, please be *kind* to me ... I'm getting over New York flu, my nose is red under my beige foundation, and bunged up like a blocked drainpipe.'

Into the vast chandelier-hung ballroom Joan Collins strode (to a whispering chorus of 'I can't believe she's 56, isn't she *amazing*) her slim voluptuous figure clad in a chic, black raw-silk suit, drawing gasps of admiration.

'Who does she think she is, for heaven's sake, Salman Rushdie? A Booker Award contender? A Real Writer enriching people's souls with inspirational literature?' hissed a bespectacled hackette with showy gums. 'Shush,' hissed a hundred others, gazing in awe upon the author of *Prime Time* ('the ultimate Hollywood novel'), the story of a talented, beautiful and romantic soapstar whose very life is at stake as one man, with madness in his heart, watches her from the shadows.

In two days the book had jumped to number three in the best-seller list. A staggering 200,000 copies had been printed. On publication day the author caused chaos in Harrods, selling 1,000 signed copies in one hour . . .

Everyone says it's hard work writing a book. It isn't.

'Hi, I'm sorry I'm late, but I'm at death's door,' quipped Joan Collins, ever the professional, ever the trouper, fluttering lashes like muddy spiders' legs as the popping flash bulbs ricocheted off the Art Deco mirrors. 'Take a good look at my book,' (she raised it above her head) 'God, I feel like Mike Tyson . . .'

The slit of her black silk Emanuel skirt was just high enough to reveal a trim, elegant thigh. Suddenly she coughed. A snapper with adenoids and a bulging Adam's apple flashed and drew breath at her beauty, capturing her flesh, her brunette loveliness, forever, with each click of his shutter. Cold rage gripped her. 'Don't take photos of me coughing, baby,' she snapped. 'Can I offer you anything, Miss Collins?' entreated a Claridge's lackey. 'Just some Ribena, please.'

She sat behind a trestle table massed with microphones, nervously licked Dior lipgloss and waited for the hard-hitting questions. 'Is Chloe, your novel's central character, the talented, beautiful and romantic woman whose marriage is breaking up as her career takes her to the heights of stardom, based on you?' rasped The Barracuda.

Joan Collins's laugh made the chandeliers shiver. 'I'm getting rather fed up with being asked this question. Comparisons are odious. Chloe is ambitious, romantic, spirited and rather nice, just like me. I intended her to be the best fictional creation since Scarlett O'Hara. I know there is a tendency to put yourself in your first novel and there are certain parts of me in all the female characters. A lot of my subconscious came out when I was writing. It took me three-and-a-half years by the way. Heavens, I'm very bad at doing this sort of Press conference, I must say.'

Again the chandelier-shivering laugh. Suddenly the lights dimmed. They came up again. The harassed Claridge's lackey looked panic-stricken. 'Something up with the fuse-box,' he muttered, 'Nothing serious.' Joan Collins clenched her hands until her long, elegantly-manicured nails tore into her palms. She must think positively. She must. She must. She *had* to get to the top of the bestsellers. She needed it now more than ever.

Did she ever get writer's block? bawled the bespectacled hackette. 'Yes. But I stopped writing and started again when I was in the mood. I write in a different way to other authors. I've no set routine.'

Does she have any tips for aspiring writers? 'Yes. I do. Everyone says it's hard work writing a book. It isn't.' ('Try telling that to Margaret Drabble or Penelope Lively,' muttered The Barracuda.) 'I gave up basics like cleaning my teeth and brushing my hair to make time. Everyone has a book in them. Excuse me just for a moment.' She sipped some water. The silence was broken by scraching pens and photographers' bleepers.

How much advance did she get paid? 'I'm not replying to that,' snapped Joan Collins, voice twanging like an untuned violin (speaking of which, turn to page 26 of *Prime Time* and you'll find a typical Collins metaphor: 'He played her like a Stradivarius, every part of her body was afire with an intensity she had never felt before,' etc etc).

Will she give up starring in *Dynasty* now she's a best-selling author? 'Maybe. Seven years is long enough to play one role. And I'm fed up with having to overcome people's preconceptions, they assume I'm this horrible bitch Alexis . . .'

Will *Prime Time* win the Booker Prize? Joan Collins' reply was drowned out by tumultuous laughter. She either said: 'What's that?' or 'What a cat.'

The ordeal was over. Hot tears pricked the back of her lids. Her throat felt constricted. How long had this gone on? 'Thank God the sleazebag rag reporters are going,' sighed Joan Collins, forgetting for a split second to hold her chest out. As she checked her whirlwind schedule of signing, interviews and chat shows and glanced at another 500 copies of *Prime Time* waiting to be let loose upon the world, she overheard The Barracuda's voice booming from the ladies' powder room. 'Prime Time is trash, it's trash with knobs on, it's trash wearing wet-look lipgloss and diamante ribbons in its hair.'

A strangled gasp. A gurgle. The sound of someone (possibly the bespectacled hackette with showy gums) shouting: 'Shut up, you snooty cow. I can't wait to buy a copy.' And footsteps racing down the marble corridor. Joan Collins gave a little moan of ecstasy.

'And is there honey still for tea?' she murmured, her publicity lady's arm encircling her waist, their hands clasping in a firm, confident handshake.

I gave up basics like cleaning my teeth and brushing my hair to make time. Everyone has a book in them.

Prime Time (Century Hutchinson, 1988).

John
Francome

To be honest, my heart's not in this famous author racket. I'd rather be successful at training racehorses than be a successful author.

*J*ohn Francome is the most successful National Hunt jockey ever. He has ridden 1,138 winners, was champion jockey seven times, is the only jockey ever to have ridden more than 100 winners in five consecutive seasons, and was awarded the MBE for his services to racing. Last year, aged 32, he retired from racing to take up horse training and has just made what his publisher refers to as 'a stunning debut as a writer of fiction'.

Francome's first novel, *Eavesdropper*, is described on the dust-jacket as 'a fastrunning, effortlessly authentic racing thriller in the Dick Francis tradition'. It is being launched with a staggering £30,600 promotion campaign: a 'national author tour', a 'win a day at the races with John Francome' competition and displays of Francome's photos in book-shops nationwide. It is rumoured that he has already notched up £100,000 in advance payments.

In short Francome's book is being hyped with such extravagance that one might well conclude that a major talent has burst on to the British literary scene. On the other hand one might conclude that there is something a trifle suspicious about *Eavesdropper*. Particularly if one scrutinizes the book's dust-jacket.

To begin with we are told that '*only* an insider like John Francome, National Hunt's favourite son, could have devised and written *Eavesdropper*'. Yet there, as bold as brass on the front cover underneath John Francome's name (in large letters), are the words 'and James MacGregor' in much smaller ones. This suggests to me that far from John Francome 'an insider' being the *only* one to devise and write the book, the aforementioned James MacGregor had a pretty big hand in it as well.

In fact, as I wait for Francome in the plush Carlton Tower Hotel (Knightsbridge) where we have arranged to meet to discuss his 'stunning debut as a writer of fiction' the suspicion crosses my mind that maybe he didn't write *Eavesdropper* at all. Maybe the publishers are using his name and fame and personal charisma as a front for a book penned by the mysterious James MacGregor about whom we learn nothing from the dust-jacket other than he is 'happily married and lives in London'.

As I sit there, a teatime piano tinkling irritatingly, I try to psych myself up for a confrontation. 'Look, John,' I will say as soon as he emerges from his chauffeur-driven limo through the swing doors, 'I have a hunch that you didn't actually write this book.' I rehearse this sentence several times, but when Francome suddenly arrives and saunters across the Chinoiserie lounge looking sexy enough to make a woman's nipples pucker, all the heavy, investigative questions I've prepared go right out of my head.

'Hi there,' says Francome in his Wiltshire accent, flashing gorgeous teeth, 'nice to meet you. I fancy a cuppa, how about you?' Utterly disarmed I say 'yes please' and rustle my notebook trying to look businesslike.

'What do you think of the book, then?' asks Francome, tucking into a prawn mayonnaise sandwich. 'Did you find it a bit boring in the middle?' This is a tricky one. Do I grasp the nettle and say, 'Frankly, John, I could smell horse manure on every page, and oh, by the way, I have this hunch you didn't write this book . . .'

Playing for time, I mumble something about not, actually, being a great one for racing thrillers in the Dick Francis tradition, 'racing thrillers aren't really my cup of tea, if you know what I mean . . .' Francome leans forward and interrupts: 'To tell you the truth I think *Eavesdropper* is a bit boring, now I've read the finished version. I didn't write it all, of course. I just did the racing bits.' Another flash of the gorgeous teeth. 'Really? Tell me more.' I say, feeling a great sense of relief.

The candid Francome continues: 'I wrote it with my friend, Tom Shields, a barrister who once acted for me. He writes under the name of James MacGregor and maintains a low profile because it wouldn't loqk good for his professional image . . .

'I wrote quite a lot of it. In fact I never thought I had very much imagination and quite surprised myself. I did all the racing bits, Tom did all the court scenes, then he went through the whole lot in longhand, editing it, making it gel . . .

'I would think we wrote about half each and knocked it out in three months. We had a lot of bad weather in January, and I couldn't do anything with the horses so I got stuck into some writing. I can write anywhere as long as it's not in front of a window. Tom and I are going 50:50 on the money.'

By now you will have gathered that Francome is nothing if not frank. Helping himself to another prawn sandwich he reveals that he left school at the age of 15 with two O-levels (metalwork and cookery) and rose from stable lad to champion jockey faster than you can say 'They're off!' Yes, he's met the Queen. And Prince Charles. And had a private dinner with the Queen Mother.

We had a lot of bad weather in January, and I couldn't do anything with the horses so I got stuck into some writing.

As for the MBE he says: 'It was very nice being honoured but I'm not the sort who is impressed by that sort of thing. I hate being recognized. I like to be one of the boys.

'I'm one of the boys at the fish-and-chip shop I own in Swindon. I bought it in partnership with another ex-jockey. This is the first year I haven't been in there working. I really enjoy it, putting on the old white apron, filleting the fish, slapping it in batter, slicing the chips . . .'

Attempting to steer the conversation back to his 'stunning debut as a writer of fiction' I inquire whether the creative writing process interferes with his horse-training commitments. 'It sure does,' replies Francome, tucking into a slice of fruit cake. 'Writing just doesn't fit in at all with the horses. My day starts at 6.45. I go to the yard, check with the head lad that the horses are all right, then we pull out on to the gallops at about eight.'

He adds that people should never believe anything spicy or scandalous they hear about the National Hunt world. And that he's been happily married to wife Miriam, 'one in a million', for ten years. And that he leads a very quiet life. 'Whatever you might have read in the papers you don't get groupies in racing. It's too cold for all that. If I get any fan letters they're from grannies.'

When I ask him whether he received an advance of £100,000 for the book he replies: 'No comment.' Despite several increasingly desperate promptings he has little to say about *Eavesdropper* itself which, even as we are speaking, is being rushed out in special editions by a book club, serialized in a national newspaper, and is providing some thriller fan with the opportunity of winning a day at the races with John Francome.

Francome just sits there looking restless, as if the gallops are calling. 'To be honest', he sighs, being so honest that his publisher and the publicity people who contrived this interview will feel like tearing their hair out, 'my heart's not in this famous author racket. I'd rather be successful at training racehorses than be a successful author. That's the truth.'

Eavesdropper (Macdonald, 1986).

Jonathan King

MY MAIN AMBITION IS TO GAIN RECOGNITION

AS A GREAT WRITER.

*I*f people could die of excess personality Jonathan King would have expired years ago. Unstaunched, it oozes like perspiration from the pores of this 36-year-old, megamedia Whiz-kid and first-time author as he ushers me into his bijou mews cottage, past 'Celia' his suspender-wearing shop window dummy, past flying ducks, and framed gold discs, bellowing. 'We tycoons are very busy people, so don't panic.'

Ten minutes with JK leave you limp. Phones jangle, stereos blast, a Mickey Mouse cartoon blares unheeded from a vast television screen and JK, wearing a T-shirt with the Manhattan skyline glitter-sprayed across the chest, unwraps packages containing the latest chart-bound sounds.

'I believe you rocketed to stardom at the age of 18 with your hit song *Everyone's gone for a moon'*, I shout, consulting my background notes as JK carries on two simultaneous converstions holding a phone to each ear while casting his eyes over the evening newspaper headlines.

'Gone *to* the moon, Everyone's gone *to* the moon', he corrects me, slamming down the phones and fidgeting with his infra-red remote control keypad. 'It was instant stardom, offers flooded in. At one time I had 20 records in the Top 30 under different names. When I was 22 I was running Decca Records. The rest is history.' Or hysteria.

By the age of 25 he owned 'the most lucrative independent record company of all time'.

Female fans used to hurl their knickers at him. Groupies beat a path to his front door begging for autographs, for locks of his hair, for fragments of his clothing. JK dashes to his photo collection and shows me a vast blown-up black-and-white picture of himself in his 1967 heyday, emaciated-looking, slightly spotty and wearing Buddy Holly specs.

'You looked a real little wimp in those days, didn't you,' I say, with a chummy little laugh. 'No,' replies JK, with an un-chummy little frown, 'I think I looked strikingly hand-some, veering towards God-like, possibly too macho . . . but I handled all the fame and adulation with ease, had no major problems and soon developed my legendary taste for a highly extravagant lifestyle.'

These days his 'highly extravagant lifestyle' involves commuting between his two luxury homes in London and New York. 'I think of myself as a truly bicontinental communicator. I spend three weeks at my cosy, snug house here and three weeks at my cosy, snug apartment in Manhattan. It takes eight hours door-to-door, on Concorde, during which time I do my budgets and listen to cassettes on my personal stereo headphones.

'I love New York. My father was a New Yorker which means I have mixed blood in my veins . . . I'm making myself sound like Dracula, aren't I? But New York is a place of wonderful contrasts, of opulence and squalor. If you want to be a heroin-addict-meths-drinker slumping in the gutter there's nowhere better to be in than New York. The laid-back New Yorker doesn't get all heavy and self-righteous like the upright Londoner. He says "We have the responsibility to see that this guy leads as happy a life as any heroin-addict-meths-drinker can live".'

The podgy JK finger is kept on the pop pulse of two continents by buying American newspapers when he's in London and British newspapers in New York. He says that he can chat about Ken Livingstone or Mayor Ed Koch with equal authority. He's as *au fait* with New York fashions, vandalism, social trends and gossip as he is with what's happening on The Scene in London. He employs full-time secretaries and charladies in both homes. His Rolls-Royce and TR7 wait for him in London. His Cadillac waits in New York. Clearly the man who brought to Britain deely-boppers, the Rubic cube and *The Rocky Horror Show*, to name but three of his triumphant 'firsts', is not short of the odd few bob.

Neither, one must suppose, is he short of intellect, having left Cambridge University with an MA in English literature. 'Ah, Cambridge,' he sighs brushing his hair and opening four letters. 'When I left, Prince Charles followed me into my undergraduate rooms . . . I left a little note to greet him which said "Your Highness, as a King steps down a prince comes up – welcome to Trinity", and I'm certain he read it because a while later when I was standing up for the national anthem at a Royal presentation wearing my silly, multi-coloured wig, he winked at me in a conspiratorial manner. I'm a great fan of the Royals. I know they all sit reading their Sunday papers and having a good old giggle at what's written about them.'

He says that these days, having become a sort of 'father figure' for the younger generation, his advice to youth the world over is to make the most of education. 'Maybe exams are not all that important. If I'm honest my MA has done me no practical good at all, but it did give me the chance to appreciate English literature and although I am a world-famous rock star and TV celebrity, it is not commonly known that my ultimate ambition is to be a world-famous writer.'

At this point JK springs up to locate a copy of what he refers to as his 'brilliant novel' entitled *Bible Two* (Star Books). Published last year, it is so appalling, so mind-numbingly banal that one suspects that the Cambridge don who tutored JK through his degree in English literature might very well shoot himself through the head were he to read it. *Bible Two* might best be described as scrappy without the 's'. Which is the sort of joke Jonathan King might make, but not about himself.

The story concerns a buffoon millionaire called Jonathan Farting who, living in a world peopled by nutcase tycoons, whiz-kids, TV moguls and porn merchants, lusts after a shop-window dummy. Thirty thousand copies have been sold so far and a second novel is already in the word processor.

'I wrote it very quickly. Inspiration comes to me in high-speed blasts. Writing gives me more satisfaction and pleasure than anything else I do,' says JK, scrawling with a blotchy Magic-Marker 'To Val, please review this!' on the flyleaf. 'Anything?' I inquire, managing at last to get a word in, 'Even sex?'

'That goes without saying,' snorts JK. 'As a matter of fact I'm still a virgin ... but I do cherish my personal relationships. I have close friends in both countries. My mother is a dear friend and handles my company affairs. I love living on my own but I also love knowing and relating to people.

'When I die I'd like to think that I've made a lot of people's lives much happier simply by knowing them. To tell the truth, I am well aware that I am vastly disliked by the public as a whole, people *detest* me ...' He breaks off to hurl a brick at the TV screen. I nearly fall off the settee with shock. Fortunately it's a rubber brick. It bounces off the TV screen. JK chortles until his flying ducks rattle on the pine-panelled walls explaining, 'It's a "telly brick". Another of my "firsts". A friend gave it to me specially to throw at the screen when people like Paul McCartney come on, because I loathe them so much.

'I loathe Paul McCartney's music too . . . but I'm sure, if he's got any taste, he loathes mine. Paul and I have never got on very well, but I cherish a little secret that I inspired his great song *Yesterday*. We were at a night-club and he suddenly grabbed me saying "I have to get to a piano", much as someone with dysentery might say "I have to get to a toilet". Fortunately I had a piano in my little office round the corner.

'We drove there with him dum-de-dumming in the back of the car, with a song definitely coming on and to my alarm the office-door lock had jammed. "Break the door down," he screamed insanely, so I did. In he went and I left him to it. Only the sound of assorted piano-key jinglings could be heard. I am pretty certain it was *Yesterday* he was composing. Actually we'd probably be delighted to see each other if we were suddenly to meet. In the 1960s we rock stars were all one big happy family; we all take great delight in each other's continued success and mourn those who happen to fall by the wayside.'

During this soliloquy my gaze wanders to a bizarre lump in JK's sock. 'Ah ha,' shrieks JK, 'you've noticed where I keep my wallet.' This habit, he explains, is one acquired in New York where one learns never to carry one's wallet in one's pocket. 'Unfortunately if, like me, your wallet bulges with credit cards it stretches your socks and I have to keep throwing them away. Actually, the only place I've ever been mugged is in London. The New York sock trick works a treat over there, but now I've told all I expect the world's muggers will go straight for my ankles.' He adds that the ultimate answer to the mugging menace is a special leather leg-wallet – another first – which he intends to introduce to Britain in his new series of *Entertainment USA* (BBC2).

According to JK this show is consistently in the BBC's top three. He maintains that it manages to convey the 'genuine feel' of various American cities to people who can only dream of going there. As he says: 'I've departed from the tired old format of interviewing "Famous People" – Rod Stewart, David Bowie and so on are all crashing bores. Instead I look for "personality scoops". Last series the hit of my show was a gay transvestite nun from San Francisco called "Sister Boom Boom' who arrived on his motorbike in his habit and who was standing for the council elections against Diane Feinstein, a hard-nosed lady with hair like steel, who is being tipped as the next US vice-president.'

JK flicks the infra-red remote control keypad. *Sixty Minutes* flashes on with a chilling news item about a new-born baby found dead in a litter-bin. The camera pans across a high-rise estate of indescribable desolation. 'Oh heck,' grumbles JK flicking back to Mickey Mouse, 'I don't wish to know about such horrible happenings. Those awful estates are places I go out of my way to avoid.' Miffed, he polishes his specs, makes a couple of phone calls and hurls his rubber brick.

'Look,' he says, 'I've done it all. Twice. And I'm getting better all the time. I've got the golden touch. Recently there was this guy, Howard Jones, trying to get a hit disc. I gave him a few hints and two weeks later he was in the charts at number two, going round telling everybody that all you need to do to achieve success is to touch the hem of my garment.

'No, joking apart, my main ambition, is to gain recognition as a great writer. You *must* plug my book. It's absolutely wonderful. That's why you're here. Here take three copies, give them to your friends. I've been consistently outrageous and controversial for 18 years and now I'm trying to be a bit less aggravating. I'm going to refrain from saying off-the-cuff things such as "Anyone who believes in God must be a total moron", which is what I said recently on a radio show and caused a fuss.'

With the words 'total moron' ringing in my brain I fled from JK's opulent bachelor abode, from 'Celia' the suspender-belted show-window dummy, from the 18 telephones and all the electronic artefacts crucial to a mass communicator, and headed off to a workman's café for a reassuring pot of tea.

Bible Two (Star Books, 1984).

KINGSLEY AMIS

I find all these new feminists revolting. Revolting.
They are all lacking in a sense of humour.

Kingsley Amis ('a master technician of the English language' – publisher's publicity blurb) has chosen his club, the Garrick, for this interview. It's a forbidding, gloomy, gravy-brown, men-only place hung with drab oil-portraits. It smells of mothballs, halitosis, drying umbrellas and stale cigar smoke. On the way there, by bus, I had read a magazine article written by Amis in which he ranted about the way women have infiltrated traditional male citadels like clubs and pubs. 'One of the great advantages our civilization has enjoyed over the American version', thundered Amis in his article, 'is that here it's been taken for granted that the husband is going to slip off to his club, or pub and see the lads . . . but now Englishwomen are beginning to restrict this. They have decided they don't like men getting away from them . . .' As I stand, waiting to be checked over by the man-at-the-door of the Garrick Club, I look at various old dodderers shuffling about clutching copies of the *Daily Telegraph* and find it difficult to imagine any woman giving a damn if they got away from them.

Up a wide flight of stairs where I peer through panelled doors and catch sight of men snoozing on leather sofas or skulking towards the bar. Opening time, I think, and my spirits rise. I'm feeling sick. I'm feeling nervous. Boy, am I feeling *nervous*. The only Kingsley Amis work I can remember (apart from *Lucky Jim* which I found a bit schoolboyish) is a poem which goes: 'That time you heard the archbishop fart/you did quite right to say:/and should the ploughboy turn up gold/the news would make our day:/But when the ploughboy farts henceforth/Forget about it, eh? (From: *Advice To A Story-teller.*) I feel particularly nervous because it has been impressed on my by his publishers that this man Amis is a literary giant. A *LITERARY GIANT!* And I hate his new book, *Stanley And The Women. HATE IT*. I read it, and read it again and concluded that it had been written by someone who harbours a pathological hatred of women.

If you are an ageing male-chauvenist pig you will love Amis's new book. If you are any other sort of reader it will make you cringe. Why send *me* on this interview? I asked my editor. 'Because you're the only one who reads books in this office, for Christ's sake. Everyone else watches videos. Or they're on holiday, or busy, or scared shitless of Kingsley Amis. The man is a literary giant, a wonderful character. Take the bull by the horns.'

Let's get this over very quickly. I've a very important lunch, don't waste any of my time . . .

I was also feeling sick because Amis ('the epitome of what was best, sharp, flippant in the 1950s' – publisher's publicity blurb) hates being interviewed. 'Be warned, he's a real old devil, he abhors interviews,' warned his publicity person over the phone. So why has he volunteered to do one, then? She gave one of those upper-class giggles common to all publisher's publicity persons: 'Publicity of course. Most writers are prepared to suffer in the cause of self-promotion. You should consider yourself jolly lucky that he's offered *you* half an hour. Believe me he's turned dozens down . . .'

Into the 'morning room'. Amis is there already, sunk into a button-backed chair. *'Let's get this over with quickly,'* he says, in a rapid, phlegmy voice, *'I've a very important lunch, don't waste any of my time . . .'* By now I am feeling numb with nerves. I stall for time by rummaging in my bag for notebook and pen. Any minute Amis will ask 'Did you enjoy *Stanley And The Women*?' and I'll panic. 'Did you enjoy *Stanley And The Women?'* asks Amis. I panic. This is how the interview proceeds:

VH   'Er, well, I must admit I found the main character a bit of a chauvinist. I wasn't too keen on the female characters either. They're all daft, psychotic, scheming or dangerous, aren't they?'

KA   'Hmmmrrggh.'

VH   'I mean, it's sort of difficult to enjoy a novel whose main message is, as I see it, that all women are totally mad.'

KA   (Taking deep breath. Spraying the air with spit.) 'Women are hell. In lots of ways. A lot of the time.'

VH   (Wondering where to go from there. Sit tight? Nod your head? Control the beads of sweat breaking out on upper lip?) 'Hmmmrrggh.'

KA   '. . . Obviously mine is not a book that is likely to win many prizes for fashionable social attitudes. Obviously you are entitled to your interpretation. HMM. Hmm. However, *if* you can be bothered to look it up you will see that the doctor in my final chapter far from saying all women are mad says precisely the opposite. He says that they are all too monstrously, sickeningly *sane* and that's the whole trouble. He in fact says "if only they *were* off their heads then we could lock'em all up, bung 'em in a strait-jacket, cut 'em off from society. But they're not . . ." In other words he is asking whether there are, perhaps, more insidious forms of insanity than madness.'

VH (Gobsmacked. Seething. Felt-tip pen smouldering as it skids to a halt.) Amis blows his nose noisily. VH is desperate for a drink. As it is Amis's club and women aren't allowed to buy drinks in men's clubs, it's up to him to suggest one. Will he offer to buy VH one? Not on your life. Stingy old sod. Not even coffee. There is a general clinking of glasses and geriatric belches and slurping sounds to right and left.

KA 'Glad to see you don't use a tape-recorder. Can't stand the things. Did you find *Stanley And The Women* funny, incidentally?'

VH 'No.'

KA 'Hmmmrrggh. Well that's not surprising. I'm not going to explain the humour to you. It is impossible to explain anything to women these days. I find all these new feminists revolting. *Revolting.* They are all lacking in a sense of humour.'

VH 'Oh come off it. What about Fay Weldon? Jill Tweedie? Germaine Greer? They are marvellously witty when they get going.'

KA 'Germaine Greer?! (eyes, like pickled onions, pop out of their pouches). She's a *fool* about women's equality. Mind you, she's very bright. No, not as bright as all that, now I come to think about it. She's got a very ordinary mind. I once did a book programme with her and she put on a very feeble performance.'

VH 'Don't you think she writes – '

KA 'I recall a dinner party where Germaine Greer hogged the conversation with a medical monologue. She talked for one hour about the female breast without once mentioning the fact that it is an object of desire to most men. She concentrated entirely on diseases of the breast, horrific details that turned everyone entirely off their food . . .

naturally I had very little to contribute to all of this and at the end she turned to me and said, very nastily, I thought, that cancer of the male breast is on the up and up too ... absolutely characteristic of these bloody feminists, devoid of tact, timing, humour, and a crashing embarrassment to everybody.'

VH 'Speaking of tact, timing and humour, I'm finding it rather difficult not to – '

KA (Looking at his watch. Holds it against his ear. Shakes it.) 'Get on with it, time's nearly up . . .'

Obviously mine is not a book that is likely to win many prizes for fashionable social attitudes. Obviously you are entitled to your interpretation.

VH 'In *Stanley And The Women* the male characters share an agressive attitude towards women and an almost prurient obsession with sex. One character says "I've been going out with the same one (woman) for 10 years now. No point chopping and changing. They're all built the same," and another says: "In fact women only want one thing, for men to fuck them." This strikes me as "boy talk", maybe sharp and flippant in the fifties, but dated now. Do these attitudes echo your own?'

KA (Nodding vigorously). 'I sometimes think like that. Yes. I think most men do from time to time . . . So that makes me a real sex maniac, I don't think. Do for heaven's sake realize that a novel is not necessarily the last word on the subject.'

VH 'The dust-jacket blurb – '

KA 'Which I helped to write, yes, go on.'

VH 'Did you? I've often wondered whether authors write their own dust-jacket blurb . . . On yours it says that the novel "negotiates brilliantly the difficult course that runs between tragedy and helpless laughter". I must admit that I didn't laugh once. In fact I was deeply depressed when you introduced the teenager who has a schizophrenic breakdown. It was most unfunny.'

KA 'Nonsense!' (all the old buffers with their noses in their Scotch stare blearily in his direction). 'It has its funny parts. The mad youth's absurd delusions are funny. Can't you *see* that tragedy and humour can be very close? Comic moments can be made of the most tragic happenings in our lives.'

VH 'Such as a 19-year-old going hopelessly insane and spending the rest of his life zombie-like in institutions?'
KA 'Certainly funny. Great potential. Maybe you're not up to comic fiction. Maybe your sense of humour never matured. When you get a bit older you'll get rid of some of your silly ideas . . .'

That is the end of the interview. 'Didn't you find old "Kingers" a great character?' asked my editor next day. 'A great character,' I replied. On my way out of the Garrick Club I found a copy of the *Daily Mirror* in a waste bin in the ladies powder room. Kingsley Amis is that newspaper's poetry editor. The *only* newspaper poetry editor in Britain. What an opportunity. On page 13 underneath a picture of the Queen Mother is 'Poetry Corner' with this anony-mous verse: "Hooray, Hooray/the first of May/Outdoor sex begins today.' Yes. Well. Very fifties, very public school. Maybe Amis has been overworking lately.

Stanley and the Women (Hutchinson, 1984).

Laurie Lee

> I never intended to be a
> writer. I left the village school
> at 14. I just scribbled for my
> family and girlfriends.

*I*t is three years since Laurie Lee invited anyone to his attic hideaway in Chelsea, a place full of locked rooms containing rejected manuscripts and other men's mad wives. Or so he says. He also says he doesn't own a telephone, so when one bleeps as we are matily clinking glasses to toast the forthcoming BBC television film of his classic *As I Walked Out One Midsummer Morning*, I tactfully disregard it.

Lee ignores it too. He gazes evasively through the window, the cracks of which are ineptly sealed with shrivelled brown sticky tape, and he enthuses about the view. 'I watch Concorde go over, a beautiful sight, and Prince Andrew dipping his helicopter over the palace to wave to Ma'am, and the seagulls, a sign to batten down the hatches . . .'

Lee, poet, essayist, OBE and author of one of the most lyrical autobiographies in the English language, *Cider With Rosie*, is a bit of an old rascal. The literary world tells tales of his partiality for the hard stuff, how he fell off the podium at a poetry-reading, how he smuggles drink into readings in ink bottles.

He tells tales about himself, like the one about the day he was sitting outside the pub in his native Cotswold village, Slad, when a party of giggling schoolgirls asked 'Excuse me, Sir, can you tell us where Laurie Lee is buried?' In the polite version he replies (and you must imagine his Gloucestershire burr): 'Laurie Lee is usually buried with his nose in a pint of bitter if you'd care to join me in the public bar.' In the saucy version he replies: 'Oooh ar, come up the wood girls, and Laurie Lee will soon show you where he wants to be buried.'

You can forgive bawdiness from the man who wrote: 'Such a morning it is when love/leans through geranium windows/and calls with a cockerel's tongue . . .' And you can countenance a certain amount of intemperate rambling from the man who, at 19, left his mother's cottage to walk to London and then through Spain, from Vigo to Andalusia, playing a violin for money as he went. Not that the man will discuss either his poetry or the BBC film of that celebrated trek. 'It's fairly true to my book,' he concedes, 'they shot it last year in Spain, the young man taking my part is much better looking than I was, the music's by Julian Bream . . .' But what he really wants to discuss is his TV appearance as a guest on *Wogan* and how he got up Wogan's nose.

'I soon realized that the twinkle in Wogan's eye turns to ice if you pull his leg,' he grumbles, his own astute eyes glowering through smeared bi-focals. 'When I told him not to interrupt me, he drew back, looking coldly displeased. I'd taken along my little flute to surprise him with an impromptu Irish air. In case the excitement of listening to Wogan drove my fingering from my mind, I carried a card with instructions on it saying "Three fingers down, two fingers up". When I asked him to hold it he looked cross and suddenly tore it in half and the credits rolled up. It was the "two fingers up" he didn't like. We didn't hit it off at all.

'I began telling him how I've always depended on women as voluptuous refuges. His eyes went icy. He started to look worried. I told him how I often live alone, because unlike certain more august writers, such as Blake and Dickens, I can't work with women in the room.

'This is the reason I don't live at home all the time with my dear wife. I love visiting her, then returning to my London fortress where I work. The pleasure of welcome is only exceeded by the pleasure of saying farewell . . .'

So what is Laurie Lee *writing* these days? 'Cheques,' he replies with a wistful sniff, 'gas bills, VAT returns. I spend a lot of time answering letters from people wanting their poems published. Schoolchildren doing *Cider With Rosie* for O-level write to me. My serious objection to being on the syllabus is the daft exam questions they set. But I won't say more on that topic (scowls sheepishly) in case they take me off the syllabus and my royalties dry up.'

Obviously, 'the royalties' keep the wolf from the door, not to mention the scotch on the rocks, the book having sold two million in paperback. Lee confesses it is a mystery to him that a book about rural life before it was 'raped by the combustion engine' still attracts readers.

I hazard another query about current work in progress. He appears not to hear. When I inquire whether he's slightly deaf he replies: 'My dear daughter Jesse, who gives me kisses in exchange for pound notes, describes me to people saying "he stumbles and he's a bit deaf but he's ever so young . . ." One never says one's deaf, you know, as one never says one's an alcoholic. Incidentally, my GP recently asked me what I'd drunk that day and I replied "two beers and a short" which is alcoholic code, as all GPs know, for 15 beers and half a bottle of whisky.'

At this point, the post arrives. Lee nips into the hall, wildly slitting open envelopes until, like a sniffer-dog pouncing on drugs, he finds a cheque. I make feeble further inquiries about his work in progress as he waves the cheque gleefully like a flag. 'That's the question I always shy away from,' he replies, topping up the glasses. 'Furthermore, I don't even think of myself as a writer now. More a communicator and interpreter of something which I still think of as being magically unique, that is this world and this life which, in spite of shadows and occasional pain, has been a perpetual excitement and joy. I never intended to be a writer. I left the village school at 14. I just scribbled for my family and girlfriends. When I was in my 20s, a rather grand girlfriend found my poems on the floor and persuaded Cyril Connolly to get them published.'

Bemoaning the fact that he writes very slowly, he suddenly lets slip that the sequel to his half-a-million bestseller, *As I Walked Out*, is just nearing completion. 'It is a book of defeat, pain and disaster. About a winter when the anti-Franco side were in retreat, Franco was winning and our side had no arms. I'm also writing my deathbed confessions, but that's all I'm prepared to say. No one wants to hear an old poet rambling pompously on about his next book . . .'

Lee then says that he was 'dismayed' to see a recent reference to himself as 'the 80-year-old Laurie Lee'. He promply wrote to the editor of the newspaper concerned saying 'This is an outrage, you have ruined my love life, everybody knows I'm only 59. Kindly print an apology or send me 4 bottles of malt whisky in lieu . . .' He says he was 'thrilled' and 'amazed' to receive 4 bottles of malt whisky a week later, one separately wrapped and named 'Old Grandad'.

And that's it. He invites me to peep at a heap of letters, lists, bills and poems in a room of unspeakable chaos, and steers me downstairs and out into the gloomy street, where love is definitely not calling with a cockerel's tongue but where we spot the first handful of snowdrops thrusting up through the grime and sleet.

As I Walked Out One Midsummer Morning (Andre Deutsch, 1985).

Les Dawson

I'LL TELL YOU THIS MUCH, CHUCK, I WOULDN'T
SAY 'NO' TO THE BOOKER PRIZE.

*L*es Dawson doesn't act like a man who's about to take the literary world by storm. Shortly before we met for a critical appraisal of his first novel, *A Time Before Genesis*, he was skipping across the stage of the Palace Theatre, Manchester, in a turquoise dress and padded corset, waving a lavatory brush round his head and splitting the sides of 2,000 panto fans. I mean, can you imagine John Fowles or Anthony Burgess or even Jeffrey Archer discussing their new novels in a similar setting? Can you imagine them holding forth eloquently, as Les does, about the 'dynamics of creation' and the 'torment of the speculative intellect' while the Roly-Polys (heavyweight tap-dancing troupe all weighing 14 stone plus) thunder back and forth doing routines in the background?

'I'm just putting me trousers on,' Les yells, as I tap on his dressing-room door clutching my copy of his novel, described on the dust-jacket as 'a horrific novel of the future – is it closer than we think?' A man in a tutu twirls past. A woman dressed as Robin Hood sprints by. Then the entire cast of *Babes in the Wood* clatter along the corridor as Les shouts 'Enter!'

In I go to find our hero beaming in the glow of a hundred dressing-table lightbulbs. His hastily brushed scalp is damp, a gold ingot dangles into the greying Dawson chest hair, a splodge of cold cream gleams above the left ear. 'It's a proud moment for me to see my name on the spine of my first novel,' says Les. 'Let's hope it takes the literary world by storm. How do you rate the plot?'

This question has me stumped. The plot, it must be said, is of such exquisite intricacy that it would take a more dedicated fiction fan than I to unravel all its multi-layered twists. Promising on the dust-jacket to 'unleash forces too malevolent for the human mind to grasp', *A Time Before Genesis* is low on laughs and high on melodrama. It incorporates devil worship, Nazism, lesbianism, drugs, torture, sado-masochism, dismembered corpses, you name it . . .

The main character, Gates, sums up the book on page six when he groans: 'My problem is how to set out a full story without it sounding like the ramblings of a near idiot.' A tricky problem indeed, and one that arguably Gates or Les never quite manage to solve. But it would be undiplomatic to say so at this point in the interview so I hedge my bets a bit and reply: 'Oooer! It's steamy stuff, Les. A different ballgame to *Blankety Blank*. James Herbert'd better watch out.'

We both look solemn. Les exhales noisily through his nostrils and remarks that there's a serious book inside every one of us. Devil worship, Nazism, lesbianism, drugs, torture, sado-masochism, depravity and dismembered corpses may not be the topics that immediately spring to mind when you hear the name Les Dawson he concedes, but inside every funny man there's a philosopher trying to get out.

And how. As he explains: 'I've always wanted to write a serious book. I've long been very concerned about the conflict betwen good and evil in the universe. The way human beings seem hellbent on self-destruction is for all the world as though society is beginning to crumble.' Here Les turns to page nine and reads aloud a paragraph to illustrate his apocalyptic vision of society after it has crumbled (circa 1995):

'Many learned men still pondered the question: where had the rot begun? . . . It was the epoch of physical beauty; the body was all important and the mind wasn't nourished. "Slim, slim" – that was the dogma and many a child who had been jeered at for being a "fat slob" committed suicide in the face of such taunts. Pills to help you shed excess weight were for sale. There was an abundance of sprays to enhance the body's sexual allure. "Stay young" was the cry. Maturing women held back the encroachment of time with punishing physical exercise to the wild tempo of popular music. Drug abuse became the norm . . . one popular cabaret comedian told a joke about the weight of his wife and was imprisoned for six months . . .'

Les admits that his book makes depressing reading, that it is not intended for escapists or the faint-hearted. 'If you believe in the basic weakness of human nature,' he observes – the sound of the Roly-Polys ('ten legs that shook the world') now very audible outside his dressing-room door – 'then you have to accept that there's a certain amount of bestiality in all of us. Robert Louis Stevenson said it all in *Dr Jekyll and Mr Hyde* . . .

'The decline of the church in this country is due to the fact that people don't take the power of evil seriously any more. The old fire-and-brimstone types of preachers had a lot going for them in my opinion; they were closer to the truth than we give them credit for.

'I'm not saying that *A Time Before Genesis* will change the world overnight, but it's been important for me to get certain anxieties about society off my chest. If the critics acknowledge that the germ of a serious writer is to be found in *A Time Before Genesis* I shall be a contented man.'

Les reveals that back in the days when he was paunchless and had all his own teeth he longed to be a writer. At the age of 20 he entered his Bohemian phase, travelled to Paris to chance his arm with the avant-garde, and 'bought a couple of notebooks and found cheap digs by the river'. Did he hang out with the existentialists on the Left Bank? Les slaps his knee and emits a wheezy chuckle. 'Left Bank? Right Bank? Barclays Bank? Don't know what the hell bank it was. I didn't know Paris from Adam. Couldn't speak any French. I picked up some Spanish, though. I won't say what else I picked up . . .'

Les rolls his eyes. He places a fat finger on his nose. 'To tell the truth I always wanted to have a go at poetry but there were too many damn good poets about already. I stuck to essays, mostly, lots of phrases like "dusk bled sepia-tinged over the stagnant Seine" and such like. Nothing was ever published of course.

Les admits that he has always been a trifle addicted to purple prose. In fact *A Time Before Genesis* undoubtedly contains some of the best purple prose in the English language. Whip through it and you find such jewels as 'a biting wind was savaging our shivering limbs,' and 'the reek of narcotics assaulted his nostrils as the unholy cabal threshed in sexual frenzy to the descant of the girl's torment,' and 'where once arid land had lain, lush blooms and radiant flowers jostled for room with spreading acres of verdant kingsize vegetables.'

Purple prose apart, Les anticipates that readers will get gripped by his plot. I ask him whether, perhaps, he penned his fast-moving tale with an eye to a big screen adaptation? 'I must say it hadn't crossed my mind,' replies Les, combining several winks with an eager dig in the ribs, 'but now you mention it, I wouldn't mind a little trip to Beverly Hills.' Suddenly we find ourselves bandying names like 'Spielberg' and 'David Puttnam' and starting to make casting suggestions.

How about Joan Collins as Mrs Mainwaring? ('She was in her late 40s with a mask of grief distorting the fact that she was a very attractive woman.') And Oliver Reed as Gates? ('I began to slide into the gutter, with alcohol assisting my passage. My body could not take any more pain. Only half of my physical functions were unimpaired.') We are getting eager, so carried away, so excited that I'm almost tempted to offer to do the screenplay. As Les says there's 'big bucks' to be made in movies. More than he'll be getting from *Babes in the Wood*.

Mind you, says Les, 18 months spent hunched over a typewriter has taught him a thing or two about stamina. All the research, all the ploughing through countless tomes on satanism, the occult, Egyptology, Tibetan monks, UFOs and the Crusaders, added up to a heck of a lot of effort. *A heck of a lot*. No two ways. 'Those authors who sit down regular as clockwork and write for eight hours at a stretch are beyond me. I found it a real pain in the neck. My kids kept coming in and asking me for money as is their way and breaking my concentration. So I'd storm out to the pub.'

Speaking of which, Les says that there's just about time for a swift one before the evening show starts. He guides me through corridors, across the stage, into a lift, past two goblins, through a cupboard, up some stairs and into the bar. 'The usual,' he beams, as two panto fans ask him to autograph their *Babes in the Wood* programmes. Spotting my copy of *A Time Before Genesis*, they ask if it's as riveting as Les's autobiography *A Clown Too Many*. Les explains how it unleashes forces too malevolent for the human mind to grasp. 'Oooer!' they shriek, then giggle.

Les turns to me and confides: 'I tell you this much, chuck, I wouldn't say no to the Booker Prize. I've long had the ambition to get into the world of literature. The Booker Prize is my ultimate goal. If *A Time Before Genesis* wins the 1986 Booker Prize the nation will be stunned. Mark my words.' He can say that again.

A Time Before Genesis (Elm Tree Books, 1986).

It may surprise some people to know that I've always been very fond of reading.

Mandy Rice-Davies

'*T*he daft thing about the Booker prize-winners,' reveals Mandy Rice-Davies, patting her ash-blonde hair and dragging contemplatively on a lipstick-smeared cigarette, 'is that they're all written to a formula. To hit the jackpot they have to be a bit thin on plot, very introspective and padded out with a lot of high-class prose. They even have a sort of *smell* about them. The minute you pick one up, you think: "Oh Boy! This is *Literature*" . . .'

And it is *Literature* with a capital 'L' that Mandy Rice-Davies has invited me to her Golders Green apartment to discuss. I am not there to snoop through her bathroom cabinet, as less scrupulous journalists often do, nor am I there to winkle out further revelations about Profumo, Rachman, the mysterious Man-in-the-Mask, and various licentious cavortings in the Cliveden swimming-pool, or to make impertinent observations about her gold-plated taps, her Art Deco figurines or her scarlet BMW. Certainly not. 1986 is, for Mandy Rice-Davies, the Year of the Book. These days anyone rash enough to hark back to those scandalous events of the 1960s gets, as Mandy Rice-Davies would then have put it, a smack in the gob.

Her first novel *Today and Tomorrow*, hailed by a Sphere paperback publicity person as 'The sensational, unstoppable story of high-class seduction and ruthless international intrigue', was completed only days after she shook hands with Princess Anne at the premiere of *Absolute Beginners*, in which she has a minor role ('I'm back in the fold Val, living proof that a person can rise again after being crucified'). Make no mistake. It is as a novelist that Mandy Rice-Davies ('Call me Mandy, Val, call me anything you like so long as it's not The-Girl-Who-Brought-Down-Harold-Macmillan') wishes, in future, to be celebrated.

And it is *Today and Tomorrow* that she insists we chat about, because (and here she thoughtfully rubs cigarette ash off her mock-croc slip-ons): 'I'm very keen to make my mark as a serious writer. Get this down please, Val. *Today and Tomorrow* is a very serious book. It may surprise some people to know that I've always been very fond of reading. Certainly my taste in literature is rather good. I've read all the classics, Balzac, Hugo, Maupassant, the Russians and I've always admired good prose, writers like Durrell, Nabokov, Margaret Drabble . . .'

Today and Tomorrow follows the aventures of Amethyst Barclay (28) a freelance journalist (and fan of Ferdinand Mount's column in *The Spectator*) who is overtaken in life's fast lane by forces beyond her control. She falls for Henry Brauner, an American politician and CIA agent. At their first meeting Amethyst, sensing 'a compressed violence in him that frightens her' stands locked in his 'shocking blue stare' and is suddenly filled with wild, unfamiliar longings:

'She wanted to be dragged away by him and made love to completely and immediately. She was feeling something she had so far never felt for a man – an overwhelming physical attraction that chopped her off at the knees. Christ, this *is it*, she thought. Lust at first sight.'

Things hot up, and two pages later Amethyst is being mesmerized in the hotel room 'like a bird by a snake'. Lust conquers all: 'No, thought Amethyst to herself desperately. Not this soon – I mustn't. We ought to have a conversation first – or something.' But it is too late. Before she can say 'Hello', or 'Do you want the light on?' or even 'Have you got herpes?' which I believe is the current fashion in such situations, Brauner is plunging in and Amethyst, 'astounded by his primal power', is freaking out: 'Amethyst was roused beyond containment . . . he encountered her hotly and forcefully, bringing her to the longest, sweetest orgasm she had ever experienced.'

Next morning our heroine gets straight on the phone to *The Observer* to offer them a major profile on Brauner. Mandy assures me that this is exactly how the political correspondent side of Fleet Street works. Speaking as a NUJ diehard and as someone who was once commissioned by *The Observer* to write – possibly by the same features editor – 3,000 words on veteran youth hostellers, I feel obliged to tell Mandy that the episode lacks the ring of authenticity. 'Oh, but it's dead accurate,' insists Mandy, with an enigmatic wink. 'Fleet Street works just like that.' She has plenty of political correspondent pals, she adds. The name 'Ferdinand Mount' hovers on my lips but Mandy stays mum and says that she checked all her facts. She did her research. Here I make a mental note to stick to veteran youth hostellers and to leave politicians' profiles to the likes of Amethyst Barclay.

But sex is merely a minor distraction in an action-packed tale that zaps from Southsea, Cuba, Maida Vale and America, and covers espionage, political skulduggery, revenge, racial hatred, the Israeli Secret Service and a meeting with Fidel Castro. Mandy says people are amazed, but *amazed* that her first novel isn't a steamy potboiler. 'My book isn't packed full of sizzling sex because my head isn't full of sizzling sex,' she explains, popping out to put the kettle on, 'anyway, life's not like that. None of the women I know want it all the time, two or three times a night like they do it in books like *Lace* and *The Stud*. Besides, I think good taste is coming back. People are fed up with what I call "Flasher Fiction". People don't want all the ins-and-outs and physical minutiae. I hope you notice that my one steamy scene is all done very tastefully. That passage was very difficult to write. I re-wrote it eight times. I didn't want it to sound cheap. When I showed the finished manuscript to my publisher (Fisher) he complained that it wasn't hot enough. I screamed down the phone: "You want my character to be having orgasms bloody well falling off the ceiling, don't you?" He was dumbstruck.

'It didn't take long to deliver the goods. I soon taught myself all about plot structure and how to develop a story-line. The one thing I'm good at is telling a story. I did a lot of background research. At first I was slightly shaky on the technical side and I'm still not good at long, descriptive bits. I want the story to gallop along. Hemingway is a good example of that, he didn't go in for a lot of descriptive trivia either.'

Once the contract was signed, Mandy had many sleepless nights. No, she's not saying how much she signed for. But it's in four figures. And the paperback's in five. Her publisher was fairly enthusiastic about the final draft, although his major criticism was that 100 pages more wouldn't have come amiss.

However, as Mandy points out, *Today and Tomorrow* is only a first attempt. She is well aware of its failings. 'At first I had too few characters to keep it going. You *must* have a

> **My book isn't packed full of sizzling sex because my head isn't full of sizzling sex.**

sub-plot, and flashbacks winding through the story to keep the readers from flagging. A bit like *Hotel du Lac* . . . Let me tell you this much, Val, I'm going to write a Booker winner. Definitely. Having cracked the formula' – and here she taps the side of her nose with a long, crimson finger-nail, her words conjuring up visions of Keri Hulme, Salman Rushdie, Anita Brookner et al scribbling smugly away to this elusive 'formula' – 'having cracked it, I've already started a saga, called *The Scarlet Thread*, based on the Ottoman Empire about 1913. It will be big, mark my words, with eight major

I hope you notice that my one steamy scene is all done very tastefully. That passage was very difficult to write. I re-wrote it eight times. I didn't want it to sound cheap.

characters and plenty of sub-themes.' It will doubtless have that certain *smell* about it, too.

Meanwhile readers of *Today and Tomorrow* may detect just a hint of the 1960s Mandy in extrovert, champagne-sipping Amethyst. They may hear the Rice-Davies voice of experience speaking through this reckless freewheeler who foolishly flings herself under a politician's duvet. As Mandy says, with an enigmatic hooding of turquoise eyelids, 'Yes, there is a thread of my past experiences in the book although I've definitely never had a fling with a politician. Well, not an English one, anyway. Incidentally, I've always said I was game but not on the game. I'd like you to make that point, Val. Readers will be able to spot an autobiographical thread in the Epilogue, the way Amethyst hasn't got a bloody clue about all the drama that's going on around her. It's just like Proust, one story being told from four different angles, and Amethyst is the innocent party throughout.'

Today and Tomorrow (Inner Circle Books, 1987).

My book is about responsibility. Mine and Mick Jagger's is a wonderful story.

Marsha Hunt

*T*he first time I saw Marsha Hunt it was at the Rolling Stones' free concert in Hyde Park, 1969. There was glamorous, exotic Marsha, catching Mick Jagger's eye and sitting up on the VIPs' scaffolding tower. And there was me and my friend Beryl, crushed cheek by sweaty jowl just 40 rows back among the thronging thousands. In our cheesecloth skirts and love-beads and hippy headbands we bounced up and down screaming 'Mick, take me!' like the groupies we'd read about in the papers.

'Oh God, what has Marsha got that I haven't got?' I remember imploring Beryl as Mick released 10,000 moribund butterflies as a tribute to Brian Jones, found drowned in his swimming pool four days previously. 'Take your glasses off a minute, Val,' Beryl replied, staring at me hard and trying to spare my feelings. 'Honest. If Mick had met you first, and if you hadn't been wearing your NHS specs at the time, old Marsha Hunt wouldn't have stood a chance . . .'

Reflecting nonchalantly upon this fraught period of my youth, I ring Marsha Hunt's front door bell, 17 years after Hyde Park, with a copy of her autobiography, *Real Life*, under my arm. Mick must have climbed these very steps, and rung this very bell, I think to myself.

As Marsha welcomes me into a top-floor flat in the enormous, elegant London house she owns, sits me down, makes cups of tea and so on, it pains me to admit that maybe Mick made the right choice. There sits glamorous, exotic Marsha rapping about her raging days in rock 'n' roll and about starring in the musical *Hair*, her animated face framed by wonderful, wiry hair which cascades halfway down her slim back like hanks of glossy acrylic knitting yarn. There sit I, still wearing NHS spectacles, conscious of my split ends and raging cellulite. The mother of Mick's 16-year-old 'love child', Karis, is utterly, utterly stunning. No wonder she got Mick, and I got the village ping-pong champion.

Not that Mick is to be our exclusive topic of conversation. 'My book is about my life and he just happens to be a part of it. OK?' says Marsha, teeth flashing through flawless lip gloss. She steers the conversation towards her ghetto girlhood in Philadelphia, her riot-torn university days in Berkeley, her impecunious arrival in 'swinging London', her struggle to break into acting and singing and modelling, her marriage of

I was young and experiencing *life*. What would you have done?

convenience to an Oxford graduate keyboards player (Michael Ratledge) in order to avoid deportation . . . it is all relentlessly documented in *Real Life* and fairly fascinating as it goes, but is scarcely the stuff to keep readers on the edge of their seats.

It is not until you get to the Mick bits that things start hotting up. His Byronic presence throbs through the second half like a synchronized rhythm section. It is Mick, without doubt, who injects magic into the book, and into Marsha's life. Once Mick has shown up on Marsha's doorstep, moaning about his spots and pouring out his woes, the book begins to bounce.

'He came to me like a golden eagle with a broken wing, and I suppose he believed that I had the willingness and capacity to bandage it up and help him soar,' writes Marsha (who studied poetry at Berkeley). 'He knew that I adored him and that he could depend on me. I loved to see him run free. It was all very 60s – very Kahlil Gibran.' Broken-winged eagle Mick might have been but he certainly had his nasty little ways, not the least being his two-timing of live-in girlfriend Marianne Faithfull. Marsha's 'first-time revelations' may very well disillusion all but his most devoted of fans. Mick, it turns out, was a bit of a stingy bastard.

Consider his behaviour (aged 26) when Marsha's pregnancy was confirmed. His initial delight, his euphoric plans to call the baby 'Midnight Dream' and send it to Eton, gave way to indifference. He split without so much as a regular standing order to tide Marsha through her tribulations. As she remarks: 'After five months the baby had become my total reality, but for Mick it was just a passing fantasy . . . He was already forgetting that the baby was his idea in the first place. Oh well, boys will be boys . . .'

Girls will be girls too, of course, and there are those who might point out that you can't have your cake and eat it, and if you have your contraceptive coil removed (as Marsha did) and sleep with a notorious womanizer who hasn't so much as *hinted* at 'settling down' or even 'living together' then you want your head examined. But point these things out and Marsha says: 'I was young and experiencing *life*. What would you have done?' Well, point taken, but nevertheless there are moments in Marsha's book when you feel rather exasperated by her whingeing, self-righteous, victimized tone.

When Marsha became pregnant with Mick's child, she was 24. She had separated from her husband. She had appeared nude in *Hair*, performed on *Top of the Pops* wearing a blouse from which her breasts inadvertently poked out each time she raised her arms, done a nude spread in *Vogue*, taken acid, pioneered the British 'Black is beautiful' movement, had a Royal Crest painted on her breasts by Ralph Steadman, met Princess Margaret, and been close friends with Elton John, Marc Bolan and John Mayall to name but three. In short she'd been around. Nevertheless, she was shaken to the core when Golden Eagle reverted to Little Red Rooster, turned his attentions to Bianca, and left Marsha pregnant, unemployed and broke.

As she recalls: 'During the latter half of my pregnancy when I came off the road I did voluntary work in a children's austistic unit. I wanted to be useful and keep the rest of my life in perspective. I was ashamed to ask Mick for a contribution. When I did his £200 arrived with a sweet note saying 'I know I haven't done right by you'.

Karis was born in Paddington Hospital's public ward. Marsha's red sling-back high heels were clicking down the side exit two days later. Mick's office sent a limo to glide her home. Mick called at Marsha's place with champagne and modest gifts for his secret daughter. His chief concern was keeping the birth out of the newspapers. Marsha's chief concern was his indifference to her and the new baby.

'Something was missing when Mick dropped by that day: maybe that says it, he dropped by. He was cordial, charming and in a hurry to be somewhere else.' When he 'dropped by' ten days later, Marsha's patience had worn thin. 'I told him it doesn't take a lot to pick up a telephone. He said that he had never loved me and I was mad to think he had. The pain in me burst forth in stupid girl-tears . . . he said he could take the baby away from me if he chose. I told him I'd blow his brains out if he dared.'

Thus Mick-the-Myth is revealed as the man who done

Marsha wrong. An immature shit with flabby lips and a big bank account. Marsha, apparently, scrubbed floors, ate lentils and occasionally 'signed on' while Mick married Bianca and moved to a sumptuous South of France mansion

He came to me like a golden eagle with a broken wing . . .

lending Marsha the odd £200 whenever she plucked up the nerve to beg for it.

At one stage Karis was hospitalized in Germany for ten days, Mick promised to pay £75 towards the bill and promptly forgot. When Marsha sought legal advice on how Mick might be persuaded to provide an emergency fund for his daughter, she was told that the only legal right Karis had to any paternal contributions was through a paternity suit.

'I tried to contain my fury. There was no legal alternative to my predicament but a dreaded paternity suit. I wanted to vomit. The issue was paternal neglect. Surely a father has a binding moral responsibility when he creates a human life? After two years I had to stop pretending that Mick would assume his duty.' Legal wrangles and protracted rancour followed. Mick offered to put £20,000 in trust for Karis (which he reduced to £17,000 a few hours later) to avoid a public lawsuit. He never paid up. In 1972 Marsha finally went to court. All this is in Marsha's book. I bet it will make Mick want to spit.

Marsha insists that she was 'completely mystified' when people began to accuse her of using the paternity suit as a publicity ploy! Oh the humiliation. As she recalls: 'When it hit the newspapers, it stank. As no one had known of our friendship, the story was sensationalized. Packs of photographers sat in my front garden like crows. Bianca Jagger was quoted as saying she didn't give a damn.'

Advised by solicitors to accept millionaire Mick's offer of an out-of-court settlement of £500 a year and a £10,000 trust fund in exchange for a statement denying his paternity, Marsha told lawyers exactly where to put their tedious deeds. As she says 'While modern society condones sex without marriage, the law condemns the children born of it.' The law should not allow fathers to shrug off their responsibility. I started proceedings in 1972 and it was 1975 before I received the first monthly payment of £41.67, which then was a nanny's weekly wage.'

A further paternity suit ('I didn't want blood from Mick, I wanted adequate provision for our daughter') was conducted by legendary lawyer Marvin Mitchelson, in '79. This action resulted in Mick admitting paternity and paying undisclosed maintenance. As Marsha puts it, 'Mick need no longer have any secret pangs of guilt; he now contributes regularly towards his daughter's education and upkeep'.

Well, that was seven years ago. Mick has mellowed. Marsha has matured. She insists there is no question of her cashing in on her famous lover by writing this autobiography. Heaven forbid! She wrote the book to inspire other struggling, unwed mothers. And to jog the conscience of all absentee fathers. She resents my suggestion that *Real Life* could be subtitled A Groupie's Gripe.

'My book is about responsibility. Consenting adults are responsible for the offspring they produce. Parenthood is a wonderful bonding, and binding, a thing that nature has given us. Mine and Mick Jagger's is a wonderful story about turning failure into success. I'm sure I have my shortcomings and Mick has his. He may have had psychological problems that once prevented him understanding his child's needs but he's come to terms with fatherhood admirably now.' Looking back, does she ever think she was a bit, well, rotten to pinch Mick from Marianne (who, as it happens, took a near-fatal overdose several days after the Hyde Park concert)? No, she does not.

'I don't really think so. In '69 the sexual revolution was pumping out all kinds of variations on the male-female relationship thing.' Marsha insists she has written not one word that could cause Mick any pain. 'There aren't any lies in my book. Mick and I have been through a lot together and I would be very suprised if he was unhappy about *Real Life*. For myself, I've always put my child and work first. Nobody gave me anything. I own this house. I worked damn hard for it. Life is not supposed to be easy.'

These days Karis adores Mick. Mick adores Karis. Marsha adores Mick's latest lover Jerry Hall. Karis adores Jerry Hall. And Marsha adores Mick and Jerry's two children. They all call by for tea whenever Mick and Jerry are in London. No one mentions Marianne. Or Bianca. This everyday story of famous folk is calming down. Let us hope they all live happily ever after.

Pinned to Marsha's kitchen notice-board among the cab cards and window-cleaner addresses is a small snapshot of Mick with Karis. Marsha looks wistfully at it and sighs: 'OK, so Mick and I only had approximately nine months together,' she runs long, scarlet nails through the fabulous hair, 'but had it only been one night, it would have been enough, know what I mean?'

I *think* I know what she means. But it's only guesswork.

While modern society condones sex without marriage, the law condemns the children born of it. The law should not allow fathers to shrug off their responsibility.

Real Life (Chatto & Windus, 1986).

MY CURSE AS A WRITER
IS THAT I AM NOT READ
SLOWLY ENOUGH.

Martin Amis

Sitting on Martin Amis's lavatory I gazed down on his bidet full of books and back copies of the *TLS*, and marvelled at the strange ways of the upper-classes who obviously keep their books in their bidets in much the same manner as the working-classes keep coal in their baths. To tell the truth I was playing for time sitting there on Amis's lavatory. Taking deep breaths, dropping a Valium, running my hands under the cold tap, I was trying to cool out and curb an overwhelming urge to rush into the next room and smash the beady-eyed Amis in the face.

Look, I'd come along to this interview with an open mind. 'He's a cocky little shit,' all my bookish acquaintances had said, 'a puffed-up, self-opinionated arrogant prick,' and 'he writes anti-female books full of sexual disgust,' whereupon I'd retorted, 'Yaa, you're all jealous, that's what, just because he's written 3 novels, won the '73 Somerset Maugham award for *The Rachel Papers*, was literary editor of *The New Statesman* and is an *Observer* special writer . . .' Then they'd all laughed nastily. 'Bet you a fiver', they said, 'he'll let slip that he was at Oxford the first moment you get through the front door.'

So there I am ringing on his bell with trepidation because his publisher warned that he only grants *important* interviews. Is *Time Out* magazine important enough? I ask myself, ringing his bell louder and vaguely fantasizing, in the way we journalists do, that this literary giant might fling open the door with his Fleetwood Mac album playing in the background, his smouldering eyes might meet mine in the way Jeremy Irons' met Meryl Streep's with the sea splashing over the Cobb in *The French Lieutenant's Woman*, and with shocks like hot waves suddenly drenching our bodies we might sink on to his shag pile carpet . . . at which point Amis, short in stature and wearing the sort of corduroy jacket worn only by Young Conservatives, unbolts the door, grumbles about me being early and, as I'm following him upstairs, remarks, 'As a matter of fact I was at Oxford with your editor', in such a snooty tone that through my mind flashes the unkind thought that maybe my bookish acquaintances know something I don't know after all . . .

We spend five minutes with me wittering on about how *The Rachel Papers* still makes me laugh, and what remarkable writing it was for a 21-year-old. He must have been very brilliant in his youth, I say, to which he snaps 'Why do you put it in the *past* tense? – I take exception to that – I still am brilliant, I hope.' A slight lull in the conversation and a nervous laugh from me is followed by Amis proclaiming: 'My curse as a writer is that I am not read slowly enough. Nabokov said, "You cannot read a novel, you can only re-read it." By reading my work fast one may perceive the local effects, the jokes, the virtuoso paragraphs but one gets absolutely no idea of the novel's architecture or artistry.'

At this point, I scurry out to the off-licence for a bottle of wine. 'Make sure it's white, dry, from the 'fridge,' says Amis, after stating that there's no booze in his flat, even though on my way out I glimpse something suspiciously resembling a *full* Habitat wine-rack lurking in a landing cupboard. After a glass of wine, or two, we return to the newly Penguined *Rachel Papers*. The plot concerns the japes of Charles a posh, precociously intelligent and highly-sexed teenager determined to sleep with An Older Woman, ie Rachel (20), who wears a more-or-less empty brassiere and dirty knickers. How does Amis view his novel 11 years on?

'I haven't looked at it for five years. I felt I was a different person about three months after I'd finished it, that I was already forgetting what it's like to be quite so feverish in one's responses . . . I certainly don't disown it. Some of it I find embarrassing, but I do think it's alive, it has plenty of energy all right. I feel about my first two novels that they are *prentice* novels.'

Does he mean 'apprentice'? 'No, I mean *prentice*. I'll just check that out.' He leafs through a bulky dictionary. 'Can't find it. Oh, put "apprentice", if you like.' I scribble 'apprentice novels' and explain how, in my view, the book's weakest character is his unconvincing, token working-class git, beachball-headed Norman, the sort who chucks newspapers on the floor, undresses on the stairs, walks over the upholstery in his beetle-crushers and makes observations about women along the lines of 'Fucking slags – they squirt ponce all over themselves, spend all day wiggling their bums in fucking dress shops and spend pounds on their hair in Teazy fucking Weazy's – juskers they wear the tits doesn't mean . . .' and so forth.

'Nonsense,' snaps Amis, puffing on a stingy little roll-up, 'Norman is absolutely authentic. I've met people just like that.' After I remark that I bet he didn't meet them at Oxford, and explain how people like Norman would take one look at an arrogant, idle, spotty ex-public schoolboy like Charles and tell him to piss off and get a job, Amis snorts diabolically 'Nonsense, the working-classes are *charmed* by the likes of Charles'. I tell him that they're not, actually. Amis looks at his watch, yawns and remarks that the last time he was featured in *Time Out* it was in some meretricious piece called 'The Literary Mafia', which purported to take the lid off a mythical and incestuous Oxbridge literary clique. 'In fact, all the piece did was take the lid off the strange, corrupt mind of its author, Richard Rayner . . . Of course, one would never expect critical admiration from *Time Out*, its editorial policy seems to be that all writers are simply in the business to make a quick buck – ha – what a hellova way to make a quick buck, I don't think, sitting by yourself with a pen for three and a half years . . .'

Well, I say, it's better than being on the Tesco checkout tills. Has he ever worked nine to five? Got axle-grease under the old fingernails? Asbestos dust on the old lungs? 'I have never done a hard day's work in manual labouring terms, thank God. All jobs are murder, especially those you have to leave the house to go to, but you don't have to shovel shit to get the idea of what doing a job is really like. As a writer I convey with complete authenticity *exactly* what it's like being on the Tesco checkout tills . . . the great thing about being a writer is that one is *participating* in life . . .' I interrupt here to remark that sitting on your backside for three-and-a-half years alone with a pen doesn't strike me as participating in life, to which Amis replies: 'It's called *imaginative participation* . . . As a writer I have intoxicating freedom, I can write when I like, this is the real luck and pleasure of being a writer.'

Boldly I chip in, once again, to say how some people might consider 'imaginative participation' to be a bit masturbatory. 'To a certain extent writing *is* to do with lone gratification, it *is* the utopian handjob,' Amis concedes, polishing off the last of the wine. He's had 4 glasses, I've had one. Before I can pluck up the nerve to mention the Habitat wine rack he continues, 'You are obviously the sort who thinks a coal-miner could write a good novel or poem, someone with their heart in the right place. This is simply not so. A coal-miner may be able to appreciate a good novel or poem, occasionally, but the prerogative of being a writer is not democratically extended to all people. Education comes into it. University education. It's true that everyone has a novel in them, but it's a mere slice-of-life novel which is unlikely to have any literary or artistic interest.'

'Who says?' I say, 'What about Jean Rhys, Dickens and Colette? They didn't go to university. And what about Ginsberg, Dylan Thomas and Ntozake Shange?' 'Who?' snaps Amis. 'Ntozake Shange, she wrote *For Black Girls Who Consider Suicide When The Rainbow Is Not Enuf.*' Amis makes a sound between a snort and a retching noise. 'Yes, well, I don't think I'd like that. You're one of those people who think that if something is brimming with life it's *Art*. This is an insane view. Poetry isn't about emotion, it's about writing. Feeling things strongly is no help to a writer. You are applying a sociologist's criteria, not an artist's.'

'No, I'm not,' I say, 'I'm just applying my own criteria – i.e., if the work moves me, makes the hair of my flesh stand up, causes what Wordsworth described as a "spontaneous overflow of feeling", then surely it works as a poem? What about the Liverpool poets, Liz Lochhead, Simon and Garfunkel, Leonard Cohen?' Amis makes the snorting retching noise again. 'These things you mention are therapy not art. You have a democratized view. I have an elitist one which is the only one there is. To try and skip that stage which involves solitary study, as afforded at Oxford, and bring art to the people without proper training will fuck art up completely. In fact, that process is under way even as we speak and you, Val Hennessy, are an example of this fucking up – it appals me some of the things you say about writing. It *Appals* me. I assume you have no feeling whatsoever for literature. Your arguments are confused and undisciplined. You are chaotic in your responses, the only people who think as you do about literature are to be found in madhouses.'

It is at this point that I rush to the lavatory. Outside the door Amis's cleaning lady clatters about with the Hoover. And I haven't even *started* discussing his latest novel *Money* (*a suicide note*) to be published in September. Described on the jacket (in suspiciously Amis-ian style) as 'his most startling and ambitious novel yet' and 'hilariously shocking', it is mostly about fucking, hand jobs, and women's knickers, with some sharky descriptions of the madnesses of the inhabitants of New York – 'these are people determined to be themselves, whatever, little shame attending'. The hero, a streetwise, street fightin' film director, after many fucking, handjob and knicker adventures, lands in a tight corner with the money police.

Sitting on Amis's lavatory I ask myself whether *Money* is more than a slice-of-life novel? And is the writer (incidentally, a Fowlesesque character who steps into his own novel) in the business for more than a quick buck? Sitting there I realize that we've been talking about *Literature*. Real literature. The sort that everybody says is 'a dazzling tour-de-force' and 'muscular and rhythmic prose, containing insights from an incandescent intelligence', when they congregate at publishers' launches. From Amis I've learnt that there are rules about what it is, who can write it, and who is gifted enough to read it. According to Amis unless you've sweated over *Beowulf* and *Paradise Lost* at the right prep school, you're not likely to grasp *real literature*. Yet is *Money* real literature? Or a handjob?

And why did he say that mine is a 'sociologist's view of literature'? Is it possible, I'm wondering tentatively, that Amis's understanding of society is as limited as his view of literature? Is it not possible that Amis's understanding of literature is as particular as his view of sex? Would he have a different perspective on society and women's knickers if he'd done a sociology of literature course at a Polytechnic instead of Anglo-Saxon at Oxbridge? Would he be writing real literature if he wasn't obsessed with hand jobs? Did Terry Eagleton or Colin McCabe discuss the role of knickers in the formalist aesthetic? And why can't a coal-miner write a good novel? Presumably because coal-miners, according to Amis, can't appreciate the intricacies of the formalist aesthetic. In fact anybody not formally trained in literary criticism at an ancient university is a gate-crasher at a party; a jumped-up wally who should rot on the factory floor.

And then, of course, we'd been talking about the *pain* of writing. It is a job, Amis had said, just like any job. Well, it isn't like the job I had for six months mopping up phlegm and overflowing colostomies and sluicing the floors in a gents geriatric unit. 'You don't have to shovel shit to know what a real job is.' Oh no? It must be really arduous for people like Amis struggling with the formalist aesthetic, making certain that the right literature gets consecrated, having to endure all the champagne, publishers' launches, jiffy-bags full of review copies thumping onto their front-door mats every morning, defending the parapets of the castle of literature in the reviewing journals.

Ah, the pain of making literary judgements! It was Auberon Waugh who recently pointed out in the *Daily Mail* the heavy price that puffed-up people like Amis pay for making literary judgements. They become hideously depleted with jealousy, spite, political prejudice, class hatred, sycophancy, and even lechery what with the way they try ingratiating themselves with sexy-looking publishers' publicity girls.

So, I come out of the closet. The cleaning lady is unblocking the kitchen sink. Amis decides that he's peckish and suggests lunch at a little local wine bar. I'm paying, of course. We eat terrible gazpacho and something resembling foam rubber sick called lobster terrine. It costs £18.50. I ask Amis what exactly it means when his publicity blurb describes him as a 'special writer for *The Observer*'. 'It means I get paid 3 times as much for my journalism as you do,' he says, knocking back another glass of wine. George Melly is tucking in at the next table. Amis says that *Money* is his most important novel yet. It is a novel about what happens when people don't have Culture, and how impossible that makes it for them to understand what is going on. I ask him whether he ever thinks that novel writing is a bit pointless with Cruise poised and nuclear holocaust round the corner. 'It is a vulgar fallacy this idea that because there are atomic weapons writers are wasting time,' he replies, tucking into the foam rubber sick. 'Writers should stay off politics, to take politics as one's subject matter is an immediate humiliation.'

But isn't *Money* about sex and money, and aren't they political? Thankfully George Melly lurches across, slaps Amis on the back and noticing my reporter's notebook says 'Make the pips squeak, darling.' Pips squeak? Pipsqueak.

Money (A Suicide Note) (Jonathan Cape, 1984).

I wrote my book to show how, by becoming a prostitute, a woman can take control of her own life.

Melissa

*I*n the days of my girlhood (in Gravesend) it was easy to identify women of twilight. They loitered brazenly under lamp-posts wearing a superfluity of rouge and gold chains round their ankles. They would shout things like 'Get yer eye full,' and 'Mine ain't no different to yours except it's shaved,' as my friend Beryl and I hurried home from sixth-form hockey practice ogling in awe. They also emitted a divinely tarty pong of *Soir de Paris*. Those were the days when one could assume that any highly perfumed person with false eyelashes, a fag hanging from fuschia lips, fish-net stockings and stiletto heels was on the game. These days, of course, such people are invariably transvestites. Or trendy nuns.

Certainly Mrs Zoe Sharrock, author of *The Harlot's Room* ('the astonishing autobiographical story of a young mother who chose to become a prostitute') is something of a let-down in appearance. This 42-year-old mother of two and ex-canteen worker is of a Fergie sort of build. Wearing comfy shoes and warm winter tights she looks more like a Meals-on-Wheels volunteer than the professional who describes her occupation as 'sucking rubbered cocks and so forth'. No tell-tale ankle chain or *Soir de Paris* for Mrs Sharrock . . . the only giveaways are her tired-looking gums and slightly dingy teeth which obviously come in for quite a hammering in her line of work.

'Hi,' she says in a soft, slow, spaced-out sort of voice, raising brutally plucked eyebrows and casting a professional eye round the saloon bar in which she has agreed to meet. 'Isn't it shocking? The weather I mean.' 'Hi, it's kind of you to take time off to do this interview,' I reply.

Mrs Sharrock replies that the whole point of becoming a prostitute is to be at liberty to choose her own working hours. 'I do it because I want to. I really, really enjoy my work. I'm my own boss, see. I wrote my book to show how, by becoming a prostitute, a woman can take control of her own life and take time off work when she feels like it.' Yes, but isn't her occupation kind of squalid? Risky? And, er, degrading? 'No. Not at all. It's no more degrading than working in a factory or sitting behind an office typewriter all day. In most jobs you spend time with people you don't really like. I really, really like the people I'm working with. Prostitutes working independently choose their own rules.' They also avoid all the hassle of Income Tax, VAT, union fees and National **I really, really enjoy my work. I'm my own boss...** Insurance Contributions. Mrs Sharrock is unwilling to reveal precise figures.

The exact nature of Mrs Sharrock's work makes an entertaining, and occasionally gripping, read and is something of an eye-opener to those of us who still associate the word 'massage' with Deep Heat and muscular disorders.

Her clients, while inflicting their rank armpits, grubby groins, stale mouths, other assorted body fluids and processed-pea flavoured kisses upon her, chat waggishly about wives, money and football as she goes gladly about the job in hand. She describes, for example how 'I look at the mantelpiece while I rub some bloke's buttocks with ice brought in a Tesco bag'. One client places his penis on a chair so that she can stamp on it, another prances about in camiknickers doing bird imitations. For Mrs Sharrock it is all in a day's work and much more entertaining than being a bank clerk, say, or driving a bus. Furthermore she insists that her work experiences are 'very pure, very beautiful and very, very spiritual'. Certainly her book will have a tremendous appeal for armchair whores everywhere.

Between clients Mrs Sharrock washes her hands, paints stars on her telephone with nail varnish, reads *Time Out*, *Spare Rib* and *The Daily Mail* (not *The Literary Review*, but now she's an author I've suggested she gives it a try), watches *Crossroads*, anoints her body with fragrant oils, and sneaks out after dark carrying tied-up polythene bags bulging with spent condoms and soggy tissues. These she conceals in a dustbin hoping no neighbours will twig what's inside. Condoms loom large in the life of Mrs Sharrock who is undeniably doing her bit to solve unemployment in Kuala Lumpur. She purchases them in bulk (wholesale) via a catalogue she saw advertised in *Private Eye*. They arrive in various hues, sizes and designs including luminous ones and some that look like hot water bottles trimmed with bumpy bits. She recalls one awkward occasion: 'I'm using up these black rubbers see, while I'm waiting for my regular wholesale order. As I'm sucking this guy off he looks down and says "Do you get these from the council then? It looks like a council bin-liner!" You have to laugh.'

You do indeed. You laugh even harder (at least I do, with nervous incredulity) when Mrs Sharrock insists that thoughts of AIDS never enter her head. Sure she's had the odd dose of VD but the NHS soon sorted that out. Mind you, if a client refuses to wear a condom she refuses to perform. The whole point of condoms is that they protect prostitutes from infection.

By now the saloon bar is draughty with the frenzied flapping of eaves-dropping ears. 'I'm not a prostitute when I'm off-duty, you know,' declares Mrs Sharrock, smoothing her long, crinkly hair. 'I just *work* as one. I'm not one 24 hours a day . . .' As she starts to explain how she uses the *nom de plume* Melissa because that name expresses her 'romantic and liberated identity', I glance discreetly at the advance publicity blurb I received from the cheery young Chatto persuader called Ben in which he enthused: 'The Harlot's Room is a remarkable book, and the author perhaps doubly remarkable. In many ways it is an advertisement for prostitution! Yet it is also an astonishing and true story of a strange odyssey of health and happiness . . .' 'Would you say that your book is an astonishing and true story of a strange odyssey of health and happiness, Mrs Sharrock?' I inquire as she sips her glass of bitter lemon. 'Yes. Definitely' she replies, and recalls how 'amazed and hurt,' she was when Sheba (the feminist press) rejected her manuscript because of its glorification of heterosexual sex. Like Virginia Woolf, Mrs Sharrock insists that every woman needs a room of her own. Mrs Sharrock's own room is a 'cocoon and a sanctuary' where she becomes 'psychologically strengthen-ed' by countless 'really, really beautiful rituals'. And what happens to her children when she's working? 'Ah, well they were briefly in care as babies, and then raised by their stepmother. I do see them but we never talk about my work . . .' Mr Sharrock, it transpires, long ago 'did a runner'. Changing the subject she declares that port and egg nog (with ice) is a fantastic drink and adds that she was once raped after throwing a chair through a restaurant window. She was also raped at the age of nine by a man who, she since discovered, was her grandfather. 'It was a lovely spiritual experience. It made me feel really, really special.'

At this point I begin to feel really, really certain about Sheba's reasons for rejecting Mrs Sharrock's autobiography. I decide to call it a day. Mrs Sharrock departs with a friendly flash of dingy teeth. I immediately phone Ben at Chatto to inquire whether 'Melissa' is, perhaps, ever so slightly off her head. Ben is still cheery but guarded. 'Obviously you must form your own opinion', he ripostes politely, 'but by becoming a prostitute Melissa found a perfect life – healthy and psychologically reassuring. She suffered no violence, fear or hate. She loved it. It is this aspect that makes the book so astonishing.' Right on, Ben, I reply. Carry on bluffing like that and you'll have me recommending the book to the Youth Opportunities Programme. Bluff a bit more and it could become an essential text for the Careers Advisory Service. ('On your bikes, girls and off to the condom wholesalers.') Bluff as much as you like, but I bet you a packet of french ticklers that Melissa, doubly remarkable as she may be, is one author who won't be invited to plug her book on *Wogan*.

The Harlot's Room (Chatto & Windus, 1987).

Nancy

THE BOOK I HAVE WRITTEN IS FOR
ALL WHO ARE SICK OF BEING
TREATED LIKE OUTCASTS BY A
SOCIETY THAT DESPISES FAT PEOPLE.

ROberts

Nancy Roberts is a large lady who sails through life thumbing her nose at those (mostly construction workers) who call out 'thunderthighs', 'fatso' or 'porky' when she passes. Being fat has inspired her to write her book *Breaking all the Rules* which gives heart to fat women everywhere. Being fat isn't funny. Being fat isn't a lark. And, as she starts explaining the instant I'm through her front door, being a fat female is a fate worse than death in these skin-and-bone oriented times.

'Look, I was born chubby,' says New York-born Nancy, rolling Elizabeth Taylor eyes with fabulous lashes. 'I saw my first diet doctor at the age of eight. I spent the next 25 years of my life as a compulsive eater. Food ruled my existence. I hated my own body. My God! If people only *knew* the torment, the persecution, the *pain* we large women have to endure, they would think twice before making cruel cracks about our size.'

Torment? Persecution? Pain? Heavy stuff Nancy. Hang on a minute while I take off my coat. Give me a chance to sit down and get my notebook out, I plead, as Nancy rattles on at full-throttle, pacing about her kitchen in a shocking-pink taffeta blouse, fuchsia lipstick and huge earrings. Clearly 15-stone Nancy is no shrinking violet.

'In this world a fat man can be a bank manager or a politician, but a fat woman is just a joke on a seaside postcard. My God! It took me a long, long time to arrive at a point where I could accept that it was all right to be my size. Nowadays I am able to accept that I am a biggie. But that's only because seven years ago I saw the light.'

Nancy breaks off suddenly to make herself a peanut butter sandwich. Zapping nimbly between larder, fridge and table and causing my head to jerk right and left, right and left like a Wimbledon umpire's, she explains how fat people have to fight, yes, *fight*, to destroy the pernicious myth that fat equals greedy. Fat people often eat far less than skinny people. This peanut butter sandwich, she insists, is the first food that's passed her lips all day.

Certainly Saul on the road to Damascus was no more transfigured than self-hating, diet-obsessed Nancy in that instant, seven years ago, when she read in a paperback book that *95 per cent of dieters invariably regain all the weight they've lost on diets.* She was, she declares, dumbstruck. Yes, *dumbstruck.* Which, I can't help thinking, is a state hard to imagine if her present ebullient form is anything to go by. 'The foundations of my world began to crumble. One startling statistic changed my life. I suddenly realised that I wasn't greedy, or out of control, or lacking willpower as I had come to believe. I was simply fighting a losing battle with biology. And, what's more, there were millions of others just like me. There was no point in dieting.

'But wait a minute, I thought to myself that momentous day, if I suddenly give up dieting after all these years won't I blow up like a balloon? Well, happily, I discovered this is not so. If you give up dieting you lose your urge to binge, your weight stabilises and your eating becomes normal. This means you only eat when you're hungry.'

From that moment Nancy knew she had turned the corner. Her next cataclysmic revelation occured when she discovered that Macy's store in New York houses a department called 'Big City Woman' which stocks designer jeans for biggies. There on the rails were outsize pairs of the sort of jeans favoured by the slim and trendy. The *smallest* size on the rails was an 18.

'Now, try to understand this, all my life there had been a point beyond which no trousers would rise, and as the first pair of jeans slid past my danger zone I suddenly knew that not only would the zipper meet over my stomach, but they were going to be too big. For the first time in my life a garment was too big. I couldn't remember any item of clothing that hadn't been interrupted in its voyage up and down my frame by the swell of my ample behind. Hallelujah! I left Macy's with three pairs of jeans. I felt reborn.'

As Nancy says, she came out of the closet in both senses. She began wearing the clothes she wanted to wear. Neon-striped jeans, shocking pink jumpsuits, purple sweatpants, lime green and white striped T-shirts, aubergine ethnic robes, gold lurex caftans, sequinned turbans, bangles, beads, diamante chokers – you name it. She oozed glamour. Heads turned. She looked stunning. Her career as an actress and TV presenter took wing. Here was one of the fat of the land breaking the rules and blazing a path for the big women of Britain. Grateful fan letters arrived by the sackload.

'I was saying, by my very appearance, why the hell shouldn't we biggies wear eye-catching clothes? The thought of a 15-stone, 47-40-53 woman like me in a fire-engine red boiler suit goes against every rule, except my own. My advice to all large women is to ask yourself "How does this garment make me feel? Do I feel proud, self-confident and beautiful in it?" If the answer is "yes" then it works. And to hell with the rules.'

In this world a fat man can be a bank manager or a politician, but a fat woman is just a joke on a seaside postcard.

To hell, too, with weight-watchers, trimnastics, calorie control, cottage cheese and aerobics. Sob your heart out, Jane Fonda. As Nancy points out, 47 per cent of British women (and she considers herself an honorary British woman having lived here for 17 years) exceed size 14. It's time they hung up their leotards and faced the fact that they'll never resemble Jane Fonda. 'The book I've written, *Breaking all the Rules*, is a book about power. The power to make yourself look and feel great, to change the way you think about yourself, and the way others think about you. It is a book which will change lives.'

Sorrowfully shaking her head, Nancy remarks that large, voluptuous, Renoir-type women look gorgeous to her. They look gorgeous, too, to her husband, Uwe (pronounced Oover), a slim, dapper banker with a penchant for Chinese take-away food. He and Nancy have been together for 11 years but as she admits: 'It was not until I saw the light that our life together became truly relaxed. Until then I was always a cover-up person. I'd jump into bed and turn the light off.'

Thank the Lord, Nancy adds, that she's now learned not to cringe. She's learned to walk assertively, with her head held high, exuding dignity, sexuality and a sense of pride in her appearance. This way, she finds, construction workers seem less inclined to yell spiteful names after her. Children still giggle and shout things like, 'Cor, look at those fat legs', but she no longer allows them to ruin her day. Personally, she'll only be convinced that times have changed for fatties once large actresses manage to get cast as successful wives, lovers or executives instead of landing those inevitable 'character' roles.

Can you imagine a fat *femme fatale* in *Dynasty*? A fat Lady Macbeth? A fat Hedda Gabler? Of course you can't. In fact you're probably chuckling at the very idea. As I am until Nancy explodes: 'My God! We large people are totally discriminated against. Apart from skin colour, fatness is the most stigmatized human condition, and it's time this situation was changed.'

The thought of a 15-stone, 47–40–53 woman like me in a fire-engine red boiler suit goes against every rule, except my own.

Breaking All the Rules (Viking, 1985).

PAT BOOTH

Look, I don't like all these heavy questions,
right? What's Ethiopia and having a face-lift
got to do with plugging my book?

OH NO not *another* gripping saga of kinky sex, drugs, lust and violence among America's super-rich, I sigh, ripping open the jiffy-bag and staring glumly at my review copy of the 'sizzling best-seller' *Palm Beach*. How did it get past customs? And the sniffer dogs? A quick flip through the 340 pages confirms my worst fears. Paragraph upon paragraph of straining crotches, thrashing limbs, taut nipples, throbbing erections and lines like 'How do I look, Jimmy?' 'Knicker-wetting good' (p.53) and 'I want it here. Right here. Her hand pressed down hard on him invading his essence with the spears of pleasure' (p.29). There's a smattering of incest, homo-erotic massage, homicide, some lesbian oro-genital hanky-panky in a jacuzzi and a masturbation sequence at an aerobics class. However, as gripping sagas of kinky sex, drugs, lust and violence among America's super-rich go this one is certainly the pits.

To make matters worse, a note with the publicity blurb informs me that I am interviewing the book's author, Pat Booth (40) 'blonde ex-top model, Britain's answer to Erica Jong' at 10.30 a.m. sharp at the Berkeley Hotel and that she has sold the British rights of *Palm Beach* to Century for £100,000, the US paperback rights for £500,000, that negotiations are in progress for a US mini-TV series and the UK serial rights have been purchased by *Woman* magazine for a 'staggering, undisclosed sum'. Doesn't it make you want to spit? I finish off my boiled egg and cast a lethargic eye over Booth's hyped up biog.

Apparently this 'cockney daughter of a jellied-ells stall-holder' moved to 'glamorous over-the-top Palm Beach' after a 'glittering career as a celebrated 60s model and Kings Road boutique owner'. Her current home is 'an opulent mansion complete with pool and sliding roof which opens to reveal the stars'. Booth, who has 'infiltrated the highest echelons of Palm Beach society and survived to tell the truth about it' is quoted as saying: 'Palm Beach is like an errant lover – it has got a million different facets – like a diamond.' Her ambition is 'to be seriously rich' and to see 'endless red bodies on the Playa Bianca all reading *Palm Beach*'.

With this vile image in my head I made a quick call to the

fun-loving Colour Supplement features editor who has commissioned me to interview Pat Booth. 'This is the big one, doll. In depth!' he shrieks above the din of scratchy ballpoints. 'Hard-hitting questions, right? Like "Is Palm Beach totally evil?" "Is money a dirty word?" "Has Palm Beach been kinder to Pat than Tower Hamlets?" and "What's life like

Palm Beach is the jewel in the crown of America, it has got a million different facets – like a diamond.

in the wanton world of the seriously rich?" We're talking about 2,000 steamy words, doll, a penetrating profile, dig deep . . .'

So another bad book is let loose upon the world and off I dash, on my bike to the Berkeley Hotel where obsequious flunkeys are bowing and scraping to hungover mink-clad Americans. Booth sends a message from her suite to say she'll be delayed for 15 minutes. I take off my polyester quilted duffle-coat and cycle clips and, perching on a sofa with a pot-of-tea for one, I dip at random into *Palm Beach*. Page 11 catches my eye:

'There was a frantic intensification of movement as the lovers danced in a maelstrom of flailing limbs. Suddenly Mary-Ellen's legs seemed to lose their co-ordination as they set off in a wild rhythm, thrashing the air, shaking, twitching and vibrating as the shuddering feeling took her . . .'

Would Madam care for more tea? Thanks, all the same, but no, I mutter to the flunkey, getting stuck into page 30:

'Mary-Ellen took him into her . . . It was so right. This was the moment. The timeless moment of unity . . . Together they seemed to decide where the voyage must end, its mystic conclusion negotiated at some magic place where no thoughts lived, no words were spoken. For an eternity of time each lover was still, paying homage to the force of life that soon would move through them, bathing the fires with its balm, signifying an end, a new beginning. And then, at last, it was upon her. Creation's act, accompanied by two lovers' screams of ecstasy, harrowing, piercing, in their reality among the clamorous counterfeits on every side . . .'

Bloody hell I ask myself, stirring my tea, *why* am I reading this drivel? Why am I sitting here being kept waiting by the cockney daughter of a jellied-eels seller whose book is merely a vacuous artefact which is ready, at the drop of a pair of trousers, to be transmuted into a nasty little skin flick? Why do I condone these mucky American wet dreams which are marketed, hyped, paperbacked, sold at airports and filling stations, and re-formatted into mini-movies to be beamed down from satellite transponders along with the other 54 million soft porn video tapes rented out each year in the US? Why aren't I interviewing a *real* writer like Anita Brookner, or Angela Carter or even Sue Townsend?

At this instant Booth, preceded by her exotic perfume, totters across the vestibule. She is wearing cream silk harem pants and a hard look in her eyes. One senses she is no stranger to 'frantic intensifications of movement' and 'unco-ordinated twitching legs'. She has those sucked-in sort of cheeks which are usually the result of having had the wisdom teeth extracted in the sixties to accentuate the bone-structure. She looks like a whippet wearing mascara. Is Palm Beach totally evil? I begin, but my heart isn't really in it. 'Pardon?' replies Booth.

Is money a dirty word? 'Yer wot?' replies Booth. Well, Pat, in your book you make Palm Beach sound corrupt, diaboli-cal, like hell-on-earth. 'Oh. No. Palm Beach is the jewel in the crown of America, it has got a million different facets – like a diamond,' enthuses Booth. Yes, but what exactly do people *do* in Palm Beach when they're not fornicating, sunbathing, killing each other, undressing and dressing up . . . what exactly do they *talk* about? 'How d'ya mean, *talk*?' Well, Pat, one gets the impression from your book that America's influential super-rich don't discuss Ethiopia, for example, or the nuclear arms-race . . . Booth fidgets with a glitzy brooch that doubtless cost more than my house. 'What are you going on about for Christ's sake? Ethiopia?' she says, tapping an impatient foot. I am growing desperate. Has Palm Beach been kinder to her than Tower Hamlets? What's life like in the wanton world of the outrageously rich? Is *Palm Beach* post-Proustian soap opera, or the New Suburban Aesthetic? Have you had a facelift? These last two questions just slip out (like 'Bobby' on page 132) and Booth snaps: 'Look, I don't like all these heavy questions, right? What's Ethiopia and having a facelift got to do with plug-ging my book?' This is obviously not the moment. The timeless moment of unity. She springs up, spins on her heel, and flounces off muttering something unequivocal like:

'Piss off you ugly old bag.' One can tell she is more at home among the gentle hiss of lawn-sprinklers and the muted rustle of silk sheets than in a penetrating profile situation. The interview has lasted three minutes. 'Piss off yourself you stupid stuffed-up tart,' I feel tempted to riposte but refrain for fear of the flunkeys who look as if they're about to manhandle me through the glass doors and out onto the Hyde Park pavement.

Back home I make a cup of tea and over the 'phone bid a doleful farewell to the fun-loving Colour Supplement editor who gasps 'Oh Christ. We've bought 3,000 quids' worth of colour pix of Pat Booth at home in Palm Beach. She's a friend of the Editor. You cow. You've really gone and blown it . . .' My God, he thinks *Palm Beach* is a documentary, or an autobiography, I'm thinking as I replace the 'phone. Perhaps it *is*. A torrid tale fulfilling precisely the mimetic function of art. Appalling it may be, but nevertheless it is a book which at this moment is soaring up the British best-seller lists. It is a book which is, as Pat Booth would indubitably put it, creation's act. And it is probably accompanied by screams of ecstasy, and is no doubt harrowing, piercing in its reality among the clamorous counterfeits on every side.

Palm Beach (Century, 1986).

Ralph Steadman

SHOW MY BOOK TO ANY DOG, HOLD IT UP TO ONE OF THE SMELLY VERMIN AND I PROMISE YOU IT WILL INSTANTLY CRINGE, WHIMPER AND COWER IN A CORNER. WITH LUCK IT MIGHT EVEN CURL UP AND DIE.

Ralph Steadman is a world-famous cartoonist. He also hates dogs. He dreams of doing for dogs what myxamatosis did for rabbits. With his book *A Leg In The Wind* (and other canine curses), Steadman hopes to become the champion of all dog-haters. These are the people he refers to as 'the down-trodden, or rather, we who tread in it'.

If you happen to like dogs, and I do, being the owner of a much-loved if slightly brain-damaged cocker spaniel, you look round the grounds of Steadman's almost stately home and think 'what a waste'. The vast velvety lawns would be ideal for doggy dashings about. It is sad to wander down avenues of trees against whose trunks no fluffy little leg is ever cocked. It is disappointing to enter a spacious front hall which, while Steadman owns it, will never know the wag of a welcoming tail. You long for a friendly bark, an exploratory snuffle, a lolling tongue; instead you get Steadman crashing in with his pencil in one hand bellowing 'Please examine the soles of your shoes thoroughly before entering, the streets are fraught with danger at every step'.

We enter the splendid reception room with Steadman explaining how, with his book, he has purged himself of a lifetime's festering resentment towards dogs: 'Whenever I encounter one of the filthy yapping swine, I get the urge to kick it from here to kingdom come. When I was a small boy a stray mongrel, called Kim, attached its flea-infested self to my family. It fell in a bucket of offal and pig's blood that my father was planning to use as tomato fertilizer and from that moment onwards I despised dogs.'

According to Steadman's alleged 'research', the NSPCC could achieve 98 per cent of its work for neglected children on one fifth of the revenue this country spends on dogs. He is also certain that dogs are better fed than most children, and certainly better fed than him. 'Watch old age pensioners in supermarkets,' he rages, jabbing me with his pencil several times, 'you'll see them queuing up at the checkout with wire baskets containing one packet of cream crackers, one tin of spam, half a pound of margarine and 20 tins of Pedigree Chum.'

Whilst working on *A Leg In The Wind* Steadman recalls

how he became morose and intro-spective, his mind troubled by hateful images of dogs. He roamed his local streets and parks noting 'vile canine calling-cards' and growing increasingly appalled whenever he saw fraught mothers rushing their push-chairs home in order to avoid subjecting their infants to the sight of 'quivering, love-locked mongrels' outside supermarkets. You

> **Whenever I encounter one of the filthy yapping swine, I get the urge to kick it from here to kingdom come.**

can take it from Steadman that if there had been one heroic dog in the Falklands the media would scarcely have mentioned the troops. You can also take it from him that if his book bounds up the best-seller lists the Canine Defence League will come down on him like a ton of marrow-bone jelly.

Steadman acknowledges that his anti-dog sentiments have cost him several valuable friendships. 'Something that makes me foam at the mouth,' he says, foaming at the mouth, 'are the presumptuous, so-called friends who come to visit me and bring their pet dogs, great, slobbering unwashed balls of fluff that leap on me and dribble all down my clothes the moment I open the front door.'

My favourite cartoon from his book shows a wolflike hound thrusting its muzzle up a man's crotch, lifting him off his feet in fact, while its doting owner remarks, 'Take no notice of him – he doesn't mean anything by it'. Steadman's favourite shows a man collapsed on a sofa, cigarette snapped in two, smothered in dog hairs as a yeti-like animal bounds from his lap, its owner hovering nearby with a tea-tray murmuring 'And I thought you said you didn't like dogs Mr Wackley'. He also likes the one where a group of adults converse, sitting on armchairs, while a small dog mastur-bates frenziedly against one of their legs and its owner remarks 'He's really taken to you, hasn't he?'

'Oh God. I was laughing at the drawing board when I did those two,' recalls Steadman, baring his teeth, jerking in silent spasms, 'I was in stitches, feeling exactly like a tax inspector must feel, laughing diabolically as I went about my work.'

He adds, incidentally, that he'd like to live down the fact that he was the man who dreamed up the idea of immortalizing dead dogs in solid blocks of perspex. It was Steadman who coined the slogan 'Why stuff it, when they snuff it, get it and set it in solid clear plastic, fantastic.' He recalls how what was an ironic, even facetious suggestion, caught on in a big way with the Crufts crowd. There are now poodles preserved in perspex on the mantelpieces of a hundred stockbroker homes. Steadman's joke backfired. The dog-hater, the man famed for chucking boiling tea-bags into the air for dogs to catch, could have become rich had he patented his pet preservation plan.

I'd pour my pint over his soddin' head if I didn't want to blot my copybook in these quarters.

Together we stroll to Steadman's local with the ebullient cartoonist explaining how even this simple twice-daily routine has become an 'ordeal' since the publican bought a white Highland Terrier called Dougal. Steadman opens the pub door and Dougal starts yapping. 'Just look at the mangy swine,' hisses Steadman in a hoarse whisper, 'I'd pour my pint over his soddin' head if I didn't want to blot my copybook in these quarters.' Fortified by two pints of Brown Ale, Steadman waxes expansive. He confesses that his idea of hell is, to paraphrase Hunter Thompson, spending six months in a Mexican jail chained to dog expert Barbara Woodhouse. 'What does the terrible woman think she's doing, going on TV and blowing air up animals' nostrils? I'd like to blow up her nostrils and see how she'd react. I only have to hear her ghastly catchphrase "walkies" (and here Dougal's ears prick up and he waves his tail excitedly) and I go down with migraine.'

Perhaps it was the brown ale, perhaps it was the mellowing effect of the Real Flame ornamental gas fire, but Steadman opened a small chink in his armour by confessing that he was an avid Lassie fan as a lad. 'It's true. I have to admit it. I actually *loved* that dog. I adored every tear-jerking episode. Remember that little blond boy? Remember his trembling cry "Lassie, Lassie?" I sobbed through it every week.' In retrospect, I think it was because Lassie was so Hollywoodized. Shiny hair, perfect teeth, flawless smile. Like Marilyn Monroe she acquired that irresistible Hollywood glamour.'

Meanwhile Dougal is under the table rooting around for

crisp crumbs, making playful little pokes at Steadman's groin. 'I'd kick the bugger so help me,' fumes Steadman, 'if the landlord wasn't around ... Another thing I ought to point out is that dogs are great snoopers. They *listen*. They know what you're saying. I'll give you this tip.

... dogs are great snoopers. They *listen*. They know what you're saying.

You should never say unpleasant things about a pub, such as you're not too crazy about the bar snacks, or the noise of the Space Invader machines, if the publican's dog is in the vicinity. It somehow passes on the word in its horrible doggy way.'

Suddenly brandishing his book he insists: 'Show my book to any dog, hold it up to any one of the smelly vermin and I promise you it will instantly cringe, whimper and cower in a corner. With luck it might even curl up and die.' Okay, I say, try it on Dougal. Go on. Steadman approaches Dougal waving the book and looking, to my way of thinking, like a psychopath. Dougal sniffs at the book, yawns, rolls over onto his back with legs waving in the air, presenting his tummy for a tickle. Steadman says it makes him sick. It's all he needs to ensure that he'll be in a state of tension for the rest of the afternoon.

A Leg in the Wind (Arrow Books, 1982).

When you're six-
teen you just don't
care if pills make
your nose bleed or
you park your lunch
in a washbasin.

RICHARD

SHERIDAN

Publishers are desperate for young writers. This desperation is evident from some of the crass, ineptly-crafted first novels being promoted by reputable publishers who ought to know better. One suspects that nowadays they whip out a contract for any daft bugger with a pin through his nose and a swastika hanging off his ear who can actually hold a pencil. 'It can hold a pencil! Wow! Amazing! Quick, sign it up . . .' Never mind that its lips still move as it reads. It represents the authentic, quintessential Voicer Yoof, Okay?'

Such a novel is Richard Sheridan's *End of '77*, an everyday story of contemporary drug-taking folk, described by Chatto & Windus as 'energetic, street-wise and sassy, the first novel to give us chic-punk and street culture as they look from street-level: sordid, colourful and unmistakably alive'. For 'unmistakably alive' read 'unmistakably dead' because all the main characters spend most of their self-indulgent, appallingly pop-obsessed lives bombed out of their brains on pills, dope and Special Brew, or comatose, or vomiting in gutters. Filth, fornication and fellatio seethe on every page. If this is 'skin culture' (whatever that may be), it is not 'energetic', but obnoxious. If this is chic punk it is not 'sassy' but grotesque. If this is literature, then it has dived down the drain.

It is this last fact that bothers me. And the fact that none of the Yoof spotters at Chatto & Windus noticed that *End of '77* is as half-baked as a microwaved potato. Sheridan's background is a Yoof spotter's dream. Expelled from school at 15, he drifted into pop and bummed, drummed, and succumbed to illegal substances. He undoubtedly has something to say. A good editor, having spotted certain potential, might have been more assiduous in helping him to say it with syntax and structure. Having retched through my proof copy, and having got wind that all the pathetic middle-aged trendies who edit the style sections of colour supplements and magazines like *The Blitz*, *I D* and *The Face* were at each other's throats about serial rights, I thought it might be enlightening to go along and interview Sheridan. As doubtless we will soon be seeing him on *Wogan*, *Arena*, *Bookshelf*, if not perspiring in the studio lights with Melvyn Bragg, I figured it might be interesting to get there first.

He is a handsome (no pin, no swastika), amiable, happily-married young man who greeted me with the words: 'I was going down the cleaners to get my clean trousers and jacket but I never got it together.' He wasn't wearing any socks. It was 10.30 a.m. He was already on his second Super Lager. We conversed above the stereophonic wailing of Dolly Parton. He recalled how

Obviously, an ending was in the back of my mind but I didn't bother to write it.

'this woman' at Chatto & Windus read through his unsolicited manuscript and raved. She shouted 'I love it. I love it. And it makes me feel a hundred years old.' She, no doubt is the person responsible for the dust jacket blurb about the novel 'bringing to life an irrepressible bunch of characters in the flowering of punk'. Mind you, Sheridan is the first person to admit that his novel has its faults: 'I'm well aware that there's a certain amount of fast, almost sloppy writing. It's not too clearly thought out, partly because it started out as a short story. Also it peters out at the end a bit. Nothing is resolved. That is fairly deliberate because I didn't feel that any of the characters were at a stage in their lives when things could be resolved. Obviously, an ending was in the back of my mind but I didn't bother to write it . . . Incidentally, just because I haven't got any "O" levels and haven't read Martin Amis and Shakespeare doesn't mean I can't write a book.' A good point, that, and one I'd like to pursue, but it is difficult above the screech of Dolly Parton. 'Myself, I read about one book a year, and my favourite book of all time is *Last Exit to Brooklyn*,' added Sheridan, pulling the tab off another Super Lager.

To oldsters like me the lifestyle of urban youth, as depicted by Sheridan, is vile and degrading. To him it is 'a gas' and 'a giggle'. Those whom I regard as foul-mouthed human debris he sees simply as his generation thumbing its nose at the old, incompetent order. Our conversation continued like this:

Me: You certainly need a rather strong stomach to read some of your bleak revelations of the 'chic punk' way of life.

Sheridan: Bleak? You call that bleak? You wait till my next book. That starts with a 7-page sequence of someone dying of a heroin overdose . . .

Me: Can't wait, can't wait . . .

Sheridan: Yeah, I suppose that *End of '77* has its nasty moments. But things like that *are* going on everywhere in Thatcher's Britain; my book is super relevant to what's happening to young people. When you're sixteen you just don't care if pills make your nose bleed or you park your lunch in a washbasin. It's a glamorous scene.

Me: Are you a wiser man now you're 24?

Sheridan: You're implying that to be into drugs is not wise.

Me: Too right. Personally, I'd like to see all drug-dealers lined up against a wall and fatally stabbed with hypodermic syringes. But I notice you've dodged my question.

Sheridan: I'm being careful about my answer. Okay. Talking straight there isn't a helluva lot I'd refuse, right? Even though some of it does your head in. Quite honestly, if you were sitting there doing your crack while we do this interview I wouldn't grumble.

Me: Crack? Oh CRACK. Yes, CRACK. (Tap my nose, flash a sassy, streetwise smirk.)

Sheridan: I must admit, though, that I saw this girl on the tube a while back who used to be in my class at school. She looked very rough. One of her arms was twice as thick as the other. She'd let some smack freak jack her up and he'd hit a nerve. Her arm had gone green. It was disgusting. I could have put things like that in the book, I suppose, I could have made drug-taking look less attractive, but I was writing about a time ten years ago which for me and my mates was great.

Me: Don't you think that the sex scenes, and reference to girls as 'passing traffic' could outrage female readers?

Sheridan: I find those scenes a bit difficult to defend, but sex *was* free, gratuitous and wild when I was 16. Now I'm married I miss all that to be honest . . . when I was writing it, I admit there were times when I thought 'Doesn't that bit sound like one of the readers' letters in *Penthouse*?' I've just written a sex scene for my next book, trying to look at it from a female's point of view. That's my conscience salved, right?

At the risk of sacrificing my street cred, I'll stick my neck out and say that *End of '77* is an atrocious book. Stuff street cred, it is the frantic maintaining of street cred that is responsible for much of the trash pushed upon us in the patronising guise of 'youth culture'. The middle-aged hoaxers doing the pushing should grow up. Sheridan's novel has already won the heart of a TV producer who has commissioned him to devise a screen play based on one of its characters (skinhead, ex-Borstal boy Andy). Channel 4 are putting out feelers. Everyone with any street cred worth its salt is hopping onto the Voicer Yoof bandwagon. Let us allow Sheridan to have the last word: 'If you ask me why I wrote the book the answer has to be a mercenary one. If it makes some money then that's one less on the dole. I won't beat about the bush. I think writing for television is where the bread is. I want to steam in there. Dirk Bogarde recently said that television is lavatory paper. He's nothing but an ignorant snob. It is the most liberating art form we've got and I'm not talking about *The Benny Hill Show*. Television is where good art is going to come from. Young people, *my* generation, watch television instead of reading books. The day I spend £10 on a hardback book is the day I'm pushing up daisies.'

. . . when I was writing it, I admit there were times when I thought 'Doesn't that bit sound like one of the readers' letters in *Penthouse*?'

End of '77 (Chatto & Windus, 1986).

ROBERT

I WAS STUNNED BY BOB DYLAN. THE
GUY WAS BREATHING FIRE AND
SMOKE. EVERYONE WAS ASKING
'WHAT HAVE WE HERE?' AND FOR THE
PAST 26 YEARS I'VE BEEN TRYING TO
ANSWER THAT QUESTION.

SHELTON

*M*any people (including, perhaps, Bob Dylan) reckon that Robert Shelton knows more about Dylan than Dylan does himself. Way back in 1961 Shelton breezed into a Greenwich Village folk club and heard the then unknown 19-year-old perform. Ever since he's been trailing after Dylan in much the same way that Boswell trailed after Dr Johnson.

'I looked up on stage and saw this magic cross between a beatnik and a choirboy. He was working his guitar, using his hat as a fan, and singing his bleeding soul out,' recalls this earnest Chicago-born man with receding hair and gums, beneath whose crumpled sports jacket throbs the heart of a romantic troubador. 'At that time I was folk-music critic of the *New York Times*. My subsequent rave review is generally credited with being the piece that "discovered" Dylan. I was stunned by him. The guy was breathing fire and smoke. Everyone was asking "What have we here?", and for the past 26 years I've been trying to answer that question.'

Consequently Shelton's small Brighton terrace house overflows with Dylaniana. There are thousands of books, pamphlets, cuttings and photographs. There are six four-drawer filing cabinets stashed with accumulated research on the enigmatic star, variously described as 'Wordsworth of the microgroove' (*Esquire* '72), 'The Brecht of the juke box' (*Village Voice* '67), and 'Homer in denim' (*Guardian* '65). There are letters and original song manuscripts penned in Dylan's own hand. There is a treasured snapshot of Dylan ('he's the one wearing shades – we were close cronies at the time') at the Newport Folk Festival, with Shelton's podgy, overawed features fuzzy behind a cloud of Dylan's reefer smoke. There are envelopes full of erudite interchanges between Shelton and various British highbrows from whom he solicited serious literary analysis of Dylan's lyrics.

Anthony Burgess, for example, wrote: 'First class pop art, some might say, but he can't compare with Philip Larkin.' Professor Christopher Ricks of Cambridge University declared: 'Not all of his work is perfect. He's only as good as Shakespeare, who had a lot wrong too.' And there are all Dylan's official albums, plus hundreds of rare bootlegs – 'I had to call a halt to collecting Bootlegs,' rasps Shelton ruefully, 'or I'd have gone bonkers.'

Ask him any question concerning the life and times of the song-writer who became 'the voice of his generation' and the answer comes back quick as a flash. The love affair with Joan Baez? 'Yeah, well, Joan once told me she tried to get Bobby to look after his health, to get him to cut down his smoking, brush his teeth and all of that . . .' When did Dylan first conquer Britain? 'Spring '65 was the turning point. In March 7,000 tickets for his 10 May Albert Hall concert sold out within two hours. If one single external factor triggered Dylan's British breakthrough it was the Beatles' public endorsement . . .' What was the truth about Dylan's mysterious motorcycle accident? 'No one knows it all. No way. Late Friday night, 29 July 1966, I received a call from Dylan's distraught dad saying he'd heard a news bulletin to the effect that Bob was badly hurt in some road accident and wanted my confirmation . . .' Who was Mr Tambourine Man? 'No simple answer. He *could* be some embodiment of the muses of music and poetry, or a spirit which draws us out of our routine selves . . .' Shelton can (and does) fill you in on Dylan going down with a stomach virus in '65, on Dylan being invited to John Lennon's 22-room Weybridge mansion, and on Dylan's habit of scribbling songs on paper table napkins, wiping his mouth with them and throwing them away.

Obviously it helps to be a Bob Dylan fan when you're conversing with Shelton. He admits that those who fail to share his passion tend to drop out of his life. Like his ex-wife. 'She thought I was giving too much attention to Dylan research and not enough to her descending career as a singer. This was not the *only* reason for the divorce, but it helped.' And his ex-girlfriend: 'I lived for five years with an Anglican Bishop's daughter who quit because she wanted more people round the house and fewer filing cabinets.'

In the company of fellow-fans (like me) Shelton opens up like a Chinese water flower. When I tell him about the conversation I had during a chance meeting with Dylan during his rehearsal at Earls Court (*Dylan*: Hi. *Me*: Hi. *Dylan*: How d'ya rate the band I've got together? *Me*: Great. *Dylan*: It's the only thing I *have* got together these days.), Shelton sighs and solemnly interjects: 'Ah yes, that would have been 1980 when he was at an all time low during his Christian phase . . .' When I recall how I accidentally locked myself in a lavatory at the start of the 1980 Budakhan Tour, missing Dylan's first three songs, Shelton groans: 'I sympathize, I got stuck in an elevator during the interval of the same gig and missed four songs in the second half.'

For Shelton, the sleuthing, loyalty, scrupulous analysis and years of hanging on Dylan's every word have all paid off (emotionally) with the publication of his bulky, unauthorized biography of Dylan the passionate genius. As he explains: 'There were many problems doing this book – publisher problems, money problems

. . . people must be attuned to Dylan to appreciate the subtlety of my book. Speaking of subtlety, the people who handle serial rights wouldn't recognize subtlety if it kicked them down the stairs.

. . . and the central problem, Bob Dylan, who didn't stop changing. I was fortunate that he co-operated from the start. But he set down certain boundaries. He said: "You can't ask me about how I sleep, how I make it, and what I think I'm doing here. Other than that we'll just get along fine." '

Dylan knew that Shelton was a man to be trusted. He wasn't in the same league for example as the dreaded Dylanomaniac known as 'The Scavenger' who spent three years rummaging through Dylan's dustbins and playing his albums backwards in search of hidden meanings. Dylan came to trust Shelton to such an extent that he actually instructed him to 'put the record straight' and tell readers that he did *not* take his name from Dylan Thomas. Quite where he did take the name from Shelton is still unclear but trust was certainly established and as Shelton points out 'the guy had known me long enough not to bracket me with those reporters who believe that to go around de-nuding celebrities is a way to earn a living'.

Has Dylan said what he thinks of Shelton's book? 'We're getting on dodgy ground here . . .,' replies Shelton, perspiring slightly and taking several slugs of Scotch. 'Let's just say we had a cordial meeting in London. I know he'd received an advance copy but I didn't ask him for an opinion. He did not offer one. Knowing I was off on a book promotion tour he asked: "How long's your tour?" I replied: "Two weeks." He laughed and said: "That's a really big tour" – note the impish humour from a guy who's been on perpetual tour all his life. He then said: "It's a really big book." My interpretation of this conversation is that there would have been no cordial meeting if he hadn't liked my book.'

Dylan's work will always be open to interpretation. It will always hurl lightning into the sky.

He admits that delivering the manuscript was like ridding his neck of an albatross. He was 'highly elated' when the book received a rave review in *Time* magazine which described it as 'a thoughtful, compassionate and scholarly appreciation'.

'I like to think it's loaded with revelation. Sex, drugs, confusion, everything is there, but people must be attuned to Dylan to appreciate the subtlety of my book. Speaking of subtlety, the people who handle serial rights wouldn't recognize subtlety if it kicked them down the stairs. Bastards.'

Shelton cannot yet bring himself to dismantle the archives. He plans to leave them to a university for perusal by future Dylanologists. He says Dylan's work will always be open to interpretation. That he will always hurl lightning into the sky. 'The guy's a poet, Okay? *Tant pis*, as the French say, but as that phrase sounds like a bladder condition you'd better change *"tant pis"* to "that's the way it blows". Thanks.'

No Direction Home (New English Library, 1986).

FRANKLY, I THINK THERE'S BEEN TOO MUCH FILTH PUBLISHED.

Shirley Conran

hirley Conran maintains that too many greedy women writers have hopped onto what she calls the *Fat Filthy* bandwagon. She insists that Fat Filthies (American publishing term for steamy bestsellers) have had their day. The tide has turned. The days of the 'never-mind-the-quality-feel-the-width' block-buster have gone. Rush out for a copy of Shirley's latest tome *Savages*, and you'll have to wait till page 297 for the first filthy bit – a voluptuous, squelchy lesbian love sequence which, it has to be said, mercifully lacks the usual throb and thrust we have come to expect from the author of *Lace*.

'Frankly I think there's been too much filth published,' says Shirley, ushering me out onto the terrace of her sumptuously converted chateau on the French Riviera. Heat hits the back of my sun-starved neck, a fragrance of wild lavender tickles my nostrils. A champagne cork pops. Shirley kicks her somewhat large and bumpy bare feet in the air declaring: 'I like to be ahead in the publishing game. I *know* my timing's right. Sex is out, female assertiveness is in. Female assertiveness is a quality which is highly necessary to modern women.'

This quality, as it happens, flares from Shirley like a blowtorch. It crackles. It blasts. It scorches every one of my feeble little interjections as the ex *Fat Filthy* virtuoso starts banging on about the tribulations of authorship. I just sit there bemused wishing I had a chateau of my own and wondering why I haven't got into writing Fat Filthies as Shirley grumbles about the flack she has to face. Oh yes, people have been slow to realize there's more to *Lace* and *Lace 2* than sex. As a matter of fact it's a 'deep' book. Very deep. Shirley says that.

She's all too aware that people sneer. They frequently scoff, they even make her out to be 'the Mandy Rice-Davies of English Literature', speaking of whom Shirley would like to point out that in 1968 Mandy was raking in an incredible £5,000 a year for being villainous-landlord Rachman's mistress while Shirley Conran, fashion editor of *The Observer*, was getting a paltry £2,500. Crazy, isn't it? Shirley lets out a little yelp. She makes the same yelping noises, she explains, when the writing is flowing fast.

'I promise you, hand on heart, that I'm *never* going to win any literary awards,' she says, one hand on her heart, the other on the champagne bottle, 'yet *Savages* has already netted £2,500,000, it's been sold as a six-hour mini TV series, it's going to be W.H. Smith's book of the month, and quite frankly it's the first fiction I've *really* enjoyed writing. It's the first time I've followed my writer instincts. I'm proud of this book. Yes, *proud.*'

Savages ('the ultimate adventure for women') is set on a Pacific island. Five pampered American women, accompanying their husbands to a business conference, are marooned when their dinghy breaks down. Washed ashore, they get lost in the jungle and suffer every ghastly tribulation imaginable. Scorpions, rats, supperating ulcers, dysentery, heatstroke, murder, amputated fingers, decomposing flesh, bats getting tangled in their hair, you name it . . . And when they try to escape by boat worse is to follow with sharks, dehydration, hallucinations and cannibalism.

> I wrote the lesbian scene with great trepidation, I might add . . . I thought that it would be dead easy, that I'd just need to read *The Joys of Lesbian Sex* and chat to a few lesbians. Not on your life.

Fat it is, but definitely not filthy. Yet if you're thinking that there wouldn't be much time (or opportunity) anyway for sex in such an action-packed scenario you should hear Shirley on the subject.

She did her research. She has four suitcases full of notes. And one important fact that she ascertained is that deprivation doesn't necessarily diminish the sex urge. 'My Hollywood agent insisted there should be some lesbian content in the novel. I replied "Nonsense, the women would be far too exhausted to get up to any lesbian activities." He snapped "Check it out". So off I trotted to a psychiatrist who confirmed that fear would drive women into each other's arms after 24 hours. I didn't believe him. I dismissed him as a dirty old man, or as some sort of anti-woman type. But when a second psychiatrist told me the same thing I felt I *had* to include some element of lesbian love. I wrote the lesbian scene with great trepidation, I might add . . . I thought that it would be dead easy, that I'd just need to read *The Joys of Lesbian Sex* and chat to a few lesbians. Not on your life. It was extremely difficult to write.'

Lesbianism apart, Shirley insists that *Savages* is a meticulously researched book which may be used as an authentic jungle and sea survival manual. Her research encompassed such topics as cannibalism, how to cook rats, how to carry out a fatal stabbing ('I met several professional killers, extremely nice chaps who took their job very seriously'), and group dynamics under stress.

At a Cumbrian Outward Bound Centre, Shirley observed what happens among women when they try to grapple with the elements. 'Within 24 hours they lose all interest in their appearance. They're reduced to the *real* person behind the glossy facade. As one of my *Savages* characters comments wryly, women only act natural when men aren't around. To be absolutely frank, I was perfectly disgusted by the behaviour of some of the women at the Outward Bound course. In a mixed group they were given materials to construct a raft and I noticed how they invariably allowed the men to emerge as leaders. One of them needed to take off her track suit trousers, and she acted all coy and silly as if she couldn't get out of them without male assistance. I thought to myself, there is *no hope* for the female race if they go on behaving like that ... I also noticed that the meek girls, the types who take orders from others all the time, are full of bloodthirsty suggestions about survival, and I thought, God, I'm on the right track in *Savages*, there's a hellova lot of buried resentment in women ...'

Shirley, you gather, is certainly the sort who takes off her own trousers, thank you very much. And any buried resentment is a thing of the past. She says she's not the sort to bear a grudge. Subtlety may not be her forte, in fact she's like 'an elephant dancing through daisies' when it comes to personal relationships, but she has no real enemies apart from one of her three ex-husbands who shall be nameless and people who put cigarette butts down her lavatories. Resentment is certainly a thing of the past. As it jolly well should be what with millions of pounds and dollars earned from her books, a picturesque French chateau, two apartments in Monte Carlo and a brand new £4,000 face about which she's keen to talk. 'I deliberately came out into the open about my nip-and-tuck. It's only in England that people seem to think that cosmetic surgery should be reserved for Spitfire pilots.' She leans forward allowing me to search for invisible scars on her eyelids and under her chin. 'They shove a vacuum gadget in, whoosh, slurp, and dropped jawline and crepey bits vanish.

It's the first time I've followed my writer instincts. I'm proud of this book. Yes, proud.

I wish I'd done it five years ago when it would have cost £1,000. Five years later, gravity being what it is, and the pound falling faster than my jawline, the price had gone up to £4,000. Who do I look fabulous for, you may ask? Myself, that's who. Why shouldn't I look good? I've damn well earned the money. I'm about to go on a world book promotional tour so I want to look my absolute best.' Shirley's only regret is that an Aunt ('I could have strangled her') showed Shirley's mother an article in which the outspoken daughter confessed that she'd decided on a facelift after observing the time-ravaged features of her own mother.

One glass of Shirley's champagne and I'm practically under the rattan table. Three glasses ahead and Shirley's on ebullient top form, waxing cynical about blockbusters ('Just because people pay me millions to write them there's no reason to suppose I'll do so for ever.'); and the agonies of writing ('You have to pass through the pain barrier of being alone in a room to write'); and love ('I hope I'll never be in love again. I hate it. One mopes and becomes illogical. I'm deeply appreciative of the man in my life, I'm mentioning no names, he's the only person who's really interested in *me*, but I'm not "in love" '). She recalls a recent ladies' Rubella luncheon graced by the Princess of Wales. Shirley and Molly Parkin, another Fat Filthies authoress, were discussing the menopause when HRH interrupted them, rendering them both speechless by her charm. And it takes quite a lot to render Shirley and Molly speechless. 'The Princess was wonderful. Wonderful. Although, as Molly remarked, a good fashion editor would have taken off marks for her rather visible panty-line.'

Downing another swift glass of champagne Shirley ruefully pats her hips and says: 'If someone were to ask me what issue has caused me most anxiety throughout my life I wouldn't reply "The bomb" or "the starving brown babies of Ethiopia". The thing I have been worried about most is the dimension of my hips. And sitting writing doesn't help. A great friend of mine, Lesley Blanche, the frightfully famous novelist, looked at my behind in a rather speculative manner recently and said: "Let's face it, Shirley, ours is a very physically unbecoming profession." '

Rising unsteadily to her feet. Shirley proposes a small conducted tour of the chateau. Allowing her to lead the way for fear of her criticizing my visible panty-line, I gaze through tastefully converted doorways, at dazzling kitchen units upon which no fatty pans have ever loitered, at snowy duvet covers upon which no felt-tipped pen has ever leaked, and at flawless lavatory seats where no backside has ever sat. It is all perfect, spotless, soulless, empty. Earlier that day, when asking for directions to the chateau, an elderly local gesturing up the hill said that the house contained some of the best medieval ceiling paintings in France. 'Where are the ceiling paintings?' I ask Shirley, as she is pointing out the dungeon entrance now blocked by her deep freeze. 'Ceiling paintings?' She throws back her facelift and yelps: 'I whitewashed over them during the conversion. The locals go on about their historic value, but I knew they were fakes, of course.' Of course. 'Those are arrow slits,' she says, pointing upwards, 'and those are gaps for pouring boiling oil onto one's enemies. I must say I can think of one or two people I'd like to pour it on.' You bet. Particularly anyone who dares to suggest that *Savages* may not reach the parts that the Fat Filthies so profitably reached. Say no more.

Savages (Sidgwick & Jackson, 1987).

Sue Townsend

Of *course* my books are about
class; I've got a permanent chip
on my shoulder about class.

ev, an 18-year-old friend of mine, had never read a book until he discovered *The Growing Pains of Adrian Mole*. Okay, so it's not Shakespeare, Bronte or even Mailer, but the silent moving of Kev's lips and the occasional empathic snigger do, at least, indicate a certain burgeoning awareness of the printed word.

'Ere, you read vis bit?' Kev asks, hauling the book from one of the multi-zipped pockets of his Flip mechanic's trousers. 'April 5th. Found a strange device in the bathroom this morning. It looked like an egg-timer. It said "Predictor" on the side of the box. I hope my mother is not dabbling in the occult' – and – 'April 13th: My father ended our first man-to-man talk by saying, "Look, kiddo, don't even think about getting married until you've spent a few months sharing a bedroom with a bird. If she leaves her knickers on the floor for more than three days running, forget it!"' Kev roars. 'Wa, ha, ha, bit of a laugh, eh? Just like my ol' man. Better than bleedin' *Cider Wiv Rosie. . .*'

No one is more delighted to hear about Kev's enthusiasm than Sue Townsend, creator of Adrian Mole, mother of four and still topping the bestseller lists after 52 weeks. 'I've had lots of letters from people of all ages saying it's the first book they've ever read,' she says, 'and I've just heard that it's been made a CSE set book which is very gratifying . . .'

The likes of Kev will enjoy the book's occasional anti-authoritarian swipes at institutions like schools and social security officialdom. They will surely sympathize with Miss Elf, the teacher sacked for drawing a moustache on Mrs Thatcher and scribbling 'three million unemployed' in her cleavage. They will certainly identify with school rebel Barry Kent, who commits educational suicide by wearing his Hell's Angels gear to school.

Obviously the play-it-safe-no-controversy CSE board has not caught onto the fact that Townsend's *Mole* books are brilliant, deceptively simple assaults on the British class structure. Drinking tea backstage at Wyndham's theatre, where Townsend is supervizing her musical adaptation of *The Secret Diary of Adrian Mole Aged 13¾*, she throws a copy of *The Times* on the floor to soak up the dribbles from a leaking tea urn, and laughs: 'Of *course* the books are about class, I've got a permanent chip on my shoulder about class. Whenever I come down to London it seems like another world. I'm amazed by all the obvious prosperity, people gorging themselves in expensive restaurants, the casual attitude to money. People don't seem to realize how bleak things are further North . . .'

' "Mole" is really about the 15-year-old no-hoper who fails. He's about *me*. I went to a secondary mod. I didn't get any O-levels. I don't remember anybody *mentioning* them . . . it wasn't until five years ago that I had the nerve to "come out" and admit to the bloke I'm with that I was a secret writer. I was scared he

I can hardly believe that this pompous little wimp, who I invented on boring Sunday afternoons when my kids were whining to be taken to Safari parks, has earned me more than £250,000, so I'm told.

would laugh. It was traumatic. Like owning up to being a closet bondage freak.'

Townsend, daughter of two bus conductors, left school at 15 and worked in a shoe factory for two years, married, worked in a garage forecourt, a hot dog van, a dress shop. 'Any sort of job where I could *read*. I always got jobs where I could *read*. Next to my husband and baby, reading was my favourite thing . . .' She pauses, lighting a cigarette. I notice that *The Times* page catching the drips has a sizeable article about herself. Townsend glances at it and sniffs: 'They refer to me as "whimsical". Christ, anyone less whimsical you've never met . . .'

Director Graham Watkins dashes in to announce that the stage Adrian Mole has been rushed to hospital from his home with a suspected broken arm and is being plastered up. Hot tea gushes on to the director's foot. Expletives are muttered. The leg falls off Townsend's chair. Unruffled, she picks herself up explaining how she chose 16-year-old Schatzberger to play the part of Mole from 200 young hopefuls, mainly because he lied about his age. She says he is perfect for the part. Hilarious. He starred in a recent nine-week run in Leicester where every seat sold out in a day.

A light-bulb fuses. A picture slips off the wall. Townsend

laughs a fifty-fags-a-day laugh that sounds like a cement-mixer and says that her head still spins just thinking about the triumphs she's notched up in two years thanks to Adrian Mole. It's hard keeping track. *The Secret Diary* has been translated into seven languages, made into a BBC cassette and a TV serialization, and now Mole is making his lugubrious West End debut and the box office took £12,000 in advance takings on the day it opened.

'I can hardly believe that this pompous little wimp, who I invented on boring Sunday afternoons when my kids were whining to be taken to Safari parks, has earned me more than £250,000, so I'm told,' says Townsend, 'mind you, I draw the line at all the spin-off-merchandizing, the T-shirts, toothbrushes, duvet covers etc; my own kids have been ripped off by too much of that sort of plastic crap. I've said "Yes" to an Adrian Mole practical diary, and to anything bearing his name which may encourage people to read and write.'

She adds that it's ironic to consider the success of this conservative, reactionary and priggish literary brainchild when you consider the paltry fees she received for the previous plays she wrote, 'plays that gave me grey hair and sent me *mad* during a writer-in-residence stint at Leicester's Phoenix Arts Centre. You can imagine how rueful I felt when news came out that Mole was hitting the boards and the local paper ran an item headed "Leicester mother breaks into stage!" At that time I had already written six plays and one, *The Great Celestial Cow*, even went to the Royal Court.'

Money, Townsend says, has certainly perked life up a bit; 'I've moved out of the inner-city ghetto where we were in danger of becoming a problem family due to the fact that my husband ran off, a while back, with a nubile girl. God, have I been *broke*! There have been days when I had to take the empties back to get my bus fare to work. And I'm the world expert on retrieving 10p pieces from down the back of settees. With my '*Mole*' money I've bought a suburban vicarage about a mile from the station with lots of rooms and trees in the back garden . . . The great thing about having money is that suddenly I can buy *hardback* books and fags in cartons of 200.'

Fame, she insists, is rather daft. All at once she's an 'in' person, and she's receiving invitations to literary gatherings. 'I did one book programme. I was on with Lady Antonia Fraser and Malcolm Bradbury. I don't come over very well on telly. We had a little disagreement when Lady A was discussing her biography of George VI. She said he had made sacrifices during the war by refusing to drink the contents of his wine cellar. I said this didn't strike me as much of a sacrifice. A little frisson ran round the studio.'

In an endearing burst of candour, Townsend confesses that she's sick to death of Adrian Mole. Fed up to the back teeth. Enough's enough. After all, he's not Great Literature, and he was the easiest thing she's ever written. Just dashed him off on the back of phone bills. And what people don't realize is that he's mostly Sue Townsend: 'I'm a manic-depressive but I don't let it get me down. It's *rude* to be a manic depressive, and upset all those around you. Naturally I'm grateful to *Mole* for my change of fortune but I tell you this, whenever I feel tempted to buy a first-class train ticket I get out my copy of Engels's *The Condition of the Working Class in Britain*. It keeps my on my toes. And on the straight and narrow. It was written only 100 years ago. I reckon we all need constantly to remind ourselves that human nature doesn't change.'

The woman who is currently bigger than Ballard, Burgess and Barbara Cartland amalgamated in 1984 book sales term says that it's fine by her, seeing that it's Christmas, if we end the interview with one of Adrian Mole's (unpublished) poems. Here it is:

MRS THATCHER
by A MOLE

Do you weep, Mrs Thatcher, do you weep?
Do you wake, Mrs Thatcher, in your sleep?
Do you weep like a sad willow?
On your Marks & Spencer pillow?
Are your tears molten steel?
Do you weep?
Do you wake with 'Three million' on your brain?
Are you sorry that they'll never work again?
When you're dressing in your blue, do you see the waiting queue?
Do you weep, Mrs Thatcher, do you weep?

The Secret Diary of Adrian Mole Aged 13¾ (Methuen, 1985).

I feel very strongly that women
should write about sex.

WENDY
PERRIAM

'Gusto' is the word critics most frequently use in describing Wendy Perriam's books. They have 'sexual exuberance', 'explosive frankness', 'smouldering lustiness', but above all they have 'gusto'. There is not one paragraph, not one line that doesn't fairly pullulate with gusto. *Sin City*, Perriam's latest, has gusto coming out of its ears. So, it must be said, has its author, a vivacious, sparky-eyed wearer of scarlet lipstick who begins spouting a sex-obsessed stream-of-consciousness monologue within two minutes of our meeting.

'I feel very strongly that women should write about sex,' she announces, with an impatient, small-bosomed shimmy inside a T-shirt with LAS VEGAS stencilled across the chest.

'In fact I've been criticized for giving all the steamy details, for staying around until the afterplay. But I believe that women have been duped by male models of sexuality in literature. We've all read too many books where men and women climax simultaneously, then fall back exhausted and satiated which, of course, is rarely the case. Women take a while to calm down, many of us given the chance can achieve multiple orgasms, my books reflect these realities . . .'

Here the 47-year-old Surbiton celebrity pauses to scrutinize a menu. This is certainly one up on interviewing Margaret Drabble, say, or A.S. Byatt. I am agog. Everyone in the restaurant is agog. People are actually beginning to slobber. When Perriam remarks (in her somewhat penetrating voice) that she also feels very strongly that women should write about masturbation and that Carole's orgasmic masturbation sequences in *Sin City* are deliberately introduced to reassure closet female masturbators, there is not a dry mouth in the room.

'Everyone accepts that men masturbate but female masturbation is somehow taboo, not "nice". Yet sex surveys show that most women wank so why shouldn't they wank in fiction, that's what I want to know. Are you sure this is all right for the *Literary Review*, Val?'

Er, Well, Wendy . . . I begin, glancing at my list of prepared questions and trying to decide whether to interject with 'It has been suggested by V.S. Pritchett that the principle of procrastinated rape is the ruling one in all the great best-sellers, what is your view?' or 'Susan Sontag maintains that perversity is the muse of modern literature, do you agree?'

But Perriam waits for no woman:

'I mean I could talk about how I started out as a poet, took drugs in my youth, how I revise all my manuscripts and spend hours agonizing over the

... Ted Hughes. My God what a sexy man! He looks like a cultured bricklayer with ravaged eyes.

right words. Cyril Connolly once said, in *Enemies of Promise –* do read it, even though it's old, it's full of good ideas – he said that ten minutes' extra thought in the choice of a word or the position of a stress can make a thousand years' difference. I take fiction writing very seriously. I've even been tutor at the Arvon foundation in Devon, the place set up by the Poet Laureate, Ted Hughes. My God what a sexy man! He looks like a cultured bricklayer with ravaged eyes. Yum. Yum. Anyway, maybe what I'm about to say isn't really suitable for the *Literary Review* but I'll leave you to decide. Val . . .'

Er, thanks, Wendy. She orders fried calves' liver-and-onions, sprinkles it with salt and continues:

'You see, another thing not generally appreciated is that women, whilst having sex, can feel a whole range of emotions unrelated to the Act such as boredom, anger, hilarity, anxiety about the gas bill and so forth. We women can fuck without having our minds on it.

'Men, on the other hand, become limp the instant their thoughts stray. At least I think they do. Ask *Literary Review* readers, Val. Organize a survey and let me know the results. I'd be truly fascinated . . . (Any *Literary Review* readers eager to comply may contact Wendy Perriam c/o her publisher Michael Joseph). Mind you I do hate generalizing but in my experience men are so damn cagey that few will admit that they lose their erections if they stop concentrating on the job. Women are much more realistic and humorous about sex. They chuckle and say "I don't know what all the fuss is about" – you never hear men say that, do you?'

Er, well Wendy . . . and here a brief respite. She tucks into the calves' liver and I inform her that her previous novels, *After Purple, Cuckoo* and *The Stillness of Dancing* have a tremendous, much-thumbed following amongst various young people of my acquaintance. Indeed, when asked how they rated Perriam's works they replied: 'Wohr! Hot stuff! Knickers off and down to it, no messing about with poncy old scene-setting. Right on!' *Sin City* definitely comes into the 'Wohr! Hot stuff!' category. It tells the story of two mental hospital patients, Norah (hospitalized since baby-hood and whose sole visit to the outside world had been a day-trip to Littlehampton) and Carole (an 18-year-old manic-depressive who has only had sex 8½ times) who win a holiday-for-two in Las Vegas. These innocents, in an out-of-the-frying-pan-into-the-fire situation, plunge into a steamy world of strippers, gamblers and mass fornication. Norah comes to a sticky end, Carole comes sticky and moaning, and love conquers all including one set of male genitals mutilated during the Vietnam War.

As the dustjacket blurb warns 'This book, daringly unin-hibited, is not for the prudish'. It is however, a milestone for contemporary fiction because, according to Perriam, it is the first novel in which AIDS awareness ('You can check this out, Val, but I'm 90 per cent certain.' 'Er, thanks, Wendy . . .') flits through the heroine's mind. On page 143 Carole, contemplating a quickie with Milt, agonizes:

'I can't. I daren't. Those AIDS advertisements have all come screaming back – gruesome tombstones inscribed with four dire letters, posters planted everywhere DON'T DIE OF IGNORANCE! If I'm going to die of AIDS I've got to have a fag first . . .'

Perriam is understandably proud of this literary first:

'*Sin City* is definitely the first novel which actually quotes the AIDS adverts. AIDS has caused confusion amongst novelists. I inserted the AIDS reference at the last minute when the novel was at proof stage because I move with the times and I reckoned that Carole may be extremely impul-sive and randy but like any young woman in 1987 she would not go to bed with a pick-up without considering the AIDS risk. Anyway let's get on to brothels . . .'

Las Vegas brothels are where Perriam conducted much of her *Sin City* research. The reason she's wearing her Las Vegas T-shirt, she explains, is because she's just been photographed by *The Standard* who were very keen on the Las Vegas angle:

'This *Standard* photographer, all creased-looking as if he'd been sleeping in the car all night, and Irish, shook my hand so hard I was in pain. He dragged me off to a building site near Fleet Street and said "This will only take five mintues" and I must admit that through my mind raced the thought that he was a rapist and not a *Standard* photographer at all . . .'

'However, the Las Vegas brothels were extraordinary. They smelt of meat stew and reminded me of my convent boarding school. The girls – pinefresh and faces scrubbed so I couldn't believe they were hookers – had teddy-bears in their rooms and snaps of mums and dads on the wall. In the action rooms there were ghastly satin heart cushions, naked lady lampstands, enormous vibrators, and pingers outside the doors like microwave oven pingers so that clients know when time's up. You would have died laughing to see the brothel torture-chamber, a sort of fantasy dungeon with cardboard skeletons, racks, thumbscrews, girls wearing Nazi gear.

Sin City is definitely the first novel which actually quotes the AIDS adverts. AIDS has caused confusion amongst novelists. I inserted the AIDS reference at the last minute when the novel was at proof stage because I move with the times . . .

'I offered my husband, Alan, two girls as a treat so he could tell me what happens but he turned me down. He's a typical Surbiton person. He prefers feathered birds to the other sort. If a great spotted wagtail flew past he'd rush after it I'm afraid. But I won't go into my marital miseries . . . One girl started rubbing her naked tits across his tweed jacket, placed his glass of beer inside her G-string, but I'm sorry to say it just put him off his beer . . .'

Sensing by now a veritable loss of interview control on my part and wondering whether this is what Virginia Woolf must have been like on a bad day I make doomed efforts to elevate the conversation. I mention Fay Weldon, I quote Colette, I even inquire whether Perriam's Las Vegas experiences convinced her of the exploitation of women. At this she roars: 'Exploitation? Heavens, in a way *I'd* like to be a prostitute. A lot of women have prostitution fantasies, you know. And sado-masochistic fantasies. What the hookers told me about the torture chamber sessions was absolutely killing. They love every minute . . .

'. . . Men ask to be dragged round by their tongues, have their testicles slammed in drawers, pins stuck in their pricks . . . apparently if you stick a pin into an erect penis the blood gushes out in gallons . . .'

Gripping my knife and fork, white-knuckled, I push my plate to one side. I push my interview to one side. The gusto grates on the ears of fellow-diners who are hurling black looks across the water-jug. But Literature's answer to Dr Ruth rants on regardless:

'For me to become a prostitute would be like saying "Ya Boo" to my Reverend Mother. The nuns brought me up to think sex was wrong. All that induced guilt spoilt it for me. In a way many Catholic girls long to do vile things as a revenge. Quite honestly I'd love to visit a brothel for women. Imagine it, all those studs just waiting to do anything a woman fancies. Fabulous. Terrific. As a matter of fact there's one in Hamburg. Oh, Val, let's go! together! Let's! We could have such a laugh, such a terrific time. Imagine it!' Er, Well, Wendy.

Help! I'm rather busy for the next few years . . .

Sin City (Michael Joseph, 1987).